# FACES OF JESUS

## THE CONTRIBUTORS

**Hugo Assmann**, a Catholic theologian, is a professor at the Methodist University of Piracicaba in his native Brazil. His works include *Theology for a Nomad Church* (Orbis).

**Leonardo Boff** is a Franciscan priest and a professor of systematic theology at the Petropolis (Brazil) Institute for Philosophy and Theology. His previous books include *Jesus Christ Liberator* and *The Lord's Prayer* (Orbis).

**Georges Casalis**, a French Reformed theologian, is a professor of systematic theology at the Reformed Theological Seminary, Paris. His previous work includes *Correct Ideas Don't Fall from the Skies* (Orbis).

**J. Severino Croatto** is professor of Old Testament studies at the Instituto Superior Evangélico de Estudios Teológicos (ISEDET) in Buenos Aires. In English he has published *Exodus: A Hermeneutics of Freedom* (Orbis).

**João Dias de Araújo** has been a pastor of the Presbyterian church in Northeast Brazil for over thirty years. He is also a lawyer for CEDITER (Comissão Evangelica dos Direitos da Tierra).

**Ignacio Ellacuría**, born in Spain, has lived and worked in Central America for some thirty years. He is professor at the Universidad Centroamericana José Simeón Cañas in San Salvador.

**Segundo Galilea** is a Chilean priest who does grassroots pastoral work in Santiago. His works in English include *Following Jesus* and *The Beatitudes: To Evangelize as Jesus Did* (Orbis).

**José Míguez Bonino** is professor of systematic theology and ethics at the Instituto Superior Evangélico de Estudios Teológicos in Buenos Aires, Argentina. His other works include *Doing Theology in a Revolutionary Situation* and *Toward a Christian Political Ethics* (Fortress).

**Pedro Negre Rigol**, a Spaniard, holds graduate degrees in theology and sociology. Formerly the secretary of studies of ISAL (Iglesia y Sociedad en América Latina), he now resides in Barcelona.

**Lamberto Schuurman** was born in Holland. An ordained pastor of the Reformed Church, he has served as professor of systematic theology and as dean of the Instituto Superior Evangélico de Estudios Teológicos in Buenos Aires.

**Juan Stam** is professor of theology and ethics at the Baptist Theological Seminary in Managua, Nicaragua. He also works with the pastoral team CELEP (Centro Evangélico Latinoamericano de Estudios Pastorales) in San José, Costa Rica.

**Saúl Trinidad**, a Peruvian, is a pastor of the Evangelical Methodist Church of Costa Rica.

**Raúl Vidales** is a Mexican theologian and sociologist. He regularly collaborates with DEI (Departamento Ecuménico de Investigaciones) in San José, Costa Rica.

# FACES OF JESUS

## LATIN AMERICAN CHRISTOLOGIES

*Edited by*
*José Míguez Bonino*

*Translated from the Spanish by*
*Robert R. Barr*

ORBIS BOOKS
Maryknoll, New York 10545

First published as *Jesús: Ni vencido ni monarca celestial*, copyright © 1977 by Tierra Nueva, S.R.L., San José 28, Piso 6, 1076 Buenos Aires, Argentina

English translation copyright © 1984 by Orbis Books, Maryknoll, NY 10545

Manufactured in the United States of America

Manuscript Editor: William E. Jerman

**Library of Congress Cataloging in Publication Data**

Jésus, ni vencido ni monarca celestial. English.
  Faces of Jesus.

  Translation of: Jésus, ni vencido ni monarca celestial.
  Includes bibliographical references and index.
  1. Jesus Christ—Person and offices—Addresses, essays, lectures. 2. Theology, Doctrinal—Latin America—History—20th century—Addresses, essays, lectures. I. Míguez Bonino, José. II. Title: Faces of Jesus.
BT202.J43613   1983      232'.098      83-19375
ISBN 0-88344-129-2 (pbk.)

# CONTENTS

*Introduction*

# WHO IS JESUS CHRIST
# IN LATIN AMERICA TODAY?

## *José Míguez Bonino*

Some years ago, Emilio Castro suggested the question in the title of this Introduction as a theme for ecumenical study. Naturally the question itself is open to various interpretations. It can be understood as a dogmatic, normative question ("How is Jesus Christ correctly to be understood?"), as a descriptive, analytical question ("How is Jesus Christ *de facto* understood in Latin America today?"), or even as a theological, confessional question ("How is the working, efficacious power of Christ present in Latin America today?"). Of course these three levels intersect—as we know, the distinction between description, analysis, and praxis is necessarily a theoretical abstraction from a single indivisible reality. The chapters of this volume are separate articles, written from various viewpoints, each centering on one or other of these three interpretations of our question. But like the questions, the articles all intersect in the concrete reality of Jesus. Whether they treat our theme at the interpretive, the descriptive, or the practical level—or, perhaps more accurately, from the historico-biblical, theological, or pastoral viewpoints—they meet in Jesus Christ from every angle of approach.

### IMAGES OF CHRIST

Parts 1 and 2 of our book are devoted to identifying the christologies that have been present in Latin America throughout history. Our authors approach this in either of two ways. The first way is descriptive—an attempt to sketch the "image of Christ" as seen, experienced, and described in various sectors of the population at various moments of history. Here the possibili-

1

ties are almost infinite. For part 1 we have selected three articles, each in a different area: popular culture (João Dias de Araújo) and "liberal Christianity" (Leonardo Boff) in Brazil, and Protestant preaching in Latin America (Saúl Trinidad and Juan Stam).

In part 2, the articles take their point of departure from these popular images, but subject them to a psycho-social and theological interpretation. That is, they ask how these experiences of Christ actually operate, what functionality they have. The initial result of these reflections seems fairly homogeneous. The classic images of Christ in Latin America seem quite adequately defined in Georges Casalis's typology: the "conquered" Christ, suffering and passive, and the "celestial monarch" Christ, the almighty Pantokrator, assimilated to the conquistador—to which, in a further stage, a Christ of private piety, the intimate, subjective Christ, must be added. Saúl Trinidad's radical conclusion seems to be justified throughout part 2:

> Both images . . . are faces of a christology of oppression: the Christ of "established impotence," of a resignation that refuses struggle because it has already been alienated and conquered, and the Christ of "established power," suggesting a subjugation that has no need of struggle, because it has already overcome.[1]

## THE REVOLUTIONARY CHRIST

Trinidad's conclusion implies still another christology as its point of departure. A "christology of oppression" is suddenly confronted with the "Christ who conquers death," the "revolutionary combatant." Casalis explicates this counterposition in his article. But where does this "other Christ" come from? A first answer is, from the gospels. This theme has been the object of heated discussion among New Testament specialists during recent years. Once the political dimension was taken into account, it was inevitable that questions would be posed about the relationship of Jesus to the agitated political scene of his time, his attitude toward freedom movements such as that of the Zealots, the political character of his trial and execution, and his relationship with the "poor of the earth" (*'am ha'arets*). We have no intention of presenting a review of these studies in the present volume. The works of Hengel, Cullmann, and others offer an adequate survey of the question. But in view of the relevance of the theme for some of the most burning questions in Latin America today, we have included articles by Ignacio Ellacuría, Segundo Galilea, and Severino Croatto that deal with Jesus' relationship to politics.

## WHERE CAN WE FIND THE REAL CHRIST?

The three articles just mentioned finally force us to face a deeper hermeneutical problem. They show us that there is no such thing as a simple transposition of the "Christ of the gospels" into the present day. In the first place, is there such a thing as a single "biblical image" of Jesus? And if there is, can it be recovered? Even without succumbing to Bultmann's radical skepticism, we have to admit that biblical studies show not only that we have various christologies already present even in the New Testament, but that it is impossible to "go behind" these images, which already contain theological interpretation, in order thus to arrive at a "historical Jesus." What the New Testament gives us, as we weary of hearing, is a message, not a biography.

Nevertheless recent Latin American theology has gone beyond the simple grasp of this fact. The doubt cast by Assmann on the possibility of using exegesis to settle the conflict of interpretations is reinforced by work in the sociology of knowledge. Why do we find different, even conflicting, christologies even in the Bible, if not because they correspond to total concepts of reality themselves originating in defined and specific social praxes and ideologies? If we find middle-class and revolutionary Christs in Latin America today is it not because there are middle-class Christians and revolutionary Christians? And why does each of these two views enjoy its own self-consistency, its own rationality, forming the framework of a particular religious focus? Could there be any meaning in an idealistic search for a theological image of Christ divorced from these historical realities?

Sociologist Gilberto Díaz, dealing with the theme in a Mexican setting, proposes an interesting working hypothesis. Díaz proposes three points of reference: (1) magical, dominating the rural scene, (2) subjectivist, among the urban middle classes, and (3) historico-political, in movements for social change. We may hope that categories of interpretation, manners of conceiving the presence and power of Christ, and the expectations of piety, as further research in this field will reveal them, will confirm or correct this hypothesis. In the presence of a positive result, we would have, so to speak, three distinct "projections" of the figure of Christ.

## HOW SHOULD INTERPRETATION BE DONE?

Of course, a disquieting question remains. Does all this mean, in the last analysis, that Christ is but a projection of determinate social conditions, and the reflection of these conditions in ideology? In that case christology would be either nothing but a manner of speaking, or a form of the projection of such conditions and ideologies. In any case it could serve only to legitimate— or perhaps to provide a thrust for change, by way of a utopian vision—social contexts where religion and piety are still alive and influential. Christology could serve only to justify an already existing historical praxis. The reading of the Bible could then serve no purpose but to "read such and such a view into" (*eis-egesis*) the text.

None of our authors adopts this kind of mechanism. Assmann and Negre, in particular, are at pains to demonstrate a much more nuanced and dialectical relationship between conditioning and consciousness, and hence the possibility of breaking out of the vicious circle of simple legitimation and determinism.

The problem is deeper and more promising than such a unilateral and mechanistic view would seem to offer. Schuurman's article, especially, shows how a new consciousness of the historical situation functions as a hermeneutical key to the recovery of themes and echoes in the biblical message that had been concealed or bracketed. It is as if current historical consciousness and commitment could generate a new receptivity, stretch our capacity for the "hearing" of the word. But this rather subjective manner of expression is not adequate. As Croatto reminds us, the texts themselves do not present us with naked historical facts, but with rereadings of these facts from a point of departure in a particular situation—a situation consisting of the founding events of the faith and of the believing community. And such rereadings are no arbitrary superimposition upon the facts, for the texts have a "reserve of meaning," a certain virtuality that later situations enable one to discover and activate, but not change. A hermeneutics that respects not only the original historicity of the text but also the singularity of the reader's locus—hence a hermeneutics incorporating careful exegesis and historico-social analysis as well—is the only one that will permit access to this "reserve." In classic theological terms, it is the distinction between scripture and tradition. We can cast the old polemics aside, and hope to arrive at a new understanding of both channels of revelation. For if as Christians we believe in the power of the Holy Spirit, and in the historical, dynamic presence of Christ, then the present historical condition is not a "profane" datum, introduced arbitrarily into the interpretation, but an opportunity, a call from the very God who is present in the event testified to in the text. This is the nature of the rereading, within the Bible itself, of events such as creation or the exodus. The requirements and safeguards of this hermeneutics are of great importance for a nascent Latin American theology.

## TASKS REMAINING

The articles presented in this volume do not claim to be the last word in christology. Rather they are an invitation to reflection. They set tasks before us. In some cases these tasks have scarcely been begun. By way of conclusion I shall take the liberty of pointing to some that seem to me to be urgent and basic.

1. The study of "christological images" in the various forms of piety prevalent in Latin America offers a first, and very important, area of endeavor. By "christological images" here I mean not only the traits of the Latin American Christs (in their various local manifestations, including saints and virgins, or any personages to whom supernatural powers are ascribed and who assume a christologic character), but of the possible transformation of an alienating piety into a mobilizing one. (This observation is not to be confused with a search for short circuits, real or imaginary, consisting in the utilization of popular devotions for purposes of social transformation.)

In this connection, José Comblin has called attention to the profound element of "protest" (or "diffidence," or "rejection") with respect to the established order—sometimes even the ecclesiastical—present in certain popular religion, particularly in Afro-Brazilian messianisms. The theme is not a new one. Valcárcel has made a fine presentation of this dimension from the sculptures of the *"mestizo* Christs" of colonial Peru. Pedro Negre further explores this vein, in his attention to a certain "irony" in popular religious culture as well as in the Christ of the gospels himself. Assmann had already published on this theme, proposing an interpretation of the dynamic potential of popular religion, as an unleashing of the protest of the oppressed—which has been projected utopically in religious imagery—in order to reintegrate it into historical praxis.

What is the answer? It seems to me that the articles in this volume chart two complementary courses. First, the Christ of the gospels must be rescued—along with the prophetic tradition (see Ellacuría's article) and its mighty charge of humanizing potential—by means of a critical and topical rereading. This investigation will then provide an objective criterion whereby we can be on guard against a possible distortion—that of simple utilization. Secondly, this cannot be a mere exercise in intellectuality and erudition. In the last analysis it is active commitment itself, the historical praxis of the oppressed, which permits them to recover the Christ who transforms history, the liberator Christ who has been snatched from them. Or, to be more faithful to historical reality, it is in this living, vital response that the gospel Christ comes to meet and redeem humankind today in the concrete reality of our history.

2. Here we find ourselves confronted with a theological point of primary importance. Assmann has raised it acutely in his article. How does the power of Jesus Christ function? The theme cannot be swept aside. What is the historical correlate of the faith affirmation that Jesus Christ is Lord of history? If we cannot accept a magico-mystical, or merely subjective and individualist, projection of the power of Jesus and the action of the Holy Spirit, and because on the other hand we do dispose of certain instruments (imperfect, to be sure, but no less real for all that, and surely not something we can turn our backs on) for grasping the dynamics of historical existence, then how are we to understand the modus operandi of the power of Christ? Surely not by dehistoricizing it, snatching it out of the political conflicts, economic processes, and ideological confrontations of that history. Surely not by snatching it from the creation of culture. And surely not by rendering it an empty cipher, a form of *speaking about* this historical process.

3. These questions demand the reconsideration of certain classic aspects of christology. Lambert Schuurman, for example, sketches a new christological formulation that abandons the language and the ontological, essentialist categories of classic christology and restores a "functional and practico-political" language corresponding to the New Testament tradition. When Christ is inserted into this context, christological discourse takes its place within a "protological" frame of reference—that is, it stands in relationship with a

dynamic project of creation as the reaffirmation and reactivation of the mission conferred on us of transforming the world and of developing our own humanity. Naturally, this demands the radical restructuring of theological themes such as reconciliation, eschatology, and ecclesiology—categories traditionally incorporated into a static and ontological christology.

Perhaps this opens up the possibility of rereading even the dogmatic tradition of the church itself, and indeed Juan Luis Segundo has made a useful and meaningful beginning in various of his writings. Does not the problem of the "power of Christ" to which we have alluded raise the problem of the ancient disjunction between an eternal, impassible God, beyond all possibility of contact with history, and the historical media (saints, holy places, rites) which de facto acquire a "functional divinity," but a functional divinity divorced from the ethical and personal nature of that God? Have we not come up with a new Arianism? Have we not transported old dichotomies to a new, intrachristological plane? We seem to have both a Christ who is the Second Person of the Trinity but historically inoperative, and localized "Christs" from whom actions (magical, perhaps) are looked for in the natural, human world. Is this not precisely what is denied by the dogma of the Trinity, which affirms the "consubstantiality" of the historical Jesus (with all his content) with the Father? Do we not discern here the possibility of affirming—without division, without separation, and without confusion—the "consubstantiality" of the power of the risen Christ, and the historical mediation in which the practice of Christianity, and of humankind in general, has been expressed?

This much is certain: we are not concerned to search out a new path to an old, irrelevant speculation. Surely it is not via any recourse to a facile textual hermeneutics, or a reformulation of doctrines or concepts, that we shall come to "know" who Jesus Christ is today in Latin America. In the terminology of faith, we surely have to say that only *he himself* can reveal his presence: "I am who I am" (or perhaps better, "I am the one who will be there," or "I am the one who will be") is valid for christology too. And that self-manifestation occurs in the context of an active obedience, as highlighted in the Johannine writings of the New Testament. The reflection we offer here, in partial, fragmented form, is possible only because certain Christians, among many others surely, have set out in search of a new land—and have discovered Jesus Christ walking before them and beside them.

# NOTE

1. Saúl Trinidad, "Christology, *Conquista*, Colonization," below, p. 60. His reference is to Hugo Assmann, "The Actuation of the Power of Christ in History," below, p. 136.

# PART ONE

*The Christs of Latin America*

*Chapter 1*

# IMAGES OF JESUS IN BRAZILIAN LIBERAL CHRISTIANITY

## *Leonardo Boff*

### WHAT IS "LIBERAL CHRISTIANITY" IN BRAZIL?

When I speak of "liberal Christianity" in Brazil, I am not using the expression in the meaning it acquired in the Europe of the nineteenth century—a Christianity liberated from revelation and from the organs of the interpretation of that revelation, and linked with rationalism and the notion of progress.[1] I am using it instead in a positive and broad sense as denoting a certain form of living the Christian faith in a maturity of consciousness, in frank and open dialogue with the realities of the world, with a view to a new incorporation of Christianity in a new society. Liberal Christianity, in contrast with a Christianity still bound to the old Brazilian regime, takes a critical stance in politics and economics and in the intraecclesiastical area, with regard to a rigidly dogmatic understanding of the faith.

Brazilian liberal theology has not been submitted to a thematic elaboration, yet its history goes back to the origins of our national independence. In his study entitled "El Clero y la independencia brasileña," José Honorio Rodrihgues cites the celebrated fact that "the Brazilian clergy has always been the first to promote liberal principles."[2] In Brazil, great causes have always had religious support—yesterday for political independence, today for economic independence. That is, this has been true of the lower clergy. It cannot be verified of the hierarchy, which has always had a tendency to take sides with those in power. Heirs of an Iberian, colonializing Christianity, which in turn had inherited the notion of mission as a crusade against enemies of the faith, be they Muslim infidel or Amerindian pagan, the hierarchy was

9

ever on the side of social order and discipline. Between the years 1500 and 1800 this phenomenon created among us the mentality of a "battle Christianity"—Tridentine, apologetic, and deeply conservative, both in politics and in religion itself.[3] Hence it is scarcely strange that liberators and liberals would be anticlericals, even when they were Christians. Nor need it be cause for astonishment that priests and friars were Masons, or that it was the ancient and venerable Monastery of Saint Anthony of Rio de Janeiro that spawned the liberal conspiracy against the Empire that paved the way for the Republic.

Vatican Council II and the Second General Conference of Latin American Bishops in Medellín in 1968 pointed the Catholic Church in a very different direction. They opened the way to the experience of a liberal, revolutionary Christianity, based this time on a new consensus between the base of the pyramid and its peak. In Brazil the liberal ideas of Vatican Council II on politics, conscience, the non-Christian religions, and the legitimate autonomy of terrestrial realities, were promoted by the intellectuals associated with the Centro Dom Vital. They were inspired by the French Catholic philosopher Jacques Maritain and his "integral humanism." They published a review, *Ordem*, to give voice to their new thinking. Thus what we call liberal Christianity in Brazil is characterized in the first instance by a break with a concept of Christianity as welded to the apologetical horizon of the Council of Trent and reassumed in a neo-scholasticism that articulates the faith in essentialist, static, Aristotelian-Thomistic categories—that is, within coordinates of a natural philosophy that is abstract rather than scientific or historical.

Liberal Christianity confesses the same faith, but prefers existential categories of spirit and freedom, of history and the human adventure, and explores these themes in a frank, if not always totally competent, dialogue with the human sciences. Its principal theological interlocutors are sociology and social pedagogy. Below we shall explore in more detail the new theological horizons within which the theology of liberal Christianity lives and moves.

This first break occasioned a second: an exodus from the bonds of social status—bonds with the power-support of the established order that had held the church in its grip. It was the "passover" of the church, its transition to being the church of the poor.[4] The church's new understanding of the world was seeking a new understanding of itself, a new identity, a new place from which to makes its proclamation. Now it continued to speak to all men and women, as its mission demanded, but did so from a point of departure in an ethic of its new identity—that is, from an ethic of the poor and the oppressed. This was the occasion of dissension within the church itself. Within one and the same community there now coexisted two antagonistic orientations. One element sought to perpetuate the old commitment of the church. The other, in the name of the gospel, sought a new identity, no longer to take sides with the ones in power but to walk side by side with those deprived of this power and subjected to its machinations.

So-called liberal Christianity lives in a state of crisis today because of this double break with the past. And because it lives in a state of crisis, it is very difficult to say much about it, at least much that is concrete or well defined. It is still in a process of gestation. It is still in the process of creating a new consensus.

## A THEOLOGY MORE SPOKEN AND LIVED
## THAN WRITTEN OR SYSTEMATIZED

The greatest problem, for purposes of this article, is in the lack of significant written works upon which to base a critical judgment of liberal Christianity—upon which to evaluate its reality and stance. As a result, the image of Christ issuing from the experience and articulation of this Christianity, on various faith levels, must necessarily remain somewhat problematic.

Speaking generally, theology in Brazil is not so much written, or reflectively thematized, as it is spoken and implicit. For this reason our reflections here will be based largely on the *praxis* of theology as we discover it in our theological activities, in talks, courses, meetings, and contacts with the living thought of theologians, priests, and bishops in this immense country of ours. And even so we cannot be certain that our judgments will correspond to the whole magnitude and extent of the reality. Rather we shall say that they reflect the stance of a certain thought, committed to a cause, and considering itself to be an articulation of Brazilian liberal Christianity. There are, however, certain christological texts that do have relevancy, among the writings of theologians in Brazil (although their authors are not always Brazilians), and these will serve as our point of reference. Still we must keep in mind what we have stated, that these texts do not represent the whole breadth of the reality we call "liberal Christianity," nor of the theological reflection being carried on within it.

## BASIC THESES OF LIBERAL CHRISTIANITY

In order to speak of the images of Christ in the liberal Christianity of Brazil, one must first draw the basic coordinates of Brazilian liberal theology. These coordinates, in the form of three theses, will throw light on the new Brazilian christology and on the images of Christ that may emanate therefrom.

### Thesis 1: Revelation Is Present in History Today

One of the richest theses of modern liberal theology has to do with the concept of revelation—the key to any and every Christian theology. Whereas classic theology affirms an archeological concept of a revelation occurring in the past and closing with the death of the last apostle, liberal theology emphasizes the ongoing character of the fact of revelation. Thus, as the whole of history is the history at once of salvation and perdition, so also it is the revelation at once of God and of the human being. God is the living, self-revealing God, who positively wills the salvation of all humanity. Faith is the acceptance of the divine advent and parousia in history. In history, God comes to meet us through signals, the signs of the times, which we are meant to detect and interpret as God's revelation.[5]

The sacred scriptures of the Old and New Testaments have to be situated within the vaster horizon of God's permanent, or ongoing, revelation. In themselves these scriptures are but testimonials to God's revelation. In themselves they do not constitute revelation. They constitute the human response to the divine proposal—which, being divine, is ever beyond the human word, and always retains its transcendent character. And yet the divine word is indeed incarnate in this human word, even as this latter is historically conditioned. In it, God's self-donation and self-revelation are found. But God withdraws in it, and hides, as well. The task of faith does not reside primarily and basically in interpreting the scriptures, but in interpreting life, in which revelation is given. This is what the scriptures themselves did. When we read the scriptures we are reading human life as the sacred authors saw it through the lens of faith.

Now, in which realities, in which facts and happenings, does God principally speak to us today? God speaks to us in and through everything, of course. But there are particularly critical and profound situations in which God's design is detectable more clearly and with less static. In order to identify the realities that are significant from the viewpoint of salvation, liberal theology places special emphasis on the great social marginalization of the working masses, with the corresponding systematic and structural basis of injustice, class privilege, retention of power, and accumulation of goods and money in the hands of a few. This focus enables liberal theology to come to grips with, and publicize, the aspirations of the masses for liberation as expressed in their demand for equality, freedom, and participation. This theology also denounces the system of political, cultural, economic, and religious dependency that constitutes the basis of oppression. Thus liberal theology takes account not only of the salvation that is present in history—present both as an accomplished fact and as a promise—but also of the reality of evil—as historically structured and as the source of the continuing dialectic of repression.

Another important factor—important because it is revelatory of God's design—is a certain legitimacy of secularization, seen as the rightful autonomy of an earthly reality newly liberated from the tutelage of an ecclesiastical regime that blocked the free exercise of critical and constructive reason in the name of a "natural" and a "divine" order of both nature and society. But this liberation of the world to a worldliness that is good because creation is good has been manipulated by the lords of science and technology to keep foreign peoples, in vast regions of the world, under their domination. Here again we have both salvation history and perdition history. The general socialization and accelerating planetization of the world, despite all the mechanisms of repression and manipulation, seem to signal the path God desires for greater communication among all men and women, and for their greater participation in the human enterprise.

The thematization of like perspectives implies not only a dialogue with the human sciences—inasmuch as they too are concerned with the meaning of these phenomena—it also means doing real theology, as commentary upon, and interpretation of, the revelation event, however we are able to capture and articulate that event on the level of our language and our transforming praxis.

The normative character of revelation in the form in which it is borne witness to by the Old and New Testaments is understood in Brazilian liberal theology as a historical normativity. Our history, and the history of all the Christian churches, occurs within the historical horizon that *commences* in these testimonies, and they will always constitute the fonts of our past in the faith. But this faith lives today, within our present history, as well, and constitutes the unity obtaining among the differences of language and time.

## Thesis 2: Jesus Christ Is Something More than Dogmatic Concepts

Another important basic thesis of what is called liberal Christianity consists in its posture and comportment vis-à-vis the dogmatic tradition of the church. It neither denies nor extols it. As part of the lived past of the living church, this tradition is one manner—valid in itself—of coming to grips with the mystery of Christ.[6] But the unfathomable riches of Christ are not exhausted in ecclesiastical formulas, be they ever so venerable. And this holds not only for the councils of Chalcedon or Constantinople, but even for the various christologies that are part of the New Testament.

Jesus Christ knows a parousia in every generation. In other words, each generation must come face to face with the mystery of Jesus, and in the attempt to define Jesus it will define itself. Each generation will give him its new names of honor and glory and will thereby insert itself into the christological process that began at the time of the apostles. Who Jesus is, is not a question that receives an answer academically, in the conciliar *aula*. It is by following Jesus, by trying to live what he lived and experience what he experienced, by struggling for what he struggled for, and was rejected, tortured, and crucified for, that we begin to grasp his true and profound mystery. Only at the end of history, therefore, will we be given to know fully who and what he is. Until his definitive coming, it is given to us only to assist at his manifestation as Lord of history. This is revelation today.

## Thesis 3: The Church Exercises a Historico-Salvific Function for the World

A third basic thesis of so-called liberal Christianity is formulated in its understanding of the church. The specific and proper role of the church does not consist in transmitting revelation and salvation to the world. These are always available to human beings, in history. The function of the church consists in bearing testimony to, and being a sign of, the salvation that is already present in the world. Hence what is decisive for the church is not how many human beings it can gather by means of its clerical organization. In order to discharge its historico-salvific function, a handful of human beings is enough, a *pusillus grex* (Luke 12:32) conscious of its mission, and living, as a sign, the new life that is brought to this particular manner of eschatological plenitude by Jesus Christ. However, it is not sufficient for the church to understand itself as sign and sacrament of present salvation.[7] Its consciousness and its conscience impel it to act in the world in specific ways.

The church must be the locus of freedom, of community, and of the kind of encounter that reconciles differences. The church must exercise a critical function with regard to the structures of evil inside and outside the church itself. Its prophetic mission is inevasible, for it springs from the burden of conscience. The conscience of the church must lead it to take its stand at the side of those with whom Jesus stood—the marginalized, those without voice and without opportunity. The church ought to be the advocate of their rights and their scorned dignity. Rather than busying itself about its own preservation, with the rights of the bishops vis-à-vis the pope, with papal infallibility, with the role of the priest in a secularized society, the church should dedicate itself to the basic issues of human dignity, work, peace, class discrimination, overdeveloped versus underdeveloped peoples, and so on. This is what the church exists for. This is what its historico-salvific function consists in.

These few reflections do not pretend in any way to define the total horizon in which liberal Christianity in Brazil moves and searches. Nevertheless they seem to me to constitute the general points of reference for the various currents of thought and practice. They are standards for christology, hence also for the image of Christ that they themselves suggest. For indeed there are various images of Christ, according to the particular christological orientation along which one's reflection is moving. Let us now search out their principal perspectives.

## THE IMAGE OF CHRIST IN A RENEWED CLASSICAL THEOLOGY

Theology, in recent years, especially since the war in Europe, has considerably deepened its study of the true humanity of Jesus Christ. A particularly helpful contribution was made by exegetical studies carried out by means of the techniques of "form criticism," which reshaped our view of the synoptic texts and also, just as decisively, research into the Council of Chalcedon, its antecedents, and its consequences. One fruit of this research was a work of fundamental importance for understanding contemporary Catholic christology, *Das Konzil von Chalkedon: Geschichte und Gegenwart* ["the Council of Chalcedon: past and present"].[8] As the second part of the title suggests, the aim of the book is not merely to reconstruct the framework of the past, in which is dogmatically asserted the unity of the one Jesus Christ subsisting in two natures, in the unity of the divine person of the Word, but to translate into our language today what was expressed in those classic metaphysical categories of nature and person. This work, and the studies that it occasioned, had great repercussions in Brazil. Marcelo Azevedo, S.J., president of the Brazilian Conference of Religious, published an important study in *Revista Eclesiástica Brasileira* on the fundamentals of christology. From a most incisive and perceptive analysis of the texts of Chalcedon (451) and Constantinople II (553), the author concludes:

> The work and mystery of Jesus Christ is before all else the redemption and sanctification of the human being, by that human being who, being Son of God, made himself "son of man." A theology that bore no fruit in the area of human salvation would be frustrated in its most basic sense and meaning.[9]

This attention to the true humanity of Christ had its repercussions especially in reflection upon the human consciousness of Jesus. Scholastic theology maintained that by reason of the hypostatic union Jesus was in continuous possession of the beatific vision, or the immediate presence of God. He was endowed, it was asserted, with a "natural" wisdom—that is, the property of the divine nature in which the Second Person of the Trinity subsists—in virtue of which he knew past, present, and future. However much he may have been a pilgrim, he was always "in his father's house." If this had been true, how could we affirm that Jesus was a human being like us except for sin? How could he have shared our temptations (Heb. 4:15)?

In his study of the problem Alberto Antoniazzi comes to the conclusion that Jesus did not possess the beatific vision.[10] Of course, this is not to say that Jesus was unconscious of being the Son of God or was unaware of his divine mission. Jesus' humanity was conscious of being the humanity of the Word, says Antoniazzi.[11] But this is only one point, one focus; it is not a detailed and all-inclusive vision, a knowledge of everything.

Jesus' consciousness of being the humanity of the Word confers upon him an ultimate confidence and certitude, but it does not reveal to him the details of his path and options:

> Thus Jesus appears as someone who discovers his mission and makes his options not by virtue of a plan formed by God from all eternity, but through meditation, during nights passed in prayer, upon the mission of the Son and the dispositions and attitudes of the human beings among whom he must work.[12]

Now it is possible to understand how Jesus could have had temptations:

[Temptations demand] a certain margin for illusion, for being deceived
by the demon. In any case, we have to think that Jesus had the capabil-
ity of choosing among various alternatives.[13]

This understanding of Jesus' consciousness, an awareness sunken in the half-
light and groping of any human being's earthly consciousness, permits us to
grasp the problem of the crisis in Galilee. The enthusiasm surrounding Jesus'
initial preaching was followed by his withdrawal in the face of the crowd's
rejection of him and of his calls to conversion. Everything seems to indicate
that Jesus failed to foresee his death on the cross—that he did not conceive of
it as a predetermined, fixed reality—but that his option for death arose out of
his love, from a desire to give his life for sinners.[14]

Along these same lines of concentration on the humanity of Jesus Christ,
Mateus Rocha's book, *Tu és esse homem,*[15] constitutes one of the earliest
Brazilian efforts in christology. In a still rather traditional vein, rich in the
influence of Bonhoeffer's Christ-for-others and Teilhard's cosmic Christ, is
the book by Bertrand de Margerie, *Cristo para o mundo.*[16] J. B. Libanio's
study, "Creio em Jesus Cristo," can be considered one of the best exposi-
tions of a christology of renewal that has abandoned the categories of nature
and person in their classic meaning and reinterprets them in a personalist
sense.[17] Jesus was a person who was basically free, a believer—someone who
could let himself be loved and could love in so radical a manner that he over-
came the barriers of friend and enemy. The unity of the transcendence of the
human being—as Jesus manifests this transcendence in his everlasting
searching, longing, and desiring, and as he stands open to the concrete historical nature of this transcendence as it transforms itself into action—this is
Jesus Christ, the God-Man.[18] In this humanity of his, which he lives so radically, is the Logos within creation. His humanity is not the instrument of
revelation of a Word outside it or above it; it is the Word itself as present in
history.[19]

Another line of reflection that had a notable influence on the Brazilian
understanding of the humanity of Jesus Christ was the thinking of Teilhard
de Chardin, who inspired so many Christian thinkers during the 1960s. For
contemporary thinking, the humanity of Jesus is incorporated into a trans-
formist *Weltanschauung*. It is the fruit of millennia of evolution. In virtue of
his incarnation, Christ's humanity has inherited the whole upward thrust of
the history of evolution. Through his resurrection, he has conferred upon this
humanity the dimensions of the cosmos and brought it by anticipation to its
definitive and eschatological state. Now, as the humanity of the cosmic
Christ, it is penetrated by everything, raised up by everything. Such a vision
gives new meaning to work, to commitment in a secular world that is a Christic world as well, and to respect for the value of modern civilization—which
the church had exorcised and interpreted as the decline and fall of the me-
dieval Christian *Weltanschauung*. There is good material along these lines in
Urbano Zilles, "La cristologia em uma multividência evolucionista,"[20] Euse-

bio Martinazzo, *Teilhard de Chardin: Letturas criticas*,[21] J. Jerkovic, "O Evangelho do Cristo cósmico,"[22] and L. Boff, *O Evangelho do Cristo cósmico: A realidade de um mito e o mito de uma realidade.*"[23] In this book I make use of the structuralist method in an attempt to show how Christianity should not be understood mainly as a discourse upon reality, or as a revelation for the benefit of reality, but as a structure of reality itself, always manifested in history, exhaustively and eschatologically manifested in Jesus Christ, and still articulated today under many other titles, including some that are opposed to the church and opposed to Christ. Christianity is a reality of God's creation, a creation that reaches its maximal consciousness and explication in the community of the faithful gathered around Jesus Christ.

What is the image of this Jesus? It is that of a Jesus profoundly human, participating in the drama of the human condition, both at the historical level and at the level of an evolutionary worldview—a Jesus who was being prepared at the heart of humanity, and who in the future would assume all things upon himself, to redeem and relink all things to God.

## THE IMAGE OF CHRIST IN THE POLITICAL EXPERIENCE OF LIBERAL CHRISTIANS

With Vatican Council II, emphasis began to be laid on a dialogue with reality-in-conflict, especially social reality. A certain number of themes immediately connected with christology began to influence the attitude and praxis of the clergy and to occupy the focus of its reflection. Some of these themes, such as the exercise of critical reason, polemics, revolution, and solidarity with the oppressed, downtrodden, and humiliated, began to be accompanied by reference to the behavior and speech of Christ. This is particularly striking in the documents of groups of bishops and priests, as well as in not a few pronouncements of the Brazilian Bishops' Conference.[24]

A realistic awareness of the plight of the marginalized and of the repression exerted by the government, of the suspension of basic rights and freedoms, quickened a new image of Christ—of a Christ who, faced with the social and religious system of his time, was liberal, free, and liberating, was considered a subversive (Luke 23:2), and was treated as a rebel against the established order (Matt. 5:21 and passim). More than his words, it was Jesus' attitude of freedom vis-à-vis social and religious laws, traditions, and conventions—a freedom born of a deep experience of a Father of all goodness and love, the Father of the prodigal son, the lost sheep, and the lost coin—that provoked a conflict with the guardians of the status quo. And in that status quo he perished, accused of political and religious sedition.

In this vein the theological and exegetical works of Carlos Mesters, especially his *Palabra de Deus na história dos homens*[25] and articles in *Círculos Bíblicos* (nos. 17–24 and 29–32),[26] make their statements within a context of social and political considerations elevated to exegetical functions—parameters of interpretation of the gospel texts.

The meticulous studies of Martin Hengel, *Was Jesus a Revolutionist?*[27] Oscar Cullmann, *Jesus and the Revolutionaries of His Time,*[28] and Clodovis Boff, "Foi Jesus um revolucionário?"[29]—which stands up well to its European counterparts—critically demonstrate the sense in which we should understand Jesus as a revolutionary. Clodovis Boff writes:

> Jesus was not, historically, a militant in the strict political sense, understanding politics as the superstructure encasing everything else, invested with the exercise of power over the whole of society. He did not strive to do away with all authority, after the manner of an anarchist, or to inaugurate a new authority in a rough and brutal manner. Rather he accepted established authority critically—*juxta modum*, with reservations, only so far. On the other hand if we take the word "revolution" in its broader acceptation, as denoting any radical change or structural transformation, then we would have to say Jesus was revolutionary, and more than revolutionary, for the radicalism of his message and example can transform human beings and consequently their social structures—can translate itself into social action. In this sense we could say that Jesus was the greatest revolutionary in the history of civilization, for he was not only and simply a revolutionary, but also a powerful personality who could inspire and incite human beings to action—not excluding political action.[30]

Along definite political lines in the strict sense of the word are two books by Danilo Nunes, *A pascoa de sangue* and *Judas, traidor ou traido?* [31] Combining scholarly research with romantic imagination, Nunes understands Jesus exclusively in politico-economic categories, from a point of departure in the social conflict that his liberation message is conceived of as having provoked among the poor. Jesus attacks the acquisitiveness of the wealthy who grow continually wealthier, the hypocrisy of the Pharisees, and the impiety of the high priests, with an attitude and behavior that are clearly subversive, says Nunes. Jesus' expulsion of the merchants from the temple, the author goes on, occasioned a Zealot-type rebellion by the people:

> From the moment the Nazarene interfered with the major interests of the clerical elite and the big business of Jerusalem, he was irrevocably lost. To hurl the temple merchants into the streets was above all a denunciation of the whole mercantile class, via an attack on its main representatives and thereby on the aristocracy and upper-middle class—which, seized with panic, wondered how their future survival could now be guaranteed. Jesus had wounded mammon, the demon of gold and greed, the absolute lord of the economy—and so he will be condemned to death without right of appeal by the dominant class of the old city.[32]

Jesus' whole drama, then, begins with the passage about his expulsion of the merchants from the temple. In this view Judas appears not as traitor to Jesus, but as betrayed by Jesus, for he had hoped Jesus would usher in the kingdom without giving it a political cast. And so, as was customary in his day, Judas denounces him as a false messiah. Nunes explains:

> In Judas's eyes the Nazarene was not just a charlatan, running up and down Palestine enlisting recruits for an uprising, awakening hope in the lowly masses only to desert them and leave them to swallow their frustration. The unexpected, and useless, uprising he provoked in the Court of the Gentiles, which ended in a massacre, was well calculated to bring profound discredit upon the nationalist cause. And when shortly afterward he heard the abominable heresies of Jesus' threats on the temple, as he promised to destroy it and build another in its place in three days, it convinced him that the rabbi was mad, or at least a dangerous subversive.[33]

Nunes's theses contain nothing original, for they had all been presented before, by Robert Eisler,[34] S.G. Brandon,[35] and J. Carmichael.[36] His work is that of an interested layman who is capable of intelligent use of scholarly and theological literature.

Another approach emphasizes not so much the revolutionary aspect of Jesus' message, but principally its character as liberative with respect to oppressed consciousness—liberation of all that alienates the human being and the world. A text of the bishops and superiors of the northeast of Brazil, *I Heard the Cries of My People*, is a case in point:

> Christ taught us to live what he proclaimed. He preached the human community of brothers and sisters and the love that should inspire all social structures. And above all, he lived his message of liberation himself, drawing it to its ultimate consequences. The powerful ones of his people saw in his message, and in the real love with which he proclaimed it, a real threat to their economic, social, political, and religious interests—and they condemned him to death. But his Spirit, acting today as yesterday, gives history its impulse, and manifests him in the solidarity of those who struggle for freedom in an attitude of genuinely enlightened love for their oppressed sisters and brothers.[37]

The basic image of the social and political experience of committed liberal Christianity is that of a Christ who liberates the human person, in body, soul, and all secular dimensions as well. He is not only a liberator from sin, from the vitiated relationships between human beings and their Creator, but the liberator of the totality of the concrete world here and now.

## THE IMAGE OF JESUS IN CATHOLIC CRITICAL EXEGESIS
## IN BRAZIL

Catholic critical exegesis, in the footsteps of the Protestant pioneers, has definitively discarded an ingenuous approach to the gospels as biographical texts concerning Jesus and his message. These gospels constitute a collection of short, separate compositions, containing not only the words and deeds of the historical Jesus, but also explanations, reflections, and commentaries by the first Christians.

Studying the gospels printed in four parallel columns shows us beyond any doubt that the first Christians did not limit themselves to a simple repetition of what Jesus had said and taught, but that they interpreted and explicated it as new situations and new deeds arose in their own lives.

As each composition was subjected to its definitive redaction, as a book without any immediate historical connection with the others, it acquired a general framework and a particular tone and approach that is now to be ascribed to the final redactor or evangelist. The entire process—Jesus' words and deeds, the first Christians' reflection on them, and the evangelist's final redaction—to a certain extent forms a partition separating us from the pure, living historical reality of Jesus of Nazareth. We are no longer in a position to reconstruct a biography of Jesus, or make the connections between the various historical events. On the other hand, the figure and personage of Jesus emerging from the general context and sense of the accounts can be considered historically reliable.[38]

But this understanding of the gospels obliges scholars to make distinctions that will understandably appear arbitrary and rationalistic to anyone not acquainted with this critical method. The scholar will have to say: this statement was actually made by Jesus, this other one is very probably by the community, this third one is the result of the theological reflection of the evangelist. But often enough recourse to a comprehensive view of the several gospels, lining them up side by side, will suffice to reveal these differences and the reason for this procedure.

A book that makes use of this method to draw conclusions for the reconstruction of a new figure of Jesus is my *Jesus Christ Liberator,*[39] and we shall see its basic theses below. Another work that uses all this, and describes the image of Jesus emerging from it, is that of José Comblin, *Jesus of Nazareth: Meditations on His Humanity.* In this little book, remarkable for its simplicity and immediacy, Comblin says:

In this book we intend to meditate on the human—simply human—life of Jesus Christ . . . this Jesus of Nazareth just as his disciples knew him and understood him—or did not understand him—when they walked with him in the rough valleys of Galilee, roaming the villages of Israel, when they did not yet know him as Lord and Son of God.[40]

The author is determined to concentrate on the true and complete humanity of Jesus. And there is an important theological reason for this option:

> The humanity of Jesus Christ must never be considered a garb which God put on to make himself visible. It is a truly human life, whose human significance constitutes the key to knowing the true God.[41]

This humanity of Jesus, says Comblin, can be summed up in two basic concerns: his message of liberation and his message of a community of brothers and sisters.

### Jesus and His Message of Liberation

Jesus appears as a free person among free persons who are ruled by enslaved leaders. "He died because he challenged the prudence and wisdom of the powerful, who felt threatened by his liberty."[42] Jesus' liberation activity did not have the political aim of the expulsion of the Romans, nor did it even aim explicitly at the social virtues of justice and the like. The people itself would take care of this. But the people, taught freedom by the prophets, had become the slaves of fear and of the false religious submission in which it was kept by the scribes and Pharisees. Christ's struggle was against the religion of appearances, the religion of legalism and mediocrity.

### Jesus and the Message of a Community of Sisters and Brothers

Jesus' message of a community of brothers and sisters is extended to all. It is universal. It springs not from any theoretical reflection upon the universal fatherhood of God, but from a service of self-giving to all. He receives everyone, without hurrying, without clichés, and personally. The abundance of their sufferings moves him to compassion. He appears as a saint working cures, minus the motive of self-promotion. He receives sinners. He receives just the ones for whom Jews by their upbringing felt a repugnance, such as the sick, tax collectors, foreigners, minors, and women. The novelty introduced by Jesus was to have established a rapprochement between the first commandment and the second. A single precept of loving all as sisters and brothers liberates a human being from all laws, from evil—from slavery in all its forms.[43]

### Jesus Is Not a "Religious Person"

The specific character of Jesus' relationship with God is demonstrated in these two concrete concerns of his. "The gospels do not show us a 'religious' Jesus, but a person free of rites, formulas, and marked hours."[44] Jesus' God is called Father. This Father is alive and present and is served in our service to his children, our brothers and sisters:

Jesus revealed an unknown God: a God who is not interested in cult, but in a human existence dedicated to the service of men and women.[45]

## Jesus, Preacher of Hope

With his preaching, Jesus assumes the totality of his people's remarkable hope. Indeed, he broadens it. The expression "kingdom of God" translates all hope of liberation, hope even in the midst of sufferings and temptations.

## Jesus, Trusting God and
## Not Concerned about the Future

Basically, says Comblin, Jesus knew his mission would be very brief and simple: sow the seed and die. But he was not concerned about the future. He was not concerned about the church, which would come after him. Nor do we know that he foresaw his own resurrection. Perhaps, Comblin says, he foresaw it vaguely.[46] He did foresee a presence of his in the midst of his own, but he did not specify what form it would take:

> In what he said about the church, it is clear that Jesus did not foresee the church as it is today. He could not even conceive of what the church was to become at the end of the first century. All he said about the mission to the nations, he entrusted to his disciples.[47]
> Never was there a founder so liberal to his successors as Jesus was. He entrusted to them all the organizing. He left only one very clear principle: that the organization would always be subordinate to love and to humility.[48]

Catholic public opinion was not slow to reject Comblin's picture of Jesus. Nevertheless it is enticing. It questions fundamental points of Catholic praxis: the emphasis on worship, on organization, on membership in an ecclesiastical community, on obedience, on submission, on prayer, and so on. Comblin's Jesus rejects a "religious" interpretation of Christianity and opens the way to a concretely humanitarian one. Not that it is to be a simple philanthropy. It is to be humanitarian, but with reference to the Father. It will not, however, transform this reference into a theological thesis. Instead, it will lead to a new, liberating behavior for men and women and their aspirations.

Well within the line of Comblin's thought, but with more hermeneutical than exegetico-critical concern, are the christological works of Carlos Mesters. Mesters knows the modern problems, as he shows us in his study, "Origem dos quatro evangelhos: do 'Evangelho' aos quatros 'evangelhos.' "[49] But his real concern is pastoral: How can we translate for our times, especially for those who hunger for freedom, humanity, and justice, the profound meaning that the primitive church discovered in Jesus and testified to in the four gospels?

Addressing this concern, Mesters shows his skill in existential hermeneutics. He interprets the novelty of the Sermon on the Mount as a glimpse offered to us of God's intentions for the future. He shows the divine meaning in the human content of the parables. He understands the miracles as a free sample of the future awaiting us. The meaning of life's crises, Mesters says, is illustrated in Jesus' transfiguration. His resurrection gives birth to our radical hope.[50] Mester's essay on the liberation that Jesus brought to the people of his time is of an exceptional theological and pastoral quality, within a perspective of a theology of freedom.[51]

Oppression weighed heavy on Jesus' contemporaries, says Mesters. Searching for security, they had enslaved themselves to laws and now had begun to enslave everyone else. All lived under an unbearable burden, theologically defended by the theologians of that day and age. Jesus breaks free. He breaks free of the divisions created by selfishness and the human need for security. He breaks free of the observance of the Sabbath, fasts, alms, fixed prayers, and temple worship. He breaks free of a distinction between neighbor and nonneighbor, between the legally clean and unclean, between the saint and the sinner. Jesus' radical criticism on these points led to his death. But he created a new state of affairs, says Mesters. He cherishes human beings, he allows them to grow, he defends them against criticism by those who maintain a situation of oppression. Law exists for the human being, not the human being for law. The objective of the law is to open the human being to God and to neighbor. Faith in humankind is the first step toward liberation:

> The freedom that Christ himself bears, and offers to others (Gal. 5:1), as a real possibility, to be gained by earnest struggle, cannot be manipulated or monopolized by any group. Christ supports no particular historical liberation movement rather than any other. No one, not even the church, can pretend to be absolute master and sole defender of the values singled out by Christ. Christ does not take his position at the side of human liberation projects in order to invest them with his authority; he takes his position at the side of men and women, encouraging them to project into the future, to go in search of freedom, to become conscious of the oppression they live under—in order to shake it off, take up their lives in their own hands, and be themselves.[52]

Mesters's exposition of these viewpoints and approaches in his collection *Círculos Bíblicos*, comprising more than forty booklets, is, in my judgment, the best thing to come out of Brazilian pastoral theology in all these last decades. Without extrapolating beyond the horizon of faith, and without borrowing themes from other ideologies, Mesters succeeds in molding a language and a system of themes that lead readers to heighten the consciousness of their dignity before their fellow human beings and before God. These booklets are of inestimable value for education and for conscientization. In them you learn not only religion, you learn to think about life—to criticize it, to improve it without rancor, and to revolutionize it without violence to others.

## THE IMAGE OF CHRIST FROM THE PERSPECTIVE OF A HERMENEUTICS OF THE HUMAN

I have myself made a presentation in the area of christology in Brazil in my book *Jesus Cristo Libertador* (English edition, *Jesus Christ Liberator),*[53] which has occasioned discussion in theological circles as well as in the media, and which has now been translated into several other languages, including Spanish, Italian, French, German, and Japanese. My basic concern is to combine a number of different problems within a single systematic view of the whole: the modern exegetical and critical problem of the gospels, the dogmatic problem of traditional language, the hermeneutical problem, and the problem of basic anthropology. All this is to be placed within the broader horizon of the "human"—understanding "human" not in the categorical sense but in the transcendental sense, and thereby with a continuous explicit reference to mystery and the Absolute.

Jesus of Nazareth is, on a first level, an articulation of this reality of the human. The New Testament testifies to the history—and to the understanding of this history—of the mystery that is thematized in Jesus Christ. Mere exegesis is not enough at this level, however critical it may be. What is it that is proposed for our examination and challenge, what is laid open to question, in Jesus Christ? What fundamental structures, and what realities within these structures, appear in the Christ event?

### *Only God Could Be So Human*

My book is an effort to explain and defend my conviction that the divinity of Jesus is not to be sought outside his humanity. It was precisely within this humanity that God's self-revelation was made manifest; or better, it was this humanity of Jesus that was God *praesens*. My attention, then, is concentrated upon this humanity-that-is-divinity. The incarnation therefore is not a confirmation of what we knew already. It communicates something new even for God, and something that human beings did not know. Now human beings can live the event of the divine joyousness, by anticipation, inasmuch as it has become human in Jesus.

This means that Jesus' message does not fall from heaven disconnected from its human roots. On the contrary, it shoots up from the furthest depths of the human and bears that human element to its definitive, victorious, final form.

Thus Jesus' basic message, the kingdom of God, takes on, via a utopian vision, the first and most basic human yearning: the yearning for the reconciliation of all things with their ultimate Meaning and Truth, the yearning for God's definitive victory over the self-estrangements that fill history. Jesus takes up this utopia at the heart of humanity and promises its perfect and exhaustive accomplishment. It is not escape from the world, but the ultimate meaning of the world, that is the object of Jesus' preaching. " 'The time has come,' he said, 'and the kingdom of God is close at hand. Repent, and believe the good news' " (Mark 1:15). He inaugurates the reality of the kingdom by means of liberating deeds and a new solidarity among all human beings, particularly with the most dispossessed. He demonstrates the reality of the new person. He assumes the role of *the* person of the kingdom, and thereby all his activity takes on the character of crisis—judgment—for the human situation.

Along these lines, the theme of liberation reechoes—understanding liberation not just in its political and social denotation, but in its total content as genuine exodus from the human condition and eruption into God. Jesus provoked an impasse in Judaism that led to his death.

Here the historical path taken by Jesus of Nazareth is being examined under the lamp of critical exegesis, as I subject the various layers of the gospels to scientific scrutiny. I view Jesus as someone deeply involved in the human scheme of things, someone who felt his way, who believed, and who hoped; who did not know, and did not seek to divine, the ultimate will of the Father in his regard along the road of life. Rather it was he who illuminated his own way, overcoming temptations and strengthening his resolution in a particular way of life. Like all the prophets, he preached to the end without retreating, without entering into any compromise with the situation he wished to alter so that the kingdom of God could come. He trusted in God to the end, the God with whom he lived in the most intimate relationship of Father and Son, and had confidence that, in spite of the pressure of an eschatological situation, that Father would not abandon him. In my judgment, Christ did not expect death. He did expect a great misfortune—a common belief in the apocalyptic milieus of his time. But he realized the will of the Father only on the cross. And he died abandoning himself to this Father of his, in spite of his consciousness of failure.

The resurrection is the *punctum stantis et cadentis*, the very touchstone, of the Christian faith and of the genuineness of Jesus Christ as well. Without it there would be no Christ—only the prophet of Nazareth, in the line of the great religious innovators in human history. With the resurrection, which is not the reanimation of a corpse but the entry of a person into the eschatological situation with all of that person's human reality, the human-and-utopian is suddenly real: there is the "implosion" and "explosion" of the kingdom. Jesus' preaching has come true. Human destiny is good and is guaranteed, for it has been manifested in the path trodden by Jesus Christ.

With the resurrection began the christological process properly so called. The Christian communities now initiated the process of interpreting this human life. A slow, step-by-step evolution culminated, in the nineties of the first century, in the affirmation of this man's divinity—this man Jesus dead and risen again. The messianic titles of honor, glory, and exaltation had no other purpose than to shed light on, to interpret, who this man was whom the apostles had known. God, Son of God, Son of Man, and so on, are adjectival for the substantive that is Jesus of Nazareth "dead" and risen again. Nor did the process end with the primitive Christian community. It still goes on today. The question mark that is Jesus stands open to the ages.

In faith, we find the answer to the mystery of the human. It is called "total transfiguration"—insertion into the very mystery of God.

At this level, the theological problem is now posed: How is divinity as attributed to a human being to be understood? It will not be enough to repeat the venerable formulas of the faith of the Council of Chalcedon: one and the same Jesus Christ, true God and true human being, with two distinct natures, without confusion and without division, subsisting in the single eternal Person of the Word. In our day the words "person" and "nature" have acquired other meanings, no longer under the control of the church and of theology. How can we preserve the essential content of the faith of the fathers in another horizon?

*Jesus Christ Liberator* makes an attempt to build a new understanding of the mystery of the incarnation from an analysis of what we can glimpse of the mystery of the human. The incarnation is the concretion of a possibility that exists within the human—always understanding the human as self-transcendence and self-communication in all directions. The human being is a being-in-itself, to be sure, but one related with the whole of reality. And in its self-communication, it becomes human being and person. Jesus was the human being who lived his being-for-others and for-the-Absolute-Other in such a way that he was able actually to identify with them. He emptied himself to the dregs of annihilation, an annihilation he freely assumed and accepted. This, I believe, is the way to understand the possibility of being totally penetrated and culminated by the Absolute Other. Jesus gives himself totally to God, to the point of being able to subsist in him; then is realized what we profess in faith as the incarnation of God or the divinization of a human being. Jesus actualized this possibility that is inscribed within the human. And it is thus that he is the eschatological person, the consummate Adam, and the presence of the kingdom within the old world.

### Christ and the Meaning of Human Life

The incarnation, then, actualizes a possibility within the human. And so a new horizon dawns on our understanding of the destiny of humankind and the world. The human being is called to an ineffable union with the mystery of God, the God of mystery. Other works of mine, *A reseurreição de Cristo nossa resurreição na morte* ["the resurrection of Christ and our resurrection in death"] and *Vida para além da morte*["life beyond death"],[54] attempt to unveil the riches of christology for the meaning of human life. In Christ human beings catch a glimpse of their future. Accordingly the divine joyousness can be lived even today.

Discussions concerning gospel texts, or concerning this theory or that one, lose their relevancy in the face of a much more essential theme—the structure of human life as revealed in the Christ event.

The church is at the service of this revelation of the fundamental fact of faith. It is not at the service of its own preservation, or its ensconcement in the structures of the old world.

The Christ dreamed of, portrayed, and loved in my christological studies is that of the Ecce Homo—so radically human that he could only be God. He is, and continues to be, an ongoing critical memory for every human being who has ever come face to face with him. Our attempts to define him define not him but ourselves. Indeed, he is hidden in the inmost recesses of each human being. Thus, each human being is made to the image and likeness of Christ. Human history transforms itself into the history of Christ, and of his mystery that fills all things and is reflected in millions, billions of different visages— and that manifests itself in definitive form in Jesus of Nazareth, who "pitched his tent among us" (John 1:14).

## UNITY IN DIFFERENCE

In this modest essay I have sought to offer a glimpse of several different facets of Christ. Some of them, perhaps, contradict others. Nevertheless, in faith, and in a correct hermeneutics, we may behold the manifestation of the single mystery of Christ—which, being mystery, and rich with the riches of God, is not exhausted in any one image, or lost in any heterodoxy. In every image Christ is at once whole and partial—for he continues his ongoing incarnation as he enters our schemes of comprehension in every generation. He will receive many a name, and will be worshiped and loved under many an image. Still he is the nameless one and the imageless one, for he is the very mystery of God-and-the-human, fused into a definitive union with each other. What is important is to be able to see and perceive this mystery in all the images and beyond all the images. Only then will Christ be everything and in everything (Col. 3:11).

# NOTES

1. See *Lexikon für Theologie und Kirche* 6(1961): 1007-8; G. Martina, *Il liberalismo cattolico ed il Sillabo* (Rome, 1959); E. Barbier, *Histoire du catholicisme libéral et du catholicisme social en France*, 5 vols. (Bordeaux, 1923); C. Montalembert, *Catholicisme et liberté* (Paris, 1970).

2. *REB (Revista Eclesiástica Brasileira)* 32 (1972):310.

3. See Eduardo Hornaert, "A formação do Cristianismo guerreiro no Brasil de 1500-1800," *REB* 33, Dec. 1973.

4. See Cándido Procopio Ferreira de Camargo, *Igreja e Desenvolvimento* (São Paulo: Editora Brasileira de Ciencias, 1971), pp. 23ff.; F. Turner, *Catholicism and*

*Political Development in Latin America* (Chapel Hill: University of North Carolina Press, 1971), pp. 139ff., 222ff., 232ff.

5. See *REB*, the whole of no. 125 (1972), which is a collection of the principal essays on the problem of revelation that have issued from a group of theologians in Petrópolis.

6. See *REB*, no. 121 (1971), which is devoted entirely to the christological problem.

7. On this whole problem, see my *Die Kirche als Sakrament im Horizont der Welterfahrung* (Paderborn: Bonifacius, 1972).

8. A. Grillmeirer and H. Bracht, 3 vols. (Würzburg: Echter, 1951–1954).

9. "As bases da Cristologia," *REB* 17 (1957):605.

10. In *Atualização* 23 (1971): 479–90.

11. Ibid., p. 484.

12. Ibid.

13. Ibid., p. 487.

14. Ibid., p. 489.

15. São Paulo, Duas Cidades, 1970.

16. São Paulo, Herder, 1972. Eng. trans., *Christ for the World* (Chicago: Franciscan Herald, 1973).

17. *Convergência* 5 (1972):9–20.

18. Ibid., p. 18.

19. Many original works and translations have appeared in Brazil along these lines—indicative of the interest taken in christology: e.g., Karl Adam, *The Christ of Faith* (*O Cristo da fé* [São Paulo: Herder, 1962]); idem, *Christ Our Brother* (*Cristo, nosso irmão* [Petrópolis: Vozes, 1939]); René Guerra and N. Zinty, *Queremos ver o Cristo* (Rio de Janeiro: Agir, 1963); Michel Quoist, *Christ Is Alive* (*Cristo está vivo* [São Paulo: Duas Cidades, 1971]); R.L. Bruckberger, *The History of Jesus* (*A história de Cristo* [São Paulo: Herder, 1969]); Paul Gauthier, *O Carpinteiro Jesus de Nazaré* (São Paulo: Ed. Loyola, 1972); W. Breuning, *Jesus Cristo o Salvador* (Loyola, 1972); A. Manaranche, *Creio em Jesus Cristo hoje* (Loyola, 1973); F.X. Durwell, *The Resurrection: A Biblical Study* (*A resurreição de Jesus, mistério de salvação* [São Paulo: Herder, 1969]); J. Doyon, *Christologie pour notre temps* (*Cristologia para o nosso tempo* [São Paulo: Paulinas, 1970]). In a less orthodox vein: Erich Fromm, *The Dogma of Christ* (*O dogma de Cristo* [Rio de Janeiro: Zahar, 1967]). Special mention should be made of the excellent book by H. Richard Niebuhr, *Christ and Culture* (*Cristo e a cultura* [Rio de Janeiro: Paz e Terra, 1967]).

20. *Vozes* (Petrópolis) 60 (1967):99–118.

21. Rome, Herder, 1965. It subsequently appeared in Portuguese: *Teilhard de Chardin, Ensaio de leitura crítica* (Petrópolis: Vozes, 1968).

22. *Vozes* 62 (1958):224–56, 306–20.

23. Petrópolis, Vozes, 1970.

24. By way of example, see "Aspirações de Sacerdotes de Volta Redonda, S. Paulo y Río de Janeiro," *SEDOC* 1 (1968):394–99; "Carta aos Bispos reunidos em Brasilia," *SEDOC* 3 (1970):479ff.

25. Petrópolis, Vozes, 1971, 2 vols.

26. Petrópolis, Vozes, 1973, pamphlets 1–40, and supplements 1–5.

27. *War Jesus Revolutionär?* (Stuttgart: Calwer, 1970), Eng. trans., *Was Jesus a Revolutionist?* (Philadelphia: Fortress, 1971).

28. New York, Harper & Row, 1970.

29. *REB* 31 (1971): 97–118.

30. Ibid., p. 118, and in the anthology *Signos de liberación* (Lima: CEP, 1973).

31. *Judas, traidor ou traído?* (Rio de Janeiro: Gráfica Record, 1968); *A pascoa de sangue* (Rio de Janeiro: Expressão e Cultura, 1971).

32. *Pascoa de sangue*, p. 142.

33. *Judas, traidor*, p. 247.

34. *Jesus, Basileus oder Basileusas?* (Heidelberg), 2 vols., 1929–30.

35. *Jesus and the Zealots* (New York: Scribner's, 1968).

36. *Leben und Tod des Jesus von Nazareth* (Frankfurt am Main: Fischer Bücherei, 1968), Eng. trans., *The Death of Jesus* (New York: Macmillan, 1963).

37. *SEDOC* 6 (1973):627.

38. For a good initiation into these problems, see A. Läpple, *A Mensagem dos Evangelhos hoje* (São Paulo: Paulinas, 1971). In the same critical line, a monumental christology has been published in Portuguese in the collection *Mysterium Salutis*, III:1–4 (Petrópolis: Vozes, 1973). See also R. Schnackenburg and F. J. Schierse, *Wer war Jesus von Nazareth? Christologia in der Krise* (Dusseldorf: Patmos, 1970), Port. trans., *Quem foi Jesus de Nazaré?* (Petrópolis: Vozes, 1973); Gunther Bornkamm, *Jesus von Nazareth* (Stuttgart: Kohlhammer, 1956), Eng. trans., *Jesus of Nazareth* (New York: Harper & Row, 1961).

39. *Jesus Cristo Libertador: Ensaio de cristologia crítica para o nosso tempo* (Petrópolis: Vozes, 1972), Eng. trans., *Jesus Christ Liberator: A Critical Christology for Our Time* (Maryknoll, N.Y.: Orbis, 1978).

40. *Jesus de Nazaré* (Petrópolis: Vozes, 1971), Eng. trans., *Jesus of Nazareth: Meditations on His Humanity* (Maryknoll, N.Y.: Orbis, 1976), p. 1.

41. Ibid., p. 7.

42. Ibid., p. 37.

43. Ibid., pp. 66–91.

44. Ibid., p. 99.

45. Ibid., p. 112.

46. Ibid., p. 165.

47. Ibid., p. 166.

48. Ibid.

49. In *Deus, onde estás?* (Belo Horizonte: Vega, 1972), pp. 123–32.

50. Ibid., pp. 133–208.

51. In *Palavra de Deus,* vol. 2, pp. 133–81.

52. Ibid., p. 180.

53. *Jesus Christ Liberator* (Maryknoll, N.Y.: Orbis, 1978).

54. *A Resurreição*, 3rd ed. (Petrópolis: Vozes, 1974); *Vida para além da morte,* 3rd ed. (Petrópolis: Vozes, 1974). See also my "O Jesus histórico e a Igreja," *Perspectiva Teológica* 5 (1973): 157–71.

*Chapter 2*

# IMAGES OF JESUS IN THE CULTURE OF THE BRAZILIAN PEOPLE

*João Dias de Araújo*

A study of Christ's image in the popular mind is of crucial importance for the work of theology in Brazil. The popular religious expressions of folklore, fiestas, music, literature, all the arts, demonstrate the extent of the "feedback" we have in the communication of the ideas, sentiments, and attitudes of the religion that has been sown in our land.

Current emphasis on the indigenization and contextualization of theological thinking is the result of a particular stance being taken in theological circles. Theologians have come to realize that it is impossible to study theology *and* ignore the cultural ambience in which theology develops and grows. If we are interpreters of the word of God and we speak to the Brazilian people, then we cannot ignore the religion and the culture of the masses. For eleven years, as professor of dogmatic theology in Recife, I have been attempting to establish a correlation between what we could call popular theology and biblical theology—a correlation between the Brazilian God and the God of the Bible, between the Brazilian Christ and the Christ of the Bible, between Brazilian religious anthropology and biblical anthropology, between Brazilian soteriology, ecclesiology, and eschatology, and biblical soteriology, ecclesiology, and eschatology.

## NEW METHODS

Methods have changed with respect to the study of the figure of Christ in Brazilian Protestantism. For nearly a century it was the polemical posture that dominated. Books, pamphlets, leaflets, sermons, hymns, Sunday school classes—all sought to ridicule the worship of the saints practiced by the Catholic majority. With the advent of the ecumenical movement, however, and the celebration of Vatican Council II, a new focus appeared. Now the emphasis is on how to make Christ central to the devotional life of the people. In the Catholic Church, not only the hierarchy, but the theologians and intellectuals as well, are concerned today about the place of Christ in popular piety and are making an effort to correct the distortions our catechesis has produced across the board. It would seem, then, that the moment has come for Catholics and Protestants to make common cause in presenting the figure of Christ to the people of Brazil. A practical demonstration that we are living in a new era is the cooperation of the Catholic hierarchy of Brazil and other Latin American countries with Protestants in the distribution of Bibles and New Testaments. The great Catholic movements of today are deeply committed to centering the spiritual life of the faithful on Christ.

## THE BIBLIOGRAPHICAL PROBLEM

The bibliography on this theme is vast, and it is scattered throughout a multiplicity of works not specifically concerned with the people's image of Christ. I have supplemented my personal experience with three groups of sources:

1. General works on Brazil and the characteristics of Brazilians.
2. Pamphlet series.
3. Books, booklets, hymnals, catechisms, and other works of a religious nature.

In this essay I shall attempt to describe some of the characteristics of the Brazilian Christ as they are observable not only in popular Catholic thought, but also in popular Protestantism, as well as in the spiritist and Afro-Brazilian cults.

One fact must be pointed out right from the start. There is a popular church in Brazil that is very different from the official church. As one celebrated Catholic theologian, who knows Brazilian Catholicism very well, put it, "Popular Catholicism has always existed in relative independence of the official church."

It is this *sertão,* "hinterland," Catholicism that Ariano Suassuna describes in his *Romance de la piedra del Reino* ["romance of the rock of the kingdom"]. One of the personages in the book, exasperated by the attempt of a priest to "correct" popular belief, remarks that it "shows that a purely Roman, orthodox, official Catholicism spells death for the Sacred Crown of the *Sertão"* (pp. 37–38).

There is also a popular Protestantism, represented especially by the Pentecostal movement, and a popular spiritism, found in the Amerindian and African *mestizo* cults.

We must also call attention to the fact that all authors, Brazilian and foreign, in the area of the psychology of the Brazilian people, focus on piety as one of that people's basic characteristics. Hence something remarkable about Brazilian religion: Brazil is the largest Catholic country in the world, the largest spiritist country in the world, the country with the largest number of Pentecostal sects in the world, and the Latin American country with the largest Protestant population. To boot, it is the country that has produced a great syncretistic religion—Umbanda, the fruit of the popular experience of four centuries of religious pluralism.

In the following pages I shall sketch five outstanding characteristics of the Brazilian Christ: (1) a dead Christ; (2) a distant Christ; (3) a powerless Christ; (4) a Christ who inspires no respect; (5) a disincarnate Christ.

To be sure, these five characteristics fail to exhaust so complex a theme in the religious archipelago that is our Brazil. They do not go beyond an effort merely to make a beginning in a study of the Brazilian Christ.

## A DEAD CHRIST

One of the distinctive characteristics of the Brazilian Christ is that he is usually represented as having died. The very widespread use of the crucifix has contributed heavily to this form of his representation. We recognize the profound spiritual riches of the crucifix, for it exalts Christ's death and his sufferings on the cross. But we cannot fail to note that in the mind of the people it has produced a deformation of its symbolic message. Crucifixes, whether they hang around the neck, on the walls of homes and schools, from bedsteads, or in shops and churches, have created in the mind of the people the image of a Christ who is dead, nailed to wood, rendered incapable of reacting, wasted by the forces of evil—defeated.

This message of the crucifix has been a great generator of the fatalism and conformism that are so deeply rooted among the people of Brazil today. Here is how a popular poet describes the dead Christ in his "Las siete espadas de los dolores de la Santa Virgen María" ["seven swords: the seven sorrows of the Blessed Virgin Mary"]:

> Her eyes fixed on her dead child Jesus,
> beneath the cross our Lady sat.
> Five thousand five the wounds so cruel
> in that poor body numbered she.
> Five thousand twelve were all the thorns
> she plucked from him; five thousand drops
> of blood, all dried now, draped him shroudlike.
> Those hands pierced through, those bones disjointed,
> those two fine feet, bare, spiked to a beam,
> his breast agape where the lance had gone,
> and both his eyes asleep in death.

Another important view of the dead Christ is seen in the celebration of Holy Week, which in old Brazil, especially in certain localities of the interior, could always count on a great attendance. The figure of Christ is carried in procession, supine, to the accompaniment of many a vivid expression of unutterable suffering. Museums of sacred art in Bahia and Recife have galleries reserved for the dead Christ. It is not hard to imagine, as we look on these representations, the impact they must have had on popular piety.

The stations of the cross on the walls of churches, the religious ceremonies of Holy Week, prints and paintings in religious art, which have always exalted Christ's death and sufferings above his victory in resurrection, inculcated in the minds of the most humble the idea that their Christianity was more one of Good Friday than of Easter Sunday, as John Mackay observed in one of his books on the Iberian Christ.

In terms of the religious majority, we can state that we have a Christianity in Brazil that places more emphasis on the passion, sufferings, and death of Christ than on his victory over death, his ascension, and his office of priest and intercessor—our advocate, the living Christ of the New Testament.

Besides the ethical overtones that this figure of the dead Christ can arouse, and has in fact aroused, in the minds of the people, there is a very particular eschatological aspect. Messianic movements have never centered on the person of Christ. Whenever it is a question of the "end of the world," it is the figure of Don Sebastian that appears. And the poet sings:

> The end of the world is here!
> What terrible turmoil I see—
> so I've gathered my net
> and packed my sack
> and wrapped me in my coat,
> for the long journey I take.

The name of Christ never appears in this poem on the end of the world by Manoel Tomás de Assis.

Due to this lack of emphasis on the resurrection and the ascension, the Christian doctrine of the second coming of Christ, the parousia, is practically unknown to popular piety. Brazilians are totally ignorant of the most basic tenet of the Christian church. One hears only of heaven, hell, and purgatory. In practice, it is Saint Peter who sends you to heaven and Satan who casts you into hell. And José Costa Leite tells us:

> . . . Hell
> is really an elegant city:
> Lucifer, its prefect, plants
> gardens, and builds grand squares,
> lays pavement,

and pipes for running water. . . .
Till the dawn of Pablo Alonso
will Lucifer dance and sing.

Another passage recounts Lucifer's visit to heaven. There he speaks with Saints Peter, Zulmira, Panta, Bernard, Richard, Francisco de la Peña, Thomas the Apostle, Juvenal, Moses, Jacinta, Augustine, and Francis of Assisi. The name of Christ is never mentioned.

## A DISTANT CHRIST

Another characteristic of the Brazilian Christ is that he is a distant Christ. By "distance" here I mean the spiritual distance symbolized in the physical distance of the Christ of the Andes, high up on the mountain peak. By "spiritual distance" I mean that the person of Christ does not occupy a central place in the spirituality of the majority of the people. He is not a close and intimate figure of devotional life. This fact derives from three historical factors:

1. The religion of the Brazilian Indians. In the view of a number of contemporary anthropologists, the Amerindians were animists—that is, they attributed souls to all the forces of nature, as well as to objects. This is said to be the root of an "Amazonian matriarchate." As Raimundo Morais has put it, there was "a Day Mother, a Night Mother, a Land Mother, a Water Mother, and so on and so on."

2. The religion of the Africans. The African cults were rich in divinities—the *orixás,* considered to be protectors and intermediaries with an inaccessible divinity.

3. Portuguese Catholicism. One of the predominant traits of Portuguese Catholicism is a devotion to saints and special patrons.

These three elements had a great influence in the process of the removal of Christ from popular piety. Each city and village has its patron or protector. Brazil has a patron. Each of the faithful has their own special saint. Thus the various Madonnas—Our Lady of Nazareth, of the Apparition, of the Immaculate Conception, and so forth, are the people's favorites. Other personages as well, not recognized as saints by the Catholic Church, have become objects of the people's devotion. Don Sebastian was worshiped as a god for many generations, right up to the twentieth century. Father Ciceró Román Batista still enjoys a place apart in popular devotion. Antonio Conselheiro was considered by the people to be the Holy Spirit. Today it is Friar Damian. All these outstanding persons, these leaders, are considered saints and even gods. Of Father Ciceró the poet says:

In the Garden of Paradise shall be
a day of feasts of light—

there my Patron will stand
with his eyes of blue,
all robed in white,
in Jesus' place.
"Juazeiro," he's called
by the pilgrims who come.

When it is Jesus who is chosen as the saint of anyone's devotion, his person appears altogether devoid of any real forcefulness—he is Good Jesus of the Grotto, Lord of a Happy Death, Good Jesus of Pirapora. Many of the more ignorant think Christ was born in Bahia, for they do not know where Judea is.

As I stated in the beginning, this phenomenon is of concern to the Catholic hierarchy not only in Brazil but throughout Latin America. In the working paper of the Second General Latin American Bishops' Conference, held in August 1968 in Medellín, we find an analysis of the religious situation in all the countries of Latin America. Part of the conclusion runs as follows:

A large number of baptized persons do not attain a conscious and mature faith . . . [and] go through life without being truly converted to the gospel, without a personal encounter and commitment with Jesus the Savior. A weak faith is incapable of enlightening new problems confronting adult men and women.[1]

Further on, among the recommendations for action to be taken, the document states:

As a result of changes in Latin America, we are realizing the urgency of a new type of pastoral action relevant to each situation.[2]

After this working document had been studied, one of the conclusions drawn was the following:

This evangelization of the baptized has one concrete objective: that of bringing them to a personal commitment to Christ, and a willing surrender in obedience to the faith.[3]

The concern is altogether justified. Christ is the great absent one, unknown to the people. Raimundo Morais says:

Amazon theogony, imbued with the Catholic hagiography transmitted by the Jesuits, then with the fetishism introduced by the *Afer,* the African, continues to distinguish itself by a predominance of goddesses, to the point where they are projected back into the Catholic religion itself.

The patron of the capital of Pará is Our Lady of Bethlehem—but she is assisted by Our Lady of Nazareth, who boasts of more miracles and a greater following. The patron of Manao is Our Lady of the Immaculate Conception. A random survey of the saints of the towns of Pará will yield a preponderance of female saints.

Thus Christ remains absent from the people's devotional life. He is replaced by other personages who are considered to possess the divine favors, and who thereby detract from the presence of Christ.

## A POWERLESS CHRIST

Due to the first two characteristics, the Brazilian Christ continues to be considered powerless to effect particular miracles or cures. This is abundantly evident from popular pamphlets. Before me as I write I have three, whose titles in English would be "The Girl Who Was Changed into a Cobra" (because she doubted the powers of Father Ciceró), "The Protestant Who Was Changed into a Black Vulture Because he Had Tried to Kill Friar Damian," and "The Encounter of the Christian Changed into a Beast of Burden with the Christian Changed into a Burro" (both because they had refused to believe in the powers of Father Ciceró). Great powers are attributed to charismatic figures or other sacred personages, but Christ appears as having little power of his own.

In moments of difficulty it is to the saints that requests are directed. In fact Christ needs help from the so-called divine forces, or powerful *orixás*. In the pamphlet about the girl who became a cobra we have an example of the notion that when Christ acts he needs at least thirty collaborators. It cannot be doubted that popular piety considers Christ as anything but mighty. Sometimes Satan is considered *O Salvagem,* the Savage. At times, belief in the power of the evil spirit has been so strong that Satan has played a role in human life nearly as important as that of God. A popular poet describes Satan's mighty powers by placing these words on his lips:

> Lord am I of propaganda,
> lies, deceits of every kind.
> Wielder of this perverse talent,
> every nation I've laid low.
> Power in religion, too,
> plenipotentiary, I!
> I am mightiest, it is I
> who give commands or do forbidding.
> Will you know, then, why my legions
> abound in every wretched land?
> I've given the reason. . . .

Again Christ is thrust aside as powerless. In Ariano Suassuna's *Auto de la Compadecida* ["decree of the Lady all-compassionate"] it is the Blessed Virgin Mary who presides at the spectacle of the Last Judgment.

## A CHRIST WHO INSPIRES NO RESPECT

It is true that this aspect of powerlessness can be conducive to a greater intimacy with Christ, but it has a negative aspect at the same time. For many, Christ does not deserve the same respect as other saints. In fact he deserved less respect than Satan. While Suassuna's *Auto de la Compadecida* was playing in Recife, the star, Aurora Duarte, made several statements to the press to the effect that she did not feel worthy to play the Blessed Virgin. The actor who played Christ, who is represented as black, had no such misgivings.

At the carnival dances in the town of Caruaru one year, as the hour of midnight approached the orchestra interrupted the carnival music with Roberto Carlos's song "Jesucristo, estoy aquí" ["I'm here, Jesus"]. Without missing a step, the dancers danced now to this music and lyrics—and insisted on hearing them over and over till sunrise, refusing carnival tunes the rest of the night. The incident made the Recife newspapers.

It has been observed that crucifixes, images of the Sacred Heart, and printed pictures of Christ are displayed not only in homes and businesses, but in bars, gaming houses, and bordellos. In some bordellos of the Northeast there is a crucifix attached to the head of the bed or the wall of the room.

Gilberto Freire informs us that, in old Brazil, elixirs purporting to cure syphilis were sold in houses of prostitution. The labels bore the likeness of the infant Jesus. "Holy cards," too, were available, bearing the image of the baby Jesus surrounded by cherubs and advertising the elixir as a cure for syphilis—adding that if Christ were alive today he would recommend it himself.

In central Brazil one hears the expression, "Go to Christ," with obscene connotations. There are also regions of Brazil where to "put on the airs of Christ" means to act like a fool.

In many bars and roadhouses of the Northeast, the figure of Christ on the cross appears on walls surrounded by the figures of nude women.

All this betokens a lack of respect.

## A DOCETIST OR DISINCARNATE CHRIST

In Protestant and spiritist milieus, as well as among Catholics, one observes a tendency to a certain docetism. Among the Protestants, emphasis on Christ's divinity has been so strong that it led to a deformation of his human nature. This is a docetist or disincarnate Christ.

In Catholicism, this disincarnation of Christ finds expression in the substitution of the saints for Christ as patrons in popular devotion. Christ is a wan, womanish figure, altogether estranged from daily life.

In the Umbanda and other Afro-Brazilian cults, the disincarnation of Christ finds substitution in the *orixás*. In some groups of Kardecist spiritists there is still the idea that Christ has neither body nor soul, for he is simply the manifestation of the a peri.

In popular Protestantism, as well as in the sects, due to the enormous influence of pietism, a marked dichotomy has been maintained between Christ's humanity and his divinity, with the emphasis on the latter. Other dichotomies arose as well: between the individual and the social, the material and the spiritual, the secular and the religious.

Incorporation in Christ, for a Protestant, takes place more at the individual level, in spirit, in the distinctively religious sphere, occasioning a moralistic attitude and an intraworldly asceticism with emphasis on the certainty of having been "saved"—of having a sure place in heaven.

In catechisms, hymns, books, and sermons, we ever meet the figure of Christ disincarnate—the figure of the "sweet Rabbi of Galilee," half human, half angelic—and not the Christ of flesh and blood whom we see in the gospels.

## NOTES

1. CELAM, *The Church in the Present-Day Transformation of Latin America in the Light of the Council,* 2 vols., ed. Louis Michael Colonnese (Washington, D.C.: USCC, Latin American Bureau, 1970), vol. 1, *Position Papers,* p. 160.

2. Ibid., p. 164.

3. Ibid., vol. 2, *Conclusions,* p. 142.

*Chapter 3*

# CHRIST IN LATIN AMERICAN PROTESTANT PREACHING

## *Saúl Trinidad and Juan Stam*

### CHRIST, THE POWER OF GOD FOR SALVATION

It would be unjust not to recognize that, in spite of its christological deficiencies, Protestant preaching has been "the power of God, saving all who have faith" (Rom. 1:16), even in its weakness and folly.[1] Christ's visage has been reflected in our broken mirrors and distorted portraits—a token of the grace and sovereignty of our Lord.

1. Generally speaking, Protestant preaching has offered the believer a real, personal Christ. One comes to know him as a friend and a force in one's life. Pentecostalists know how to speak very realistically of a Jesus of Nazareth who heals, who saves, and who bestows power. They often say, "We feel the Lord's presence," or, on the contrary, "Jesus is not here tonight."

2. Protestant preaching has proclaimed a Christ who forgives, who justifies from sin, and who removes burdens of conscience, guilt, and eternal punishment. He has been a vital factor in very real personal problems thousands of times. Often, however, this soteriology has wavered between cheap grace at one extreme and legalism at the other.

3. Protestant preaching has proclaimed, and generally lived, the reality of a Christ who is mighty enough to transform our lives, especially with regard to the vices—drink, adultery, tobacco, drugs. Our churches are peopled with trophies of the grace and power of Christ. But, to tell the truth, they are also peopled with paradoxes—alcoholics (not just recovered alcoholics) who are in the church but who live the life of the periodic drinker, or who solve their

39

problem only with the help of psychiatry or Alcoholics Anonymous; the inevitable sexual scandals, not only among the young, or new believers, but among elders and sometimes even missionaries; or on the other hand, marriages (who knows how many?) that barely "hold together" because their serious problems are never addressed. And then there are the faithful who have abandoned all their "vices"—only to turn into perfect, and insupportable, pharisees!

Of course, problems are inevitable in any human community. But at the same time they constitute an index, and a revealing criticism, of the gospel of the Christ we have been preaching—as well as an antidote for an over-simplified, unrealistic triumphalism.

4. It can also be said that for many persons in Latin America our proclamation of Christ has reawakened a sense of the meaning of existence and has fitted them out with a life purpose, offering them friendship instead of loneliness and affording them joy and gladness, especially in worship. For many of the very poor, the church has been a "refuge" from the misery and sorrow of daily living. But physicians, teachers, and other professional persons too, have found new goals in our proclamation of Christ, along with the means of serving God and neighbor. This is reality, and one can find it in every country and congregation of Latin America. These Christians are "living epistles," written by the living Christ.

## CHRISTOLOGICAL IMAGES IN LATIN AMERICA: DEFECTIVE MODELS

1. The first "christological image" we encounter in our critical analysis is the *Santa Claus Christ*. The renewal movement has vigorously denounced this deformation and has advocated replacing the traditional "gospel of Father Christmas" and cheap grace with the "gospel of the kingdom." But others see in this focus on demands and discipleship a denial of grace in favor of works. An international evangelist, expressly contradicting renewal thinking, once exclaimed: "Yes, the gospel is gift! That's it exactly! Praise the Lord! It is the gospel of the gifts, the gospel of God giving—and giving, and giving some more!" (quoted in Pereira, *Los efectos de la Cruzada Costa Rica '72* ["the effects of the 1972 Costa Rican Crusade "].[2]

A student commented:

Certainly very pretty, but it's only a half-truth. This is a "Father Christmas Christ," one who comes to give only because he's so rich. He has lots of capital. Christ becomes a commodity, and the highest bidder gets him. All we hear is, "Who wish to receive Christ as their personal Savior, and not have to go to hell? Who wish to be healed this evening? Let's see the hands." Those in need accept this gift of a witch-doctor Christ, and every time they see the minister it's "Reverend, I hurt here," or, "Reverend, please put your hand here and say a prayer." The church starts looking like Jesus the Witch Doctor's hut. Jesus, working cures? Sure he does, but cures aren't all there is—and they're certainly not supposed to be legal tender.

2. All this becomes more dramatic when Jesus is presented as if he were a *beggar Christ.* "Don't cause Christ to suffer any more . . . he's waiting for you with open arms . . . don't make him wait. Surrender your hearts to him!" This is a *Christ of convention*—that is, persons accept him if it suits them, if he offers them something they want. Otherwise he can just keep standing there, or go next door. One offers oneself to Christ in the terms of the marketplace, as when vendors hold up their wares and call to someone to please buy something, even as a favor.

3. The Santa Claus Christ is also presented as a *magic-potion Christ,* for solving all your problems, a *deus ex machina.* He comes to spread peace, love, and felicity, the automatic solution to every problem, as these extracts from a sermon exemplify:

> Christ seeks to enter into the human heart, says the evangelist. When Jesus enters a sinner there is direct contact with God. Jesus takes over that person's interior life, and he or she receives the supernatural power to conquer temptation. . . . God wants the sinner to be at peace, to have joy and gladness, love and happiness. . . . God provides for your needs. . . . Are you sick? Sick with sin, sick from nerves, sick from anything? Then know this, that God has prepared for you a perfect heaven, a place of peace, love, happiness, and justice.[3]

There is truth in all these statements. But this sort of preaching leaves christology mutilated. Jesus gives, yes, but he also makes demands. He demands discipleship—service, sacrifice, and obedience. Often enough the converts this preaching makes expect only to receive, receive, receive. Receive everything! Fewer responsibilities! But actually these are the querulous. They are very "delicate." When trials come, or when their superficial prayers fail to receive automatic answers, they opt out.

This Christ also appears in slogans such as "Christ is the answer"—or even, "Accept Christ and end your problems." But Jesus never offered a life free of problems. Quite the contrary! As Arrastía puts it, "He promised to keep us not *from* problems but *in the midst of* problems."

Arturo Hotton was asked, "Is Christ the answer to problems of Latin America?" He answered:

> No. Latin America has many problems, and to preach the Lord Jesus as the sole answer to them all is dishonest. Christ gives us new life, transforms us so we can carry his blessing to the world—but there are economic problems that call for economic solutions, political ugliness that

demands political methodologies, sociological problems that require methodologies for solving sociological problems. Christ redeems human beings—makes them a blessing at the right time and place. But it is dishonest to proclaim Jesus as the magic formula for all the problems of humankind.[4]

4. Another christological image frequently heard from Latin American pulpits is one we might call the *passport Christ*—Christ as a kind of air-mail lottery ticket. When the only preaching is "Accept Jesus as your Savior and you shall have entry to heaven," heaven appears as an escape from earth, an evasion of life. Heaven-centered preaching is an implicit contradiction of the Word who left heaven and took flesh in order to live on earth. Christ is only incidental to this kind of preaching in any case. It makes use of a *decontextualized Christ,* a heavenly Christ who is soon to come and "kidnap" his church. You meet this "heavenly," overspiritualized Christ in the clouds, not on earth or in history. He is foreign to every human reality—removed from the world of our needs. What a tremendous contrast this neo-Docetism is to the historical Christ, the Christ of the synoptics!

5. Nor is it unusual to hear in sermons, or gather from them, the message of an *asocial Christ,* a divisive Christ. The convert is required to withdraw from the world, and this means from all family, social, cultural, and political bonds. Disciples of the "asocial Christ" are dislocated, cut off from their cultural ambience, locked up in their individualism. They feel deprived of the possibility of having social relationships outside the church, for "whoever make themselves friends of the world become the enemies of God." The "divisive Christ," far from lending meaning to converts' human relationships, separates, decontextualizes, and estranges them.

This dualistic Christ traces a blind frontier, a kind of Maginot Line, between two worlds—the profane and the religious. This basically neo-Platonic dichotomy has its adherents in both public and private life. In theology it yields us the "dogmatic Christ," and in ethics the "legalistic Christ," or the Christ of prohibitions, of negative answers.

6. At times, especially more recently, our preaching has put extreme emphasis on the *cosmic Christ* alone, a Christ of faith and glory but deprived of any connection with the historical Jesus. This is both a tremendous truth and a tremendous lie. It is biblical and unbiblical at the same time. The cosmic Christ, the glorified Christ, *is* cosmic and glorified thanks to his historicity, his incarnation, his human nature as a real person of flesh and bone. It is thanks to his death and saving sacrifice that he has been elevated to the cosmic Christ. A Christ who has only to do with the spiritual—ecstasies, exorcisms, charisms, pardon, and so on—and little or nothing to do with the historical, concrete, existential human being, is a mutilated cosmic Christ.

7. Nor do we lack an image of the *Christ of Calvary* alone, the Protestant answer to the crucifix. Sermons become saturated with the Christ of the passion, of Calvary, and of death, a Christ failed and resigned, more inspiring of

compassion and pity than of celebration. At bottom he seems rather more like a "hero" who valiantly succumbs in battle and nothing more. No one disputes that the redemptive sacrifice is fundamental to the Christian faith. But a Jesus who is only a Jesus of Calvary is no longer Christ. It is his triumphant resurrection that gives meaning to his liberating passion.

This image of the "Christ of sufferings" could make it seem as if the Christian's lot were to suffer more than anyone else. Many have made this interpretation, to the point of thinking that God sends these sufferings as tests of Christian faith—or worse, that God demands, in the name of the humiliation of the *kenosis* of Christ, resignation and passivity in the face of injustice and outrage. Followers of this Christ actually come to enjoy their sufferings, as if Christ were a masochist.

Here again, what we are facing is precisely the lack of an integral view of Christ's incarnation. Christ was born and lived a fully human life before he expired on the cross. And after dying he rose, as Lord of all might and principality. But the Lord's resurrection and ascension to the right hand of the Father with power, glory, and empire are not very much preached. When the lordship of Christ is preached, there is a tendency to present it as an overspiritualized concept—cosmic but not historical, heavenly but not walking in the streets of Recife or Buenos Aires. The *Kyrios Christos*, even as a *Kyrios Kaiser,* has by no means served to dethrone the "lords" who dominate in Latin America.

8. The *guerrilla Christ* is another model that has appeared from time to time down through the centuries—as in the Crusades, or with Thomas Münzer—and has recently reappeared in numberless graffiti and slogans all around us. This image is a tremendously attractive one for some, just as it is blasphemous to others. But much as one can admire the total commitment, to the very death, of a "Che" Guevara, or even recognize that persons such as Camilo Torres or Nestor Paz Zamora sincerely based their guerrilla commitment on the teaching of Jesus, demonstrating a strange sort of "revolutionary saintliness," it is still naive to speak of a "guerrilla Christ"—even if he is pictured with a beard. He may have been subversive for the prevailing unjust order of his day, and he was often confused with the Zealots. But the fact remains that when the time came, he rejected this option. The picture of Christ in the scriptures is not that of a guerrilla.

9. For some the "guerrilla Christ" may be needed as a corrective for another image—a much more common one, but one just as false: the *middle-class Christ*. Colonialism carried to Latin America a Christ who is ever disposed to bless the status quo, a sweet, soft Christ who always goes the second mile, always turns the other cheek, and who soothes souls—but who never denounced injustice or led a demonstration or grabbed a whip to spill everything over in the temple. And at the same time he is a Christ whose generous gifts appeal to a consumer society, and who actually demands very little—no drinking, no smoking, tithing, going to church, saving souls—so much so that "refuge in the church" can be a form of escape from the more radical

demands of the "world." Perhaps this is why a union organizer in Costa Rica complained to a Protestant minister, "I notice every time one of our members converts to your church he breaks ranks with us."

## CONCLUSION

Evidently, a profound christological task lies before the Christian church. Instead of finding a single, definitive image of Christ, it ought to expect to find, and should explore more broadly, the many facets and viewpoints the New Testament offers—the synoptics' Son of Man, John's *Logos,* Paul's *Kyrios,* and the conquering warrior of Revelation. At the same time it should critically examine the distorted images that have sadly so abounded in its message until now.

It is difficult to resist a conclusion in the following vein. Protestant preaching has by and large been characterized by a functional Docetism in its christology (as also, basically, by a deism in its doctrine of God, a dualism in its concept of the human being, and a legalism in its ethics). The "heavenly" and "spiritual" Christ has been real and personal for believers. But he has not been Jesus of Nazareth in all his humanity and historicity. The church has maintained the humanity of Jesus as orthodoxy and the incarnation as dogma. But it does not appear to have taken the reality of the incarnation seriously—as a demand, a call to de-gnosticize our faith and to convert it into discipleship and practice, in collaboration with the Lord, in the historical and salvific undertaking that gives meaning to history from its beginning to its end.

A student in a christology class, who was studying patristics at the same time, discovered by himself something of this new reality of Christ and the challenge of finding a new language to proclaim him. He concluded a long review of the christological controversies with the following reformulation of the Apostles' Creed—in terms very modern, meaningful, and personal:

I believe and I live in God the Just One, the Liberator,
    who created the world and my neighbor,
and in Christ of Nazareth, his only son,
    and my only head,
who was born of a woman like my mother,
suffered under the oppressor's might,
was despised, marginalized, and crucified.
He descended upon the mechanisms of power,
    staged a coup d'état,
    and is in command, together with God the Just One, the Liberator.
And soon, when everything is under control,
    he will pass judgment on rich, poor, and indifferent.
I believe in the church, which lives in the world and for it,
    in liberation from alienation,

in the equality of human beings,
in the Prince of Peace,
and in the new life dawning on the horizon of history.

Amen.

# NOTES

1. It has repeatedly been asserted that the preaching of the Protestant churches in Latin America has been predominantly christological, perhaps even "christomonistic." This assertion is not sufficient. One must determine the explicit content and the implications of this preaching—what they denote and what they connote. One must determine the historical functioning and effect of these messages, along with their ideology. The authors of this chapter conducted a research seminar at the Seminario Bíblico Latinoamericano in San José, Costa Rica, using collections of gospel sermons aired over Faro del Caribe ["Caribbean beacon"], some of the research by Dr. Pablo Pretiz of INDEF, also in San José, other research done in Chile by the same team, the theses of Guillermo Cook B. (*El Movimiento de Renovación en San José*) and José Pereira de Souza (*Los efectos de la Cruzada Costa Rica '72*), and, finally, the seminar papers and discussions themselves. What is presented here is a kind of preliminary redaction of this material, along the lines of approach used in the seminar and often enough in its own wording.

2. Pereira, *Los efectos,* p. 92.

3. Sermon quoted by Pereira, *Los efectos,* pp. 78–79.

4. Arturo Hotten, *Acción en Cristo para un continente en crisis* (Bogotá: CLADE, 1967), p. 91.

# PART TWO

*The Meaning of
the Latin American Christs*

*Chapter 4*

# CHRISTOLOGY, *CONQUISTA*, COLONIZATION

*Saúl Trinidad*

## ANTECEDENTS

Any representation or image, be it conceptual or material, is the product of a synthesis of ideas, feelings, and historical situation. For the Spaniard, eight centuries of continual agony—in the original sense of "struggle"—with the Arabs produced a tragic concept of life, a terror of extinction, and a sin-tormented conscience. All this in turn led to a kind of "redemptive masochism"[1] and kindled the high passion that is a fundamental Spanish trait.

The Spaniard is an *apasionado* of life and immortality. This great passion for "universality" led Spaniards to "absorb the universe, individualize it, remake it to their own concept of abstract unity." Christianity never managed to make a dent in this Spanish mind-set. Spain "brought Christianity under its domination," to the point of "appropriating God."[2] As Unamuno put it, Christ was made prisoner in Spain. And there came to be a kind of expansionist, military theocracy, reaching a point where being Spanish and being Christian were identical.[3]

Rendered homogeneous by Christianity, this thirst for expansion, domination, and grandeur fed on the internal conviction of a temporal "messiahship." The result was the Spanish "messiah":

These [sentiments] profoundly influenced the Spanish concept of Christ. . . . Apart from them the Spanish Christ and the religion that centers around him cannot be understood and evaluated.[4]

**49**

Then that Spanish messiah's christology, driven by the desire for glory, gold, and religion, was set loose in the New World.[5] It is this christology that I shall concentrate on in the following pages.

## IMAGES OF SPANISH CHRISTOLOGY

Unlike our Western colleagues, we Southerners have no systematic christological treatise:

> At most we have notes on church history. Generally we have to reflect, and make deductions. That is, we have to "explicate" the christology that is implicit in the Latin American ecclesiastical process.[6]

### Dolorous and Defeated

If we attend merely to the physical traits of the Latin American Christ images, portraits, we confront someone who has died as the victim of a tragedy:

> In most instances, he appears as one on the point of death—his eyes rolled up in their sockets, his face turned down to the earth, and his whole body exhibiting the havoc wreaked upon it by the blows of his torturers.[7]

Miguel de Unamuno describes him:

> This Christ, immortal as death itself, does not rise again. For to what purpose? Death alone was what he awaited. Down he flows, from his mouth half agape, black as the mystery indecipherable, to nothingness, and never arrives. . . . This corpse of a Christ, being a corpse, has no thoughts. It is free of the pain of thought, of anguish, of the soul overwhelmed with sadness. After all, he did ask the Father to remove the cup of pain from him—. . . and now how is he to suffer its thought if he is but dead flesh, drenched and scabbed with blood—curdled, black blood? . . . This Spanish Christ, which was never alive, black as the mantle of earth, lies like a level plain, horizontal, stretched out soulless and hopeless, its eyes shut against the sky that stings with rain, and scorches the bread.[8]

This dead or dying Spanish Christ was here in Latin America. Well he reflects his eight centuries of struggle, agony, and suffering under the oppressor. This christology will win still more strength from the event of the Christ of Calvary, but it will have no part with the resurrected one. This is a christology calculated to impel a human being to search out happiness in suffering.

We meet another projection in Velázquez's "Cristo crucificado." Moreno Villa describes it:

This Christ seems wrapped "in a deep sleep, rather than having died a bitter death." Other authors say that this Christ is too cold—they want one more tortured, with more tragic a body, and suffering on the cross, or already dead but with the signs of his organic convulsions still in his bloodied flesh.[9]

But Velázquez did not accommodate himself to this manner of dramatic, gesticulatory painting. His christological conception leads him to the secure, to the placid—and this is why his crucified Christ cannot be anything other than an image like this, an image "of reposeful expression, harmonious of line, lovely in form, refraining from awakening any memories of horror, but 'solacing and strengthening' us as he bathes us in his love."[10] This is the Christ of romantic mysticism, inspiring a sort of tranquility of eternal ecstasy.

## A Christ in His Mother's Lap—and His Guardians' Power

The Christ child ("Baby Jesus," as we say), inoffensive and sweet as any baby, lies in his mother's protecting arms:

[She] is never far away, a woman of ordinary stature, dressed in violet, and with her bosom pierced through by a sword, whose point appears protruding from her shoulder. What a desperate mother![11]

This Christ has not yet learned to speak. His babbling is incomprehensible. And sometimes his demands are not heard, either. Still less can he reproach his guardians, protesting their abuse of power, their greed, and their limitless injustice inflicted upon the defeated persons upon whom this light is shining.

His face wears a perpetual smile, for he is indifferent to what transpires around him. His joyfulness invites the multitude to come share his childlike "innocence." Many are they who have become his "guardians," who have "adopted" him, become his lords. And now his smile is only for them. And he seeks to settle in his "protectors' " laps, with as little inconvenience as possible. He has learned to speak their language—and even, dutiful adopted child that he is, to speak in their behalf.

The historical Christ appears in only two of his aspects, and dramatically: as the helpless and harmless child, and as the humiliated and defeated victim. He was born, he died. But he never lived. The formative period stretching from his unproductive infancy to his option for a liberating messianic passion is forgotten. Full proof is to be had in the corollary of all this, our celebrations of Christmas and Holy Week.

## The Christ of the Mysteries

In the liturgy of Spanish piety we meet another image: the Christ of magical power. We find it in the doctrine of the transubstantiation, of whose elements the Spaniard partakes, not to experience Christ's nourishment but as a "magic recipe prescribed by the church for eternal life, in order to live forever"—to carry Spanish messianism to its culmination. This is why Pizarro, Almagro, and Friar Hernando de Luque celebrated the Eucharist in Panama—to seal their pact, and to "secure strength for the undertaking"[12] of conquest, expansion, and grandeur.

## The Celestial-Monarch Christ

Christ was thought of as a heavenly monarch, to whom all things, and authority over all things, spiritual and temporal, are now transferred. Hence the legal jurisdiction of the pope, who as vicar of Christ is himself a monarch—over all men and women, animals, and lands, with the power to make "donations." That is, he can authorize the taking of new territories.

Consequently, just as Portugal did, the king and queen of Spain, once Christopher Columbus had planted the flag of Spain and the cross of Christ in the New World, petitioned the pope for title to these new lands, arguing that their most ardent desire was the extension of the church. Pope Alexander VI granted their petition in his bull *Inter Caeteris*, and gave them authority to missionize and to colonize, making them the "lords and masters" of the New World.[13]

All acquisition of goods, whether simply by taking possession of them or by the shedding of blood, was justified. So now Queen Isabella and King Ferdinand began to be "glorified," as "lady and mistress" and "lord and master" of these new lands. Columbus himself assures us of this:

I ought to be judged as the captain from Spain who carried the *Conquista* to the very Indies . . . where by the divine will I have established the *exclusive lordship of our lord and lady*, the king and queen, in a new world. Now Spain, called poor, is richest of all. The gates are open now for gold and pearls, for precious stones in quantity, and a thousand other things besides.[14]

It was in the monarchs of this earth that Christ, as a "heavenly monarch," was considered to be manifested and revealed. First, of course, came the royal pair, Ferdinand and Isabella. But then there were those surrogate Ferdinands as well—the *encomenderos,* the big landowners, the colonial officials. Lords and masters. *Their* portraits, too, were framed with gold. And they had halos, just like Christ-the-rich-and-powerful:

Thus, whoever prays before or venerates these images [of Christ and the Blessed Virgin] honors and accepts as well the power of the earthly representatives of these glorified beings.[15]

Christ is identified with the lord of the hacienda, with the *patrón*, or landlord (*papá, Tayta*), with the *jefe*—"lords" every one of them, to whom one doffs one's sombrero.

*Christ as Pacifist*

In figures like Bernardo de Santo Domingo, Antonio Montesinos, and humanist Fra Bartolomé de Las Casas—persons who stepped forward in defense of the Amerindians' freedom and human rights—we find another christological image, one very different from those already mentioned.

Bartolomé de Las Casas was an *encomendero* and colonial official—until he was changed radically by a conversation with Montesinos.[16] Then he freed his slaves and "lived for the Indians only, from that moment on."[17]

By contrast with those who saw in the natives only "beasts, or nearbeasts," Las Casas held that the Indians "were rational beings, whose lives and properties were to be respected," and proclaimed that Christ's great injunction to "go and preach to all tribes and nations" meant the American Indians too.[18]

In regard to evangelization, Las Casas said:

> Delicate, sweet, and gentle should be the manner of teaching others the true religion. It is nothing else but the persuasion of the understanding and the moving of the will.[19]

He urged preachers to be amiable, gentle, humble, and filled with love. He warned them against any ambition to dominate or exploit. Their lives, he said, ought to be exemplary ones: they should follow Jesus' example of humility, humiliation, and suffering.[20]

In this conviction Fra Bartolomé labored to soften the attitude of the exploiters. He campaigned in writings, in personal conversations, and in sermons.[21] But he was laboring in a vacuum. He was surrounded by the deaf. Valiantly he confronted those who used coercive methods in their "evangelization." Daringly he fought for the christianization of the new lands by peaceful means.[22] These bloody, lopsided wars were intrinsically unjust for him, and he declared that "no king, no emperor, not the Roman Church itself, has the right to make war on" the Indians.[23] He protested with equal vehemence the "alienation of the Indian woman, the mother of Latin America."[24] Now she was reduced to slavery.

Fra Bartolomé considered the pastoral praxis of the conquistadors a denial of the faith itself.[25] So he initiated a new style of *conquista* and evangelization, which he said was the Christian way to treat the Indians. He had hopes that the natives, seeing the Spaniards' industriousness and pleased by their advice and favors, would easily be converted to the Christian faith. But in spite of all his efforts his project failed to prosper.[26]

This christology of beneficence, and its praxis of a pacifist *conquista* and evangelization, collided head-on with the "lords and masters"—the terrestrial monarchs—and Las Casas ended as "Antichrist" and "Devil." There was even an attempt on his life.[27] He was accused of having been bribed by the tycoons of the slave traffic, and it was alleged that this was the reason why he had authorized and supported the introduction of blacks as slaves in America.

To all these charges Bartolomé responded with the theory called in moral theology the "lesser evil." That is, "seeing that the slavery to which the Indians were forced to submit held out the menace of extermination, he had proposed that Negroes be imported for the heaviest work."[28] There was also a time when he accepted as just the enslavement of Indians who had risen up against the Spaniards.[29]

This new christology presented a nonviolent, nonpredatory image of Christ, a Christ of the works of beneficence—a Christ of a character sweet and gentle, delicate and paternal. Patiently this Christ would await the fruits of his love tactics—the conversion, in the sense of voluntary submission, of the Indians, for the sake of "the salvation of their souls."[30]

With a smile of loving charity, a struggle of self-sacrifice, a father's protection, and a readiness to give himself in self-surrender, Christ now towered before the Amerindians no longer as a heavenly monarch and inquisitor, it is true, but still as a monarch—of the philanthropical stripe now, amiable, collaborating, and occasionally distributing his little gifts and gratuities. But in the last analysis the path of pacifism is but the best way to dominate, for it encourages the submission of the will itself.

Whatever the conquistador's method, violence or pacifism, at bottom the objectives were always the same—domination, extension, and wealth for the great two-headed Spain of the faith and the *conquista*. And so whatever the christological image might be, it always amounted to a single function—the legitimation of exploitive domination.

## COLONIAL *CONQUISTA* AND CHRISTOLOGY

*Overview*

The year 1492 is important for two reasons. In Spain the struggle between Christians and Muslims was over. Ferdinand and Isabella determined that a unified Spain would be only for Christ and Christians, and pushed its frontiers outward. And Christopher Columbus discovered some islands in the Caribbean.

What lands were these, where a hispanicized Christianity would take up its abode? They were the lands of our forebears, the Mayas, the Chibchas, and the Incas. In these lands were "villages, cities, and cultures, and the earth was crisscrossed with highways whose footprints their own tread would never be able to efface,"[31] as the foreign conquistadors abruptly entered this continent. These were the cultures that now came into confrontation with an Iberian civilization pregnant with a twofold culture of war and religion.[32]

Seen as a whole, pre-Columbian religions were very complex.[33] But the fundamental traits of the Inca religion are delineated by the Peruvian political scientist and philosopher José Carlos Mariátegui:

In their theocratic collectivism and their materialism [contradistin-guished by Mariátegui against "spiritualism" and "essentialism"], the Incas had virtually no concept of the transcendent, of the "beyond." . . . The Quechua religion was more a moral code than a metaphysical conception. State and church were identified absolutely. Religion and politics recognized a single set of principles and a single authority. Reli-gion was summed up in the social.

Its ends were more temporal than spiritual. It was more concerned with the kingdom of this earth than with a kingdom of heaven.

It was a social discipline rather than an individualistic discipline.

The organized form of the Incan religion was that of a social and political institution. The church was itself the state. Worship was sub-ordinated to the social and political interests of the empire. . . . The Incan religion was eager to domesticate the gods of subjected peoples, rather than persecute or condemn them. . . . It was not heavily cate-chetical or inquisitory. . . . It strove not so much to replace as to elevate the religion of the peoples it annexed to its empire.

Nor was there any violation of the sensibilities or customs of annexed peoples.[34]

## The Process of Evangelization

Evangelization began with Columbus's arrival on American shores. Then, with Cortés's Mexican landing and Francisco Pizarro's arrival in Cuzco (Peru), European and Indian were face to face.[35]

Hispanicized christology arrived in America at the hands of a mystic—Christopher Columbus:

He was one of the most remarkable Christian lay persons of all times. A careful Bible reader, he wrote long scriptural commentaries filled with prophecies of the future—of the end of the world and the establishment of an earthly kingdom. (He believed in the formation of a universal kingdom, which could not occur until all tribes and nations had been evangelized.)[36]

This description is very much idealized. But it does contain a truth. Besides being an adventurer, Columbus was a religious person. Writing a letter to Isabella and Ferdinand, he says, "I set out in the name of the Holy Trinity, in whom I place my hope of victory."[37] He makes a great deal of the etymology of his name, *Christopher,* "Christ-bearer," and (the Spanish version of his surname) *Colón,* "one who peoples anew" (almost "colonizer"). He liked to say that it was by his industry and toil that he had "discovered these nations" and that now, by the preaching that would be done in these new lands, "that other great nation, in heaven" would be populated. For, he thought, col-onialist Spain was "building a new Christian church and a happy republic."[38]

The mystical and religious side of "Christ-Bearer" Columbus is beyond dispute. Like others of his time, he was thought of as a "pure soul," who acted in strict accordance with his christological convictions. But he is scarcely the model of biblical doctrine and preaching that some writers have wished to make out.[39] They neglect the fact that Columbus's praxis, his "pastoral" behavior, is the very negation of the incarnation, indeed of the faith itself—for faith should have asked, "What does it mean to believe in Christ as I stand here before the American Indian?"

## The "Exalted Mandate" of Hispanicized Christology

"Christ-Bearer" Columbus was convinced that his name symbolized a mission of "carrying" Christ to the New World in fulfillment of the Old Testament prophecies. He writes:

> The truth is, all things will pass away, but God's word will not pass away, for all that God has spoken is to be fulfilled. "Surely have the coastal dwellers hoped in me, and the ships of Tarsis from the very first; to bear their sons from afar, and their silver and gold along with them, to the name of their God, the Holy One of Israel, who has given them glory" [Isa. 60:9]. . . . How clear it is that he meant these lands! . . . and that it was from Spain that his holy name would spread far and wide among the gentiles. . . . And after saying this by the mouth of Isaiah, he made me his messenger, and showed me where to go.[40]

Thus a supposed fulfillment of a prophecy, together with its gloss, and the symbolism of the name "Cristobal Colón"—christianization/colonization, Christ and state, faith and politics, the spiritual and the material, cross and flag—illustrate the basic intent of the explorations: grandeur, extension, and wealth.

True, the great mandate of Jesus of Nazareth is to "proclaim the good news to all creation" (Mark 16:16), but the "great mandate" of Spanish christology was thought to be to "go and impose religion, and extend the 'civilization' of the Spanish monolith to the New World, baptizing them by the power of the sword and in the name of the Trinity, subjecting them to slavery so that you can exploit them, and teaching them to keep faith with the 'homeland,' where Ferdinand and Isabella will be with you always, 'even to the end of the world.' "

This is put very well in Columbus's letter of March 15, 1493, to the royal couple, in which he prays:

> Thus, as our Redeemer has given our Most Illustrious King and Queen this victory and kingdoms of such high estate . . . may it likewise please our Lord to grant them long life and to further this so noble undertak-

ing, in which it seems to me that our Lord receives much service, Spain much grandeur, and Christians much consolation and pleasure, seeing that thus the name of our Lord spreads through every land. . . . I have commanded a cross be planted, and have notified the natives of Your Highnesses' State and See, which is Spain.[41]

In this fashion the conquistadors, monks, warriors, *encomenderos,* and catechist landholders "bore their Christ" to the New World. As Míguez Bonino puts it:

The ancient dream of a "Catholic kingdom," a unified political and religious structure ruled by Catholic teaching down to its last details— the dream that could never be realized in Europe—was transported to Latin America. "Christianization" meant the inauguration of this dream in this land—the dream of creating Christianity exemplary "from top to bottom."[42]

Naturally, the presence of other gods, other worship, would constitute a threat to "unity." They could not be tolerated. And millions of human beings were sacrificed on the altar of gold and silver. Gold and silver became the "new gods."[43]

## *The "Incarnation" of the Spanish Christ*

The moment has come for us to examine the encounter between this ecclesiastical, hispanicized christology, and the Amerindian. How did this dolorous, or defeated, or magical, or pacifist Christ, or celestial monarch, "incarnate"? How did he "indianize"? What was the manner of his *kenosis*, his identification? Did it actually take place at all?

Some, from the ecclesiastical and liturgical viewpoint, see in this encounter the source and beginning of a syncretism. And it is possible that they are correct. But the manifest inadequacy of this syncretism, if there was one, to explain the contemporary Christian identity crisis in these lands suggests another explanation. Míguez Bonino writes:

There was a tendency in the Catholic Church, when evangelization first began [in Latin America], not precisely of syncretism, I should say, but of integration. There was an effort to take certain pagan, Indian traditions and rework them, transform them in terms of Christian faith. But this is not the tendency that triumphed. The tendency that triumphed was, on the contrary, the massive rejection of everything native, based on a principle of separateness, of breach—to the point where not even native names were considered suitable to Christian theology, and the Indians were obliged to learn Latin names for all religious ceremonies.[44]

The implementation of this false incarnation took two forms. First, there were acts of the crudest political and religious Macchiavellian sort—unjust, cruel, bloody, one-sided wars and inquisitorial practices. Then, after having destroyed and annihilated "everyone who could have dreamed of, sighed for, or thought about freedom, [the Spaniards] oppressed the others with the most horrible slavery to which human beings or beasts could ever have been reduced. 'It is pleasing to God to kill and rob unbelievers,' " they said.[45]

Next, thanks to the abundance of natural resources, a second plan of spoliation was devised and executed:

> Now came the second age of the history of the colonial priesthood: the age of a placid and tranquil life on magnificent religious estates, the age of the sinecure, of affluent parishes, of social influence, of political supremacy, of luxurious fiestas—all of which inevitably led to abuses and laxity.[46]

The approach taken by this Christian faith, this christology, was a strange one indeed, very different from the character and behavior of the Indian gods Pachacamac, Huracocha, and Inti, son of Inca, the Sun.[47] And it was the very negation of Jesus Christ the Nazarene, who walked with the outcast, the downtrodden, the humiliated. He not only "lived in a culture, he was permeated by culture."[48]

Lands and families were parceled out without thought for their future even as a labor force and means of production. They were *made* to serve, the very contrary of the Christ of the New Testament accounts, who said, "The Son of Man himself did not come to be served but to serve, and to give his life as a ransom for many" (Mark 10:45).

## CHRISTOLOGICAL PROJECTION OF THE AMERINDIAN

*Christology of Resignation*

The Indians, defeated and subjugated, gaze upon the sad and defeated image of the Spanish Christ and behold, reflected there, their own selves and destiny. In the agonizing and dying Christ they confront a reason for *resigning themselves* to their lot and accepting the fate of a conquered, beaten, subjugated people. The helplessness, the uselessness, of this Christ is completely internalized, as Hugo Assmann puts it so well:

> The dolorous Christs of Latin America, whose central image is ever the cross, are Christs of impotence—an impotence interiorized by the oppressed. Defeat, sacrifice, pain, cross. Impotence, powerlessness, is accepted "undigested," recognized in advance and submitted to. Defeat is not perceived as a temporary reversal to be overcome in struggle. It appears as an inevitable necessity, as a condition for the privilege of living.[49]

One must suffer "patiently" in order to survive. "One must know how to 'live it up' in the midst of sufferings." Such alienating counsels crystalize in conformism, resignation, and "tranquil desperation" in the face of the historical reality of Latin America.

Mothers and wives, too, find motifs that reflect their sorrows:

At the side of the Man of Sorrows, Our Lady of the Seven Sorrows displays her transfixed bosom to the gaze of the multitude. For she is the personification of all the women prematurely aged by the tears they must shed for their spouses and their children as well as for themselves. Liberation struggles are very costly.[50]

This "incarnation," this identification of the two who have been vanquished—Christ and the Amerindian—finds expression in what we witness year after year in the paschal celebrations. At bottom, what does Holy Week mean for the masses? Why is so much attention paid to Holy Thursday and Good Friday ("Holy Friday," as we call it), and not so much to Resurrection Sunday? What do these great processions of millions of women, men, and children—largely miners and country folk—reveal to us? And why miners and country folk? Is it perchance that, behind all this, there lurks the conscious or unconscious acceptance of one's situation of impotence and powerlessness, of being subjugated and oppressed, of inhumanity? If so, then what do the Holy Week rites mean today? Are they symbols of the liberation of Latin America, or are they continuing to play the role of baptizing and confirming the establishment?[51]

What, then, has been the function of christology in Latin America? The first thing that stands out is its role in baptizing, sacralizing, the *conquista* and the resulting oppression, as well as making a virtue out of suffering. Suffering was supposed to lead to glory and express communion with the crucified Christ. Even the beatitudes were pressed into service: "Blessed are the poor . . . those who weep . . . those who suffer."

## Christology of Subjugation and Domination

The internalization of a christological image favorable to the oppressor is the synthetic fruit of a parallel Spanish and Incan conception of sovereignty. For the Spaniards, Christ was something of a "heavenly Ferdinand,"[52] the lord of lands, persons, and things. This authority had been transferred to the pope and to earthly Ferdinands for their "wise" administration, and they believed they had the right to take lands and make use of peoples.

The Indians, too, recognized a Supreme Being, Creator and Lord of the universe: Huracocha. They also had Mamapacha, the goddess of fertility. Administration was in the hands of *Sapallán Inca* ("Sole Lord").[53]

Great confrontations were understood as struggles among the gods. Accordingly, during the bloody and lopsided war the Spaniards waged against them, "the Indians, seeing that heaven held no thunderbolts for the conquistadors and that their God had been unable to avert the profanation of his sanctuary, were becoming gradually more inclined to pay homage" to the conquerors.[54] From now on, they will see their *Sapallán Inca* personified in earthly "Ferdinands" of earth, before whom they will prostrate themselves in an attitude of "humility, surrender, and reverence"; and their lives will be sacrificed on the altar of a new goddess: *La Conquistadora*.[55]

Representations of Christ that are not sorrowful are of someone who is rich, who is covered with gold and silver and enthroned in the heavenly regions amid cushions and columns, with a halo around his head or "wearing royal crowns like kings of Spain."[56]

Hence it is evident why the powerful, the mighty, take such an interest in "evangelization" and in the propagation of these "rare glorious Christs," these paternal Christs. They are symbols of political power and domination.

The Christ of the cross, of the death that conquers, this man of combat, "has become the archetypical beggar, some sort of scarecrow, a footstool for the feet of everybody, a compendium of miseries and a sampler of humiliations."[57] As for the Christ of the resurrection, who "got rid of the Sovereignties and Powers, and paraded them in public, behind him in his triumphal procession" of the cross (Col. 2:15),[58] they have made of him a heavenly monarch, the guarantor of his lieutenants and vicars, the kings of earth, and the oppressors who bear the title "benefactor" (Luke 22:25).

Both images, the defeated Christ and the heavenly monarch, are faces of a christology of oppression: the Christ of "established impotence," of a resignation that refuses struggle because it has already been alienated and conquered, and the Christ of "established power," suggesting a subjugation that has no need of struggle, because it has already overcome.[59]

### Christology of Marginalization

When the Blessed Virgin holds Jesus in her lap, it is she who attracts the most attention. In the colonial church of Cuzco, Peru, there is an inscription, "Come to Mary, all ye who toil and are overburdened, and she will give you rest."[60]

The baby Jesus who tried to become the Indian baby Jesus was marginalized. But the great mass of marginalized adults and children as well, the great mass of those who are not taken into account, share the situation and the lot of that other forgotten child.

And forgotten he remained, until certain "benefactors" found it convenient to "adopt" him. From then on, in the name of the marginalized child (or "poor children," as they are called), fantastic undertakings have been mounted—lucrative ones—social institutions, political groups, all under the umbrella name, "Feast of the Child," or Christmas. But these activities are not centered upon the marginalized child, but on the grand "benefactors," who are rewarded with the "blessings" (or the costs) of the Christ of marginalization.

But who is the forgotten child of Bethlehem, marginalized and made use of here? M. Grillo depicts him:

> Down white highways of night
> he comes, in search of bread and shelter.
> The prophet saw him like a rain
> of fire among the blooming cedars,
> and did foretell he was the Word
> of God, come down to the people.
> He came to illuminate us to the depths. He was the flame
> that devoured all the trembling thorns.
> God spoke among the clouds—this was his Word,
> like a blue whip of whirlwinds.
> He appeared amid a forest of hungering crowds
> gnawing their stiff and skinny arms.
> This child, the one who comes, the marginalized,
> shall cast his curse upon the books
> of scribes, and yea, upon the rich as well,
> who sow starvation by their exploitation
> of the millions of the outcast and oppressed.
> This marginalized child is light, and life—
> he came to them and they received him not.[61]

Where is *this* Christ, this *other* Christ, who says that life will be transformed, that the world will be transformed, that the world will be overcome? He said of himself:

> The spirit of the Lord has been given to me,
> for he has anointed me.
> He has sent me to bring the good news to the poor,
> to proclaim liberty to captives
> and to the blind new sight,
> to set the downtrodden free,
> to proclaim the Lord's year of favor
> > [Luke 4:18–19; cf. Isa. 61:1–2].

This Christ, who came to incarnate himself in Latin America, first passed through the West. In Spain, in the sixteenth century:

> He came softly, unobserved, and yet, strange to say, everyone recognized Him. . . . The Grand Inquisitor. . . . holds out his finger and bids the guards take Him. . . . the guards lead their prisoner to the close, gloomy vaulted prison in the ancient palace of the Holy Inquisition and shut him in it.[62]

The "Grand Conquistador" condemned him for charlatanry and disloyalty. And he remained a prisoner. As J. A. Mackay says:

> Methinks the Christ, as he sojourned westward, went to prison in Spain, while another who took his name embarked with the Spanish crusaders for the New World—a Christ who was not born in Bethlehem, but in North Africa. This Christ became naturalized in the Iberian colonies of America, while Mary's Son and Lord was little else than a stranger and sojourner in these lands, from Columbus's day to this.[63]

# NOTES

1. We find it very well illustrated in the life of Saint Teresa. See *Obras completas de Santa Teresa de Jesús* (Madrid: La Católica), vol. 1, pp. 297ff.; Eng. trans., *Collected Works of St. Teresa*, 3 vols. (New York: Sheed and Ward, 1972); and Olivera Martins, *Historia de la civilización ibérica* (Buenos Aires: Ateneo, 1944), pp. 233ff., where so-called tragic or naive mysticism is very well explained.

2. John A. Mackay, *The Other Spanish Christ: A Study of the Spiritual History of Spain and South America* (New York: Macmillan, 1932), pp. 8-9, 41.

3. See Enrique Dussel, *Historia de la iglesia en América Latina: coloniaje y liberación 1492-1972* (Barcelona: Nova Terra, 1972), pp. 55-56; Eng. trans., *A History of the Church in Latin America: Colonialism to Liberation 1492-1979* (Grand Rapids: Eerdmans, 1981).

4. Mackay, *The Other Spanish Christ*, p. 96.

5. See Justo L. González, *Historia de las misiones* (Buenos Aires: Aurora, 1970), p. 139.

6. J. Míguez Bonino, "Cristianismo en América Latina," *Orientación* 19 (Jan.-March., 1971): 8.

7. Georges Casalis, below, p. 76.

8. "El Cristo yacente de Santa Clara de Palencia," in *Andanzas y visiones españolas* (Madrid: Renacimiento, 1929), pp. 297-300.

9. "Pintura religiosa de Velázquez," in *Artes y Letras* (Costa Rica: Ministerio de Educ. Pública, 1968), pp. 28-30.

10. Ibid.

11. Casalis, below, p. 72.

12. *Cartas y testamento de Cristóbal Colón* (Madrid: Prelado, Paez, 1921), p. 53.

13. Karl Bihlmeyer and Hermann Tuchle, *Church History* (Westminster, Md.: Newman, 1966), vol. 2, p. 516.

14. *Cartas y testamento*, p. 69, italics added.

15. Casalis, below, p. 74.

16. Marcel Brion, *Bartolomé de Las Casas: "Father of the Indians"* (New York: Dutton, 1929), pp. 52-53.

17. Ibid., p. 55.

18. See Lewis Hanke, "Pope Paul III and the American Indians," *Harvard Theological Review* 30 (1937): 65-102, also cited by Hanke in his Introduction to the work of Fra Bartolomé de Las Casas, *Del único modo de atraer a todos los pueblos a la verdadera religión* (Mexico City: Fondo de Cultura Económica, 1942), p. xxi. The

article in the *Harvard Theological Review* contains an extensive description of Paul III's bull, *Sublimes Deus,* issued in 1573, the tenor of which supported Bartolomé's claims.

19. *Del único modo,* p. 9.
20. See ibid., pp. 249–303.
21. Some of his salient works in this area are *Brevísima relación de la destrucción de las Indias* (reprint, Buenos Aires, 1966); *Treinta proposiciones muy jurídicas,* Biblioteca del estudiante universitario (Mexico City: Universidad Nacional, 1941); and *Historia de las Indias y la historia apologética.* Also very important are the eight Valladolid treatises, whose titles are listed in Agustín Yañes, *Fray Bartolomé de Las Casas, el conquistador conquistado* (Mexico City: Xochiti, 1942), p. 49, n. 1. For a bibliography of Bartolomé's works, see Lewis Hanke and Iván Fernández, "A Bibliography for the Study of His Life," updated from 1954, in Juan Friede and Benjamin Keen, eds., *Bartolomé de Las Casas: Toward an Understanding of the Man and His Work* (DeKalb: Northern Illinois University Press, 1971).
22. See Yañes, *Conquistador conquistado,* pp. 10ff.
23. Las Casas attempted to demonstrate the illegality of war from three points of view: by its contrariety to the law of Christ, by the tenor of the bull *Inter caeteris,* and by the politics of the Most Catholic King and Queen and the Testament of Queen Isabella. See Venancio D. Carro, *La teología de los teólogos-juristas españoles ante la conquista de América* (Salamanca: Biblioteca de teólogos españoles, 2nd ed., 1951), p. 27; Yañes, *Conquistador conquistado,* pp. 10, 69ff.
24. Enrique Dussel et al., eds., *Fe cristiana y cambio social en América Latina* (Salamanca: Sígueme, 1973), p. 67.
25. See ibid., p. 73.
26. See W. S. Rycroft, *Religion and Faith in Latin America* (Philadelphia: Westminster, 1958).
27. See Yañes, *Conquistador conquistado,* pp. 96, 102.
28. Brion, *Bartolomé,* p. 57. It should be noted, however, that the Portuguese had been devoting themselves to this "remunerative traffic" since 1443. Certain seafarers had established trading posts whose only object was the abduction and sale of blacks. The trafficking was carried on in the open and scandalized no one. See Brion, pp. 58–60.
29. On this subject, as well as the whole ministry of Bartolomé, see the critical study of Lewis Hanke, *Las teorías políticas de Bartolomé de Las Casas* (Buenos Aires: Instituto de Investigación Histórica, 1935); idem, *First Social Experiment in America* (Cambridge: Harvard University Press, 1935; reprint, Peter Smith, 1964); and Yañes, *Conquistador conquistado,* pp. 149–54.
30. Wilton M. Nelson et al., eds., "Panorama histórico de la evangelización," in *Hacia una teología de la evangelización* (Buenos Aires: Aurora, 1973), pp. 162ff.
31. José Carlos Mariátegui, *Siete ensayos de interpretación de la realidad peruana* (Lima: Amauta, 1928), p. 183. For a broader panorama of the state of these cultures see, for the Incas, Garcilaso de la Vega, *Comentarios reales de las Incas* (Lima, 1967), vol. 1, ch. 15; Albertina Muñoz, ed., *Antiguas historias de los indios Quichés de Guatemala* (Mexico City, 1971); and Dussel, *Historia de la iglesia,* pp. 35–40.
32. See Dussel, *Historia de la iglesia,* p. 54.
33. Enrique Guang Tapia, "Teología y violencia en América Latina: análisis socio-teológico" (thesis for the Licentiate in Theology presented in the Seminario Bíblico Latinoamericano, Costa Rica, 1971), pp. 78ff., classifies pre-Columbian religion in two categories, "popular religions" and "imperial religions."

34. Mariátegui, *Siete ensayos*, pp. 162–68. Mariátegui was a most profound analyst. His openness to religion is very unusual for a confessed and militant Marxist. He not only analyzes religion in relation to its economic aspect, but seeks to recover autochthonous religious sentiments. He was committed to the search for the liberation of the Peruvian Indian.

35. See Dussel, *Fe cristiana y cambio social*, p. 77.

36. Augusto J. Kling, "El Cristóbal Colón que pocos conocen," *Pensamiento Cristiano* 78 (Sept. 1973): 106. See also Salvador de Madariaga, *Vida del muy magnífico señor Cristóbal Colón* (Buenos Aires:Ed. Sudamérica, 2nd ed., 1942); Eng. trans., *Christopher Columbus: Being the Life of the Very Magnificent Lord, Don Cristóbal Colón* (New York: Frederick Ungar, 1967).

37. *Cartas y testamento*, p. 24 .

38. Madariaga, *Colón*, p. 37. See also Mackay, *The Other Spanish Christ*, p. 46; Gilberto Bernald Cepeda, "Los efectos de la Weltanschauung calvinista en América Latina" (thesis for the Baccalaureate in Theology presented at the Seminario Bíblico Latinoamericano, Costa Rica, 1968), pp. 23ff. For a more complete description, see Juan B. Teran, *El Nacimiento de la América Española* (Tucumán, Argentina, 1927).

39. See for example Kling, "El Cristóbal Colón," who paints the explorer's use of the gospels in glowing colors, and concludes by extrapolating motivations that it seems to him Columbus must have had. But he does not question the type of interpretation and exegesis at play here, much less the structural ecclesiastical transplant.

40. *Cartas y testamento*, pp. 16, 51–52 .

41. Ibid.

42. *Polémica, diálogo y misión: catolicismo romano y protestantismo en América Latina* (Uruguay: Centro de Estudios Cristianos, 1966), p. 23.

43. See Dussel, *Fe cristiana*, pp. 66–67.

44. "Cristianismo," pp. 4–5.

45. Mackay, *The Other Spanish Christ*, p. 29.

46. M.A. Villarán, *Estudios sobre educación nacional*, pp. 10–11, cited by Mariátegui, *Siete ensayos*, p. 184.

47. The god Inti was identified with the sun. Huracocha was the creator of the Incas and Orejones (a group of aristocrats who cultivated a type of large vine). Huracocha attracted the attention of the Europeans. Both gods were recognized as beings who presided over the destinies of human beings, who gave light and heat to nations and life to the vegetable world, as well as being fathers and founders of the empire. All the temples of the territory belonged to them. See Carlos Pereyra, *Perú y Bolivia*, Historia de América Latina, vol. 7 (Madrid: Saturnillo Calleja, 1925), pp. 87ff.; William H. Prescott, *Historia de la conquista del Perú* (Buenos Aires: Suma, 1871), pp. 77ff.; Eng. trans., *The Conquest of Mexico*, bound with *The Conquest of Peru* (New York: Modern Library, 1931). Other works of Prescott on the Aztecs, on the Spanish empire, and on Ferdinand and Isabella are available in paperback editions.

48. H. Richard Niebuhr, *Christ and Culture;* I recommend this book in its entirety.

49. Hugo Assmann, "La actuación histórica del poder de Cristo" (address delivered at the Consulta de Cristología in Lima in Jan. 1974); see below, pp. 125–36.

50. Casalis, below, p. 73.

51. See Michael Schmaus, *Dogmatics* (New York: Sheed and Ward, 1971), Vol. 6, pp. 9–21 and 45–53; J. S. Charbert, "Dolor," in Diez Macho, ed., *Enciclopedia de la Biblia* (Barcelona: Garriga, 1963), vol. 1, col. 987.

52. See Casalis, below, pp. 74–76.

53. See n. 47 , above; and Prescott, *Conquista del Perú*, pp. 76–77.

54. Prescott, *Conquista del Perú*, p. 276.

55. This was the name of the famous statue of the Blessed Virgin Mary, Queen of Heaven, which accompanied Cortés. Today it is in Santa Fe, New Mexico. See Casalis, below, pp. 74 and 75.

56. Assmann, below, p. 135.

57. Ricardo Rojas, *El Cristo invisible*, 3rd ed. (Buenos Aires: Ed. La Facultad, 1928), p. 204.

58. Casalis, below, p. 75.

59. See Assmann, below, p. 136.

60. *El Cristo desnudo* (Bogotá: Gráficos Vanuus, 1971), pp. 19–20.

61. See Miguel Angel Astúrias, *El Señor Presidente* (Buenos Aires: Losada), pp. 262–63.

62. Feodor Dostoevski, *The Brothers Karamazov* (New York: Norton, 1976), pp. 229–30.

63. See Mackay, *The Other Spanish Christ*, p. 95.

*Chapter 5*

# POPULAR CHRISTOLOGY— ALIENATION OR IRONY?

*Pedro Negre Rigol*

## CHRISTOLOGY AND ECCLESIOLOGY

In his *Systematic Theology,* Paul Tillich underscores the close relationship between Christ and the church. Faith in Christ is rooted in Jesus' question to his disciples, "But you, who do you say I am?"—to which Peter responded, in the name of the Twelve: "You are the Christ, the Son of the living God" (Matt. 16:15, 16). Jesus is the "Christ"—that is, the Messiah—not that alone, but recognized and professed as such by the community of believers, the *ek-klesia,* the community of those "called apart." Without entering into any discussion of the opposite poles of the old christological spectrum, do- cetism vs. adoptionism, we can say that what constitutes and unifies this church is, in a way, the same as that which makes a human being, Jesus, into the Christ of our faith.

Just as in days gone by, today too the christological question sends us back to the question of the church of Christ, in the sense of that more or less scattered and disorganized community of his followers that the various Christian churches claim to represent. But there is a oneness of believers more basic than the unity of the organized churches, which, being institutions, claim to box in that oneness in their creeds—in "orthodoxy."

In the Middle Ages, church dogmas constituted the very root of culture— the root of the political and social oneness of nations and peoples. There was no difference between "orthodoxy" and "orthopraxis," as we would say today. But the real oneness of believers can be conceived neither as orthodoxy nor as orthopraxis—that is, neither as a merely intellectual unity nor as a practical, pragmatic one. Further, this real unity of all the faithful can be conceived neither as an intraecclesiastical one, a unity in virtue of the practice of the same rites and the observance of the same laws and precepts, nor as the broader unity of all those who, even without knowing it, are committed to the kingdom that Christ brought to this world. No, this unity, this oneness, has to be a "praxeological" one—a oneness in a praxis that includes not only the praxis, but reflection upon this praxis as well. It will be unity in a common series of actions, and in a common reflection upon this action. Or, in Paulo Freire's conception, it is "transformation of the world" and "revealing word," simultaneously.[1]

But it is here that our Latin American history today would seem to tip the balance of this "praxeological confession" in favor of action, and of an action that is conceived basically as "liberation." It was not in vain that Medellín, which championed the concept of "liberation" among the churches, said at the same time: "The present has not ceased to be the hour of the word, but it has already become, and with dramatic urgency, the time for action."[2]

## CHRISTOLOGY—THE ELITES OR THE MASSES?

Christians who have had the boldness to objectify their option for the gospel in efficacious and effective political action—knowing that the kingdom promised by Christ passes in its *entirety* through a concrete, historical undertaking, and transcends that undertaking only "from within"—discover that what they seek is common to believers and nonbelievers. They come to see that it is not a project created by the official churches, which are rather the unconscious advocates of "third positions" and "draw-match attitudes," or of discourse calculated to reconcile the all too real division of left and right. Vanguard echelons are as important today as they ever were, in the political domain as well as in the ecclesial, provided they prove able to avoid the danger of elitism.[3] Today they have a tendency to constitute political vanguards, rather than religious ones, whereas popular faith still hangs on tight to the more traditional institutions and structures. These Christian groups of the vanguard find themselves bound to the masses of the oppressed, but distant from their faith, for it is an unenlightened faith—or worse, alienated and oppressed.

If we examine the christological consciousness of the masses, the proclamation of a *Cristo Libertador* contrasts profoundly with the images of those other "Christs" of the people, which are prisoners of Catholic colonialism or of Protestant neocolonialism. The former are the dolorous and defeated Christs of Good Friday or the monarchical ones of the Spanish empire;[4] the latter are pietistic, sentimental Christs, prisoners of private religion with its uncritical ideology. "Jesus our only hope," or "Jesus our salvation," say the Protestant preachers—by which they mean individualistic, psychological salvation, lacking any repercussions on public life.

In this ecclesial context of christology, such as it is lived by our peoples today, it is not so easy to decide for the "masses" as against the "elites." The so-called christological vacuum of the theology of liberation (or rather of the theology of the vanguard) has its mighty counterpoise in the still greater christological vacuum of popular piety, with its Christs of colonial and neocolonial domination. The criticism of a possible "elitist" tone in vanguard christologies boomerangs because, more often than not, those who level it are advocates of a populist, naive pastoral approach based on the exaltation of the religious consciousness of the masses. How can the Christs of popular piety be liberated? How can their alienating and privatistic images be changed? How can we resurrect the Christ who definitively crushes the powerful of this world in order to liberate human beings from the worship of Caesar—worship of the system?

## THE IRONIC IN POPULAR CULTURE

Without denying the pessimistic image of popular Catholic and Protestant christology, I should like to point out certain of its shades and nuances that may lead us to a discovery of some possible paths of reconstruction and recovery.

One datum of popular piety and culture is devotion to Christ as the "first of the saints," or the "only saint"—depending upon whether you cite the Catholic or the Protestant version. But when we speak simply and plainly of an oppressed popular culture, we have to realize that there are ambiguities there that can be the seeds of a possible liberation. We speak too easily of an alienated culture only from the point of view of the alienating factor, and not of the alienated culture itself, as it is lived and as it expresses the life of a people fighting against the domination that is the source of its alienated culture.

A popular culture is not purely and simply a culture created by the dominant classes for the people's consumption—although that is indeed what it is fundamentally—but it is also an original expression of this same people.[5] No one imposes a culture without first believing in it, as is readily learned from Althusser's discussion of dominant ideologies. The Christs of the dominant classes do not fully coincide with the Christs of popular imagery. The dominant culture condemns the popular "subculture." The same is true with regard to piety, which is one of the nuclei of popular culture. Hence when we speak of "popular culture" (or better, "subculture"), this is a distinction to which we ought to pay close attention.

The Christs of the vanguards, like their protest songs, often fail to "catch on" among the masses, because these vanguard groups fail to take into account that their protest, even in its ideal, utopian form, is already present in popular piety, in the folklore of the people (in the case of music and song).

The piety, culture, and folklore of the people are full of these and other "ironies." These ironies fail to go beyond a merely symbolic expression of servitude or resistance. But they express the people's originality, and therefore, in a liberation praxis, must be ideologically recovered and explicated.

## FROM POPULAR IRONY TO THE IRONY OF THE GOSPEL

Exegetes today stress the socio-cultural context of the gospel. Christ's originality cannot be understood without reference to the popular piety of his time. Without being an expert in this field, I should nonetheless like to raise certain questions.

Clearly, Christ's explicit interventions in the area of politics are of little significance. In the Jewish world, even in Christ's time, politics was largely practiced on religious terrain.[6] Still, I want to point out the *irony* with which Christ makes a response whenever he steps out of the domain of religion into that of politics strictly so called.

When Christ gives his evasive answer on the question of the tribute to be paid to Caesar ("Give back to Caesar what belongs to Caesar—and to God what belongs to God"; Luke 20:25)—the tribute that the Romans impose upon those who are not actually their "vassals"—what he is doing is breezily and brilliantly extricating himself from the closed and simplistic casuistry in which his adversaries thought they could trap him. Naivety is not a trait of Christ—although political naivety was enormous in those times, in comparison with our understanding and experience today.

Subtly he confronts the political philosophy of his time—and not just a Jewish political philosophy, but a Greek and Roman one—by way of irony. He is not in agreement with the Zealots, who look for a revolutionary Messiah; but, according to Cullmann, he admits some of them among his disciples, which is going to entail all sorts of difficulties (and not the least will be the "politicization" of his message by the apostles themselves). His rejection of political authority is frank and blunt. Herod receives the epithet "fox," and Pilate, rather than being Christ's judge, is pictured in the Gospel of Saint John as being judged by Christ. He avoids coming right out and comparing them with anyone else, and yet he does condemn the shedding of the blood of the last Zealot, whom, he says, the authorities there present had murdered right at the altar. He is perfectly conscious of the political persecution that his message will stir up (of the "political strategy hidden in his religious language," as we would put it nowadays) inasmuch as his confrontations with the religious and political authorities give his public life more and more the shape of a "going up to Jerusalem" to confront all of them at once—from the cross.[7] His death outside the city, outside the *polis,* the foundation and seat of politics, is a symbol in itself.

Christ's irony bears many similarities to popular irony. Listening to his responses, the crowds perceive the condemnation of those who "tie up burdens and lay them on men's shoulders, but will they lift a finger to move them?" (Matt. 23:4). But there is another irony as well, one that goes beyond verbal or ideational triumph, and permits Christ to safeguard the transcendence of his message not only beyond history but within it. For he gives future Christian generations a broad orientation for their basic political attitude:

power exercised as service for liberation and freedom. Thus Christ's neutrality contrasts with that of the churches today and with their political stances, whether "naive or astute." [8] The christologic irony rescues the gospel message from the temptations to power to which the majority of our churches succumb—for:

1. It does not permit religion to become an abstraction that can be manipulated by the dominant classes or the status quo.

2. It does not permit Christianity to make options for its own political models.

3. It does not permit Christianity to identify with "draw-match" or "mediating" positions between good and evil (oppressed and oppressors).

I cannot develop these themes here. They may seem exaggerated if we do not take into account that the objective conditions of Palestine two millennia ago were not suited to the revolutionary changes we hope for in our own day. Speaking generally, we can say that prescinding from politics turns out to be a fiction, when we consider the political repercussions of *any* ideology and *any* praxis. Abstention from politics in the justifiable sense can be understood only as the renunciation of political activity as such, in the area of the practical organization of the taking and exercise of power. "Apoliticism" or "political neutrality" of the churches, understood in this strict sense, is to be respected, just as, in good politics, the autonomy of a union or political party is respected. But neither can it be doubted that, just as union activity presupposes a type of political commitment to which members must accede, so also religion presupposes a worldview that meditates continually on the subjects of true human history—social classes and their struggles. We have learned a great deal today about political manipulation of dogmatic abstractions, as well as about the political strategies of churches within the purely religious domain.[9] And yet, the churches and the Christs they preach turn out to be prisoners of systems far more than Christ and his primitive community were.

In the religious world in which Christ moved, and which he had the task of removing from the sway of the powers and authorities of his era, he saw greater possibilities in the simple faith of the people, and in its ironies, than in the enlightened religion of the mighty. But—and this is what is too easily forgotten by those who exaggerate the virtues of popular piety—he brought about a genuinely revolutionary religious transformation, whose sign was contrary to that of the religion of the masses.

# NOTES

1. Paulo Freire, *Acción cultural para la libertad* (Buenos Aires: Tierra Nueva, 1975), chap. 4, 5; Eng. trans., *Cultural Action for Freedom,* Monograph Series, No. 1 (Cambridge: Harvard Educational Review).

2. *The Church in the Present-Day Transformation of Latin America in the Light of the Council,* ed. Louis Michael Colonnese (Washington, D.C.: CELAM and USCC Division for Latin America, 1968), vol. 2, *Conclusions,* pp. 47–48.

3. See H. Borrat, "Para una cristología de vanguardia," *Víspera* 17 (1970): 26–31.

4. See the essays by G. Casalis (chap. 6, below) and S. Trinidad (chap. 4, above).

5. See A. Quijano, "Cultura y dominación," *Revista Latinoamericana de Ciencias Sociales,* 1–2 (1971), pp. 39–56.

6. See Juan L. Segundo, "Capitalism—Socialism: a Theological Crux" in *The Mystical and Political Dimension of the Christian Faith,* Concilium 96 (New York: Herder and Herder/Seabury, 1974), pp. 105–23.

7. This is the point upon which A. Nisin concentrates in his *Historia de Jesús a partir del Evangelio de Marcos* (Madrid: Península, 1966).

8. See Paulo Freire, "Las iglesias en América Latina: su papel educativo," in *Educación para el cambio social* (Buenos Aires: Tierra Nueva, 1974).

9. On this theme see Jean Guichard, *Eglise, luttes de classes et stratégies politiques* (Paris: Cerf, 1972).

*Chapter 6*

# JESUS—NEITHER ABJECT LORD NOR HEAVENLY MONARCH

## *Georges Casalis*

In every Latin American church, sermon, and catechism, with but few exceptions, we find two inseparable images—those of Christ and the Blessed Virgin. That is, this is what we find in Catholicism, which comprises 93 percent of the Latin American population. The Protestants, of course, who are strongest in the Río de la Plata region, Chile, Brazil, Mexico, and Cuba, have neither pictures nor statues. But their mental images correspond exactly to the Catholic ones. "More or less in the style of the Virgin," we hear.

### THE ODOR OF DEATH

A first image is that of the *suffering Christ*—the image of Jesus overcome, defeated. In most instances he appears as one on the point of death—his eyes rolled up in their sockets, his face turned down to the earth, and his whole body exhibiting the havoc wreaked upon it by the blows of his torturers. All these representations arouse a morbid fascination. They reek of death. The Blessed Virgin, who is never far away, is a woman of ordinary stature, dressed in violet, and with her bosom pierced through by a sword, whose point appears protruding from her shoulder. What a desperate mother!

"Our Abject Lord," this Christ is called. In Monserrat, near Bogotá, atop a cliff overlooking the town, the Abject Lord has a sanctuary. Beneath the main altar, lying like Lenin in his mausoleum in Red Square, you can see his glass sepulcher. And suddenly you find yourself face to face with the bloodied visage of Jesus Defeated.

When the faithful people pray before these images or venerate them, when

72

their spirit is seared all through life by a pedagogy of submission and passivity, evidently it is their own destiny that they encounter here—and worship, and accept with masochistic resignation. Indeed this Abject Jesus is nothing but the image of the conquered Amerindian, the poorest of the poor, for whom nothing has changed since Cortes, the miserable denizen of the immense barrios that fringe the great cities, where subhuman conditions defy word or concept—but viewed from afar they seem the gateway to salvation for all the exploited and starving of the countryside.

All discover a reason for resigning themselves to their lot, for accepting their destiny as a defeated and beaten people. The essence of such a religion is passivity in the face of misfortune and evil—acceptance of life as it is.

The production and distribution of such representations and images corresponds to the dearest interests of established power. Religious and political authorities have invested in them, and permit them to exist, because they hope that they will help the poor to understand the virtue of their actions and the meaning of life.

And indeed there at the side of the Man of Sorrows, Our Lady of the Seven Sorrows displays her transfixed bosom to the gaze of the multitude. For she is the personification of all the women prematurely aged by the tears they must shed for their spouses and their children as well as for themselves. Liberation struggles are very costly. In Mexico, in the mid-1970s, there was unrest among the country folk, as there always is, this time in the Veracruz area. The federal government, in the hands of the Partido Revolucionario Institucional for decades, dispatched troops, which fired upon the two hundred protesters as they were holding a meeting. Life—especially the life of anyone in the opposition—does not count for much. Instead of dying slowly of hunger, you get a bullet in your flesh. This is why women weep and suffer with Our Lady of Sorrows.

## THE WRATH OF A GOD WHO THIRSTS FOR VENGEANCE

What is our christology? Is it a teaching and a message of the suffering of a defeated humankind, or is it the reflection and liberating proclamation of human beings who combat in solidarity with those for whom they wish to open up a future?

Does Jesus' suffering have a value in itself? Can we go on representing this "dolorous" Christianity as a "failure of the cross," which cries out for reparation at all costs—or as a magical, masochistic mystery in which the shedding of innocent blood provokes the fury of a god who thirsts for vengeance?

On the very contrary, is not the cross a victory, and the crowning point of authentic solidarity? The one who dies upon it is not resigned to a blind destiny. With a consummate absence of concern for himself, has he not fought to the bitter end to free human beings from their alienation within and without? Has he not given his life that we may live? From henceforth and forever it shall be clear that only those who refuse to hold onto life for themselves can enable others to live. The reason why the cross is a victory is that it has opened a breach, once for all, in the prison wall of the selfish will to power.

In those same churches we find, as well—in fewer numbers, of course, because it is blood and death that is loved the most, unfortunately—images of Christ and the Blessed Virgin Glorified. After all we have said, it should come as no surprise to see them wearing all the insignia of the Most Catholic Royal Couple of Spain. Christ is represented as a celestial Ferdinand of Aragon, and Mary as an eternal Isabella of Castile. Their overadorned vesture, the gold of their crowns, their jewels, all this proclaims their power—a terrestrial power, which, for centuries, in Latin America and elsewhere, has planned and executed the death of aborigines, the subjugation of peoples, and the accelerating exploitation of the poor by the rich. Behold this power on a sudden transported to heaven! Thus transposed and established, it receives, from above, its legitimation and ultimate anointing.

## CHRIST AS CELESTIAL FERDINAND

If Christ is the heavenly Ferdinand, the earthly Ferdinand thereby becomes the authentic royal lieutenant of his eternal warrant. Thus, whoever prays before or venerates these images honors and accepts as well the power of the earthly representatives of these glorified beings. Hence it is evident that the powerful of this world will have great interest in the people's veneration and love for their celestial counterparts. Right along with the worship of a heavenly Christ, all political, pedagogical, and religious power—whatever be its name—is secure from all assault, forever sanctified and fortified by its throne, its couches, and its pillars. Is not its international dimension the very proof of its eternity?

Thus, just as the Christ of the passion is converted into a symbol of the secular defeat of peoples, so the Christ of glory is demoted to the rank of minister of propaganda in governments that govern by authoritarianism and torture.

In Santa Fe, New Mexico, there is a famous statue of the Blessed Virgin with the charming and meaningful name of *La Conquistadora!* This is Cortes's "Queen of Heaven," who accompanied him on his pilgrimage to our lands. With her at his side, he came from Spain in the name of God to conquer Mexico—putting into execution the greatest bloodbath in American history. To boot, as tragedy would have it, the Amerindians, in their mythology, had expected to see one day, disembarking on the eastern coasts of their lands, white gods, dispensing eternal life. And now beneath the banner of the white goddess, Christian conquistadors invaded everywhere, and the terrified aborigines quickly came to know the methods by which European empires limitlessly extended their borders.

Once again little has changed. In the mid-1970s, in Colombia, a large number of persons went on trial for the murder of some Indians. The perpe-trators—all independent farmers, white, Christian, whose goal was the ex-pansion of their property—declared unanimously and apparently with perfect sincerity: *"We did not know it was a crime to kill an Indian."* So now they have been indicted, but the trial was postponed and has yet to be re-sumed.

As I stood, in the museum of Santa Fe, gazing up at *La Conquistadora,* suddenly a shock went through me. One of her eyes had been gouged out. I felt a sudden burst of joy. Some Indian had come by here and realized that this was an image of the oppression and death of sisters and brothers, and wanted to do something to avenge them.

Why do we think of the glorified Christ as a heavenly monarch and transfer to eternity the traits of earthly kings? Is this how we justify the earthly an-guish of our peoples? Is this not the very image of all the crushing oppression carried out by paternalistic powers, so sacred and implacable? Does Easter mean that, when all is said and done, there is a heaven where oppressors are called "benefactor" as they are on earth (Luke 22:25)?

What conclusion do we draw from the fact that the risen Christ is the one who "got rid of the Sovereignties and Powers, and paraded them in public, behind him in his triumphal procession" of the cross (Col. 2:15)? Does this not mean he unmasks and denounces them, together with those structures and persons that become ends unto themselves, bringing human beings nothing but slavery and death in place of justice and freedom? In this case Easter, from henceforth and to all future time, cannot mean that he has accepted the features of abjection so that he may be raised up by the mighty, who look to nothing but to make use of him, just as they seize and make use of all else beside. If this is Easter, then we have a "diminished Christ," one rendered altogether inoffensive—or better, one become the willing accom-plice of all the blows struck against humanity, whose bloodied living theater is the world of every day.

No, the real Christ is not the Abject Lord—for the end-time is upon us, the age of the dissolution of power and the freedom of service. Or, to put it more concretely, the age is upon us when only those who follow Christ in his com-bat for freedom without seeking any personal advantage will be the ones to make history and build the future. If Christ's throne is in heaven, then there is not the slightest particle of hope on earth. But the service he renders is victory over the *world,* for he is the inexhaustible spring of all liberations, interior and exterior. *Easter is not victory over the cross; it is the victory of the cross!*

And here I pose a radical question. I ask whether the primitive church did not commit a fundamental error in formulating the profession *Kyrios Ies-ous*—Jesus is Lord. *Kyrios,* we know, was an imperial title. (It was also the translation used in the Greek Bible for the Hebrew name of God, *Yahweh*— but I cannot tarry on this here.) The Roman emperor, even during his life-time, was, if not divine, at least divinized. As a result political obedience acquired religious overtones. But here, with reason, Christians began to say that the *Kyrios* was not Caesar but Jesus. But what does this mean—the demythologization of the emperor, or the ideologization of Jesus? Or both together? Is there any way to avoid the possibility that such an imposing title may degenerate and become inoffensive—or, on the contrary, that it may gravely compromise the one who bears it? In any case, such seems to have been the process by which it came about that Jesus, who is the victorious servant, was turned into a heavenly emperor, which means exactly the opposite.

The time has come for commitment to a christology of a suffering servant who suffers because he fights. But it is clear that this would call into question, anew and radically, all the mental and institutional structures of historical Christianity. Such a reflection, concretely, could lead to nothing but a break with all the Constantinian concubinages in which the churches have installed themselves down through the centuries.

Ideologized religion is treason to humanity. The "areligious Christianity" of which Bonhoeffer speaks is a personal and communitarian adventure of living faith, in solidarity with the poor.

# PART THREE

*Christ and Politics*

*Chapter 7*

# THE POLITICAL NATURE OF JESUS' MISSION

## *Ignacio Ellacuría*

### THE PROBLEMATIC CHARACTER
### OF MULTIPLE CHRISTOLOGIES

Any theological reflection upon salvation in history demands a christ-ology. Faith in Jesus, to be sure, is one necessary element for understanding salvation history. But this faith can, and in some cases ought to, meet up with human *logos*—with human rational discourse. Faith in Jesus becomes a christology.

Now, with which *logos* are we dealing? Which rational method will be the most adequate for allowing the faith to expand to a maximal intellectual comprehension? This is the question with which we shall be dealing in the following paragraphs.

In order to respond to it, we must first recognize the fact that christ-ology, indeed several different christ-ologies, are present right in the New Testament. Both parts of this affirmation are topical in current theology, but it will be useful to elaborate on them briefly. The New Testament transmits to us not only the Jesus-faith of a primitive community, but a certain reflection upon this faith as well—more or less theoretical, more or less "log-ical," case by case—carried out either by the primitive community itself or by one of its budding theologians. Nor can this fact be passed over lightly, as if it were merely incidental. *Logos* implies situationality, and situationality delimits foci—interprets facts selectively. That this delimitation, and its correspond-ing interpretation, are doubtless justified—and even considered to be in-

spired—does not afford a pretext for denying the delimitation and interpretation. We are dealing with christ-ological reflections after the fact, not naked
historical facts.

The clearest evidence for this is in the second part of our affirmation—that
the New Testament contains different christ-ologies. That is, not only are the
facts differently selected and differently systematized—and this is already the
beginning of different christologies—but they are reflected upon in different
manners. Not that these distinct reflections are absolutely irreconcilable. But
neither are their variants to be passed over lightly. To give an example (and it
is just one example) that will be particularly relevant for our considerations in
this chapter, the christology of the gospel of the circumcision, or judaizing
current, is very different from the christology of the gospel of Paul.

This is not the place for an in-depth discussion of this often reopened and
hotly debated question. Suffice it to indicate here that the gospel of the circumcision pays more attention to the historical Jesus, as well as to his social
and historical echoes—which, by the way, are closely linked to each other.
The gospel of Paul pays little attention to the Jesus of the flesh, to the historical Jesus. It moves, rather too rapidly, to the Christ of faith. History may not
be identified with storybook narrative, granted. But neither may history keep
aloof from fact—in our case, from the visible, incarnate fact that is antecedent to faith.

The difference is an important one. It points up the fact that the diverse
christological readings of one and the same historical Jesus are due in good
part to the situation and needs of the person who has this faith in Jesus. Paul
had not actually lived with Jesus, and this lacuna in his experience did not fail
to leave its mark. That certain Judeo-Christians had *only* lived with Jesus in
the flesh, and had not managed to go beyond the materiality of his historical
comportment—this, of course, will also be a limitation. The limitations of
the distinct christologies of the New Testament must be surmounted in an
"ulterior christology," one that assumes them all and reelaborates them historically—that is, one that works out a new, historically situated, reading of
Jesus.

This is what the Greek *logos* failed to do. And yet it is this Greek *logos* that
has so long been manipulated by theologians as if it had been the only possible *logos* and the best of all possible *logoi*. This is not to deny that Greek
philosophy had much to contribute to christology. The first councils demonstrate both the advantages and the limitations of the Greek *logos* in the rational reelaboration of the Christian faith. We can go even further and admit
that the preponderant utilization of a particular Greek *logos* was perhaps the
sufficiently adequate response to a precise historical situation—the situation
of a few—in which what was important was speculative contemplation, and
by no means the transformation of society, whose subject is a whole people.

What interested this individualistic intelligentsia was a theoretical, idealist
intellection of the Christian mystery. Thus a historical answer was indeed
given to the Christ question, which included a number of permanent (but not

definitive) *logoi,* or concepts—for example, at Chalcedon. But this means neither that everything substantial in christology has now been said, nor even that advances can no longer be made along the lines of intellectual interpretation itself.

Today, we need a new christology—whose capital theme may no longer be how conceptually to reconcile (and thus to tranquilize one's intellectual concern) the unicity of Christ's person with his twofold nature, but rather how Jesus actualizes the fullness of his mission as savior of human beings. And this is no mere functional corollary of the ancient essentialist statement. Nor is it any less profound a question than the other. If history contains more metaphysical entity than static nature does, then reflections upon history must go deeper than previous questions of nature and substance—and, by definition, must be more operative and dynamic.

This new christology must accord Jesus' flesh, his history, its full revelatory value. Today more than ever before it is simply absurd to pretend to construct a christology in which the actual, historical course of the life of Jesus is not the decisive element. What was handled yesterday as a peripheral, ascetical matter (much less is done with it today), must recover its full and proper significance. Of course, one condition for this endeavor will definitely be that we carry out an exegetical and historical study of the actual life of Jesus. We must yield the right-of-way to the historical *logos,* without which every other *logos* is merely speculative and idealistic.

This historical *logos* will have to take its point of departure in the only partially known facts of the life of Jesus, to terminate in the glance of faith in which that historical life is the fullest revelation of the God confessed by Christians. Thus it must exercise the methodology of a *logos* of history, subsuming and transcending the *logos* of nature, which has a way of bypassing the *logos* of being and reality. Only a *logos* that keeps account of Jesus' historical reality can break the way for a total christology, a christology equal to the changing challenges of history. It alone will be able to reveal to us that there is salvation in history, hard by the history of salvation.

I say all this not in order to carry out what I propose, but merely to demonstrate the limitations of the classic christologies, to point a way to the possibility of transcending them—and more concretely, in order to justify the christological character of my focus in the pages that follow.

## SOCIAL AND PUBLIC DIMENSION OF JESUS' PROPHETICISM

Leaving aside certain discussions, not altogether out of place, on the precise nature of Jesus' propheticism, it can nonetheless be asserted that the prophetic dimension is a very important dimension of the Jesus depicted in the New Testament. For our purposes here, what is important is that those about him repeatedly place him in the line of the prophets. Matthew 16:14, as well as Mark 8:27–33, with their very different theological intentions, clearly indicate to us that, for the people ("What do people say I am?"), Jesus is in the same line as Elijah, Jeremiah, and John the Baptist. In a word, he is one of the great prophets. We cannot repeat here what has been said about propheticism elsewhere. But it is clear that if the crowds place Jesus in the line of the great prophets, then he must have led a prophet's life. That Matthew and Mark go further in the passages just cited, and attribute to him being the Messiah and the Son of God, does not invalidate the historical process. Jesus transcends his propheticism, yes, but he does so from a point of departure in, and an ongoing exercise of, this propheticism itself. This fact is of incalculable significance. It is via the prophetical dimension that the crowds, and his disciples as well, come to grasp what Jesus is in his ultimate reality. Hence neither can we ourselves, today, grasp this ultimate reality by seeking it somewhere out on the margin of his life as a prophet. Nor on the other hand can we duly penetrate the depths of his prophetical life without transcending it, to grasp the ultimate reality to which his prophetical life leads.

## Consciousness of Divine Sonship

The problem could, however, be further sharpened. Here we could ask one of the essential questions of christology: When and how did Jesus acquire explicit consciousness of his divine sonship—of the ultimate character of his own personhood? Christologies erected upon a Greek *logos* of nature, and insufficiently anchored to a rigorous exegesis of New Testament texts, have given aprioristic, very "unhistorical," answers.[1] A christology more faithful to the facts will suggest that Jesus acquired full consciousness of his full personal being only gradually, in and through the life in which he fulfilled himself. If this be the case, then we could affirm not only that the path of the Father's revelation passes through the life of Jesus, but that only by leading the life of Jesus ourselves, by following his life, can we reach the Father's revelation. Consequently only in following that life, and in making that following visible to others, will we be able to come to a knowledge of what the Father is, be able to proclaim, and make the Father present to a historical world.

There is no doubt that this new posing of the question would rattle all fundamental theology, and straightway reshape, in a very particular manner, the whole pastoral theology and ministry of the church. We may not forget that the predominance accorded to the sacramental sign is in the causal line of nature—whereas this new view would lead us to the predominance of the word, and of the life of a prophet, along the lines of the historical *logos*.

Hence the urgency of returning to what the life of Jesus actually was, and not so much for spiritual edification—as a point of departure for psychological relationships with him—as for its theological meaning and significance. And in this line, one capital datum is Jesus' propheticism. Even the Gospel of John does not eschew the path of propheticism as the way to the affirmation of the divine sonship. After all, John's emphasis is on the preparatory character of the propheticism of John the Baptist, together with the fullness of propheticism in Jesus himself: "This really is the prophet who is to come into the world" (John 6:14; cf. 4:19, 7:40, 9:17).

And indeed Jesus' personality and life have characteristics that clearly establish him in the eyes of the people as one of the greatest prophets. In him freedom flashes forth—in the face of traditions, and in the face of the established powers who identify their establishment with a paralyzing religious tradition. Hence the austerity of Jesus' life, his boldness in confronting the powerful of this earth, and the public character of his life to the point of its becoming a moment of decision in the concrete history of the people. In him, the power of the word, and the power of signs, have exceptional force. The word becomes the definitive herald of the kingdom—which Jesus proclaims as already present. He makes the living God vitally present among human beings. He promulgates a new morality of the heart, which transcends all our legalisms.

## Access to the Father

Let us analyze Jesus' prophetic style in somewhat more detail, from the point of view of its influence upon the shape of the prophetic element in the church.

Before all else, Jesus rejected a ritualized, dead religion. It is certain that Jesus observed the fundamental religious practices of his people. The interpreters of his life recall his circumcision, his presentation in the temple, his attendance at synagogue services, and so on. But neither is it to be forgotten that he collided with practices considered to be of the greatest importance by the legalists of his time, such as abstinence from work on the Sabbath, the washing of hands, and so on. Hence we cannot deduce any nihilism with regard to the religious element from Jesus' personal practice as it is transmitted to us by primitive tradition. But, as with the prophets, neither is Jesus an official minister of the religious establishment. He is neither priest nor levite nor anything of the kind. Instead, he is clearly distinguished from, and contrasted with, them. He does not belong to the hierarchical apparatus. On the contrary, he combats its manner of defining a human being's relationship with God.

Right from the start he places the boast of being carnal children of Abraham under interdict—that is, he interiorizes the relationship with God (John 8:39). He does not spiritualize it, but he subjectivizes it, he frees it, so that it is no longer a purely external thing. The human being must freely appropriate what is presented, for without this appropriation there is no properly human life. This is most evident in Jesus' attitude toward religious ritual, toward the localization of the encounter with God, as we observe in the passage that reports his conversation with the Samaritan woman. God will be adored in spirit and truth, not in one temple or another. For God is spirit, interiority, the interior totality present to every reality. Most precious to the Jew is a knowledge in history of who the living God is who is to be adored—not this

God's localization and cultural manipulation. Hence neither is Jesus the advocate of long, wordy prayers—especially when persons are content to implore God, without coming to grips with the will of the Father and setting themselves to bring it about.

Jesus vehemently attacks oppression by religious authority in God's name. Hence his anger at the hypocrisy of those who confuse the commands of God with human traditions (Matt. 15:1-20). He appeals to Isaiah in his condemnation of external actions that do not correspond to the truth of the heart and he proposes a program that decidedly surpasses everything ritual and legal. He attacks those who claim to carry the keys of the kingdom and who yet prevent entry (Luke 11:52)—who lay unbearable burdens upon others without being willing to lift a finger to help them. Passages in this vein are numerous.

In sum, in Jesus' mode of life and mission there is a pronounced shift of religious emphasis. Now what counts is a faith that is operative. What is important in the new covenant, in the new age, will be one's personal attitude, one's attachment to Jesus' person in faith, and consequently the following of his person in one's own life. On this personal relationship, in which following and faith meet and intersect to condition each other, will depend Christian holiness—that is, the salvific presence of God within the human being and the human being's access to God. Here again God's revelation, God's actualization if you will, in human beings depends absolutely upon the relationship of the human being with the one who professes to be the way to God, the truth of God, and the life of God. There is no other access to the Father than that shown by the life of Jesus.

## Public Discipleship

One of the basic formulations of this following, this discipleship, is expressed in the Sermon on the Mount,[2] understood not as a new law, but as a principle of discipleship, of following.[3] In this discipleship, which is visible, and not some alleged supernatural grace whose presence escapes the objectivity of personal and social consciousness, is the measure of being Christian. The eye should be fixed not on the "supernaturalness" of actions or persons, but on their "Christianity"—the following, incarnate and not in intention alone, discoverable in other human lives, of what is essential in the life of Jesus.

Now, from this perspective, Jesus is going to appear as a public force, driving forward to a thoroughgoing transformation of a public situation. The same occurred with the prophets. We need not as yet lay any emphasis upon the precise meaning of the cleansing of the temple. The deed alone, in the position it occupies in the presentation of the synoptics and John as well, demonstrates all by itself that Jesus' new manner of understanding our relationship with God is going to place him on a collision course with public religious authority. It is beyond question that the religion of Israel, even in

Jesus' time, was one of the most decisive, if not the most decisive, elements in the whole shape of public and private life. Any action touching religion was perforce an action touching public life, and although Jesus' immediate emphasis was not upon the socio-political but upon the socio-religious, his action could not have been interpreted as anything short of a grave act of interference with the prevailing power structure.

The clearest proof of this is that those who dominated the religion of Israel, and through it the social structure and life of the people, saw in Jesus, just as they had in John the Baptist, a major threat to their preeminence and power. By attacking their monopoly of faith in Yahweh, by impugning the need for their mediation in an individual's encounter with God, Jesus was undermining the power of the priestly establishment. More than this, he was placing in danger, as we shall see, the delicate balance between the people and the power of the Romans, within which equilibrium the Jewish authorities were maneuvering in order to maintain themselves in their acquired status. Finally, he endangered the source of their income, as can be appreciated in the cleansing of the temple.

Accordingly, even those who would like to reduce Jesus' activity to a purely religious one will be forced to recognize, in this first, typical deed of his propheticism, a public moment of the first importance. The priestly establishment was not purely religious; placing its false religion under interdict is automatically reason for public collision with the structure of its society. Let us not forget that in the area of the social we are dealing with structures, and that therefore the upsetting of one of its essential elements entails the imbalance of the social whole.

But there is much more than this, even in the purely prophetical activity of Jesus. His denunciations themselves are in the most typical prophetic vein. That is, besides his opposition to religious authority, his life demonstrates a determined opposition to social authority as well. His merciless attack on the scribes and the Pharisees—for practical purposes the depositories of religious infallibility and thereby the mainstay of the socio-religious structure—is already a step in the direction of a more strictly social denunciation. Without pretending to exhaust the theme of these denunciations, let us briefly underscore Jesus' position on the crucial question of wealth and poverty. And as we do so, let us not forget Luke's report that "the Pharisees, who loved money, heard all this and laughed at him" (Luke 16:14).

## Poverty and Wealth

What stands out in Jesus' preaching, for the point under consideration here, is the importance he ascribes to the theme of poverty and his presentation of poverty by contrast with wealth. It is not simply that he favors poverty as a sort of ascetical counsel, for whoever would wish to be perfect. He places poverty in dialectical opposition to wealth. In other words, it is not a matter of the praise of poverty in itself and the condemnation of wealth in itself; it is a matter of the praise and condemnation of the linear correlation between poverty and wealth. That is, Jesus condemns the wealth that causes poverty and praises the poverty that indicts the destructive existence of wealth.

The Sermon on the Mount, especially in Luke's formulation, is telling on this point. It is a radical judgment, but it is a judgment that brings poverty and its praise, and wealth and its reprehension, into relative confrontation. The poor are the fortunate, whereas the rich will not possess the kingdom of God, because they have their consolation already, in wealth. Those who are hungry will be satiated, and those who are presently satisfied shall be the ones to suffer necessity. Those who now weep shall be consoled, but those who laugh now shall know grief and tears. Finally, the attitude of the powerful toward those who live and proclaim the gospel cannot be anything but hatred, marginalization, and chastisement, as they reserve their adulation for those who, although religious in appearance, have nothing in common with the gospel. The reference to the prophets is explicit: thus did your ancestors with the prophets, the true and the false. They abused the true and extolled the false.

It is common knowledge that Luke's formulation here, as in other passages, is more radical than that of the other evangelists. For example, he does not offer Matthew's evasion, "poor in spirit." We are not concerned here with a reconciliation of the texts. For that matter Matthew's own harshness in the area of social denunciation is one of enormous vigor in its own right. (Recall Pasolini's version, which scandalized so many—not because he falsified the letter or the setting, but because the scandalized were accustomed to situate the New Testament in a mellifluous context.)

But I am concerned to stress the historical character, and change of emphasis, in the Lucan reading, which has its point of departure in a community where the problem of poverty and wealth stood in the foreground. One proof of this is the community of goods, and the sense of their strict availability according to the necessity of the community, as transmitted to us in Acts. The Lucan reading is done in the concrete situation of the community and is concretized in altogether real and effective terms, avoiding all interioristic and idealistic evasion—a reading that should be resumed today from a point of departure in the present historical situation of each ecclesial community.

The theme of poverty and wealth is therefore not an individualistic, ascetical one. It is a sociological theme, as well, and it is in this sociological dimension that its relationship with the individual's access to God is to be found. Indeed wealth is seen as one of the greatest impediments to the coming of the kingdom of God among human beings—that is, to God's becoming salvifically present among human beings. As the history of salvation progresses it becomes more and more clear that poverty, not wealth, is the locus of revelation and of God's salvation. The history of salvation becomes increasingly more radical in this direction.

The radicalization begins in the Old Testament itself, precisely through the message of the prophets. God's blessing had been seen in material things until that time in history, when it began to be appreciated that this material wealth had been amassed by riding roughshod over defenseless persons and that it led to every manner of oppression. In the face of this new historical experience, propheticism comes more and more into confrontation with wealth—to the extent that that wealth causes poverty, and not as a consideration in itself. The process culminates in the New Testament.

Thus the poverty of Jesus' life has a fundamental theological value from the very start. It is not a question of an affective, psychological reaction of wishing to be "poor with poor Jesus" in order to be "more like him." The question must be put much more radically than this. The poverty of Jesus' life has a socio-theological meaning of the first importance. It is the poverty of his life that, on the one hand, is both a condition and a result of his absolute freedom before the authorities of this world, and on the other hand is the condition of access to the only life in which God's self-revelation takes place. Hence the importance of the frequent repetition of the wealth-poverty theme in the New Testament. Both its repetition and its peculiar emphasis signify that in this aspect of life, at once personal and social, one of the essential elements of the Christian message is poverty. It is not a matter either of masochism or of class struggle. It is a matter of the real and objective locus of the divine revelation. In the struggle between poverty and wealth, God's revelation occurs plainly in poverty. It is in this light that the community of goods ought to be seen—a voluntary community, to be sure, but one most earnestly adhered to by the primitive church. It is not an installation of communism in the political sense of the term. It is an original, unprompted estimation of the optimal conditions for the proclamation of the good news to the concrete human beings of history.

I repeat, it is not a question of the abstract praise of poverty—as if the indispensable condition for the acceptance of God were to be permanent misery. Nor is it a question of an abstract condemnation of wealth, as if the enjoyment of material realities necessarily implied a roadblock across the path of Christian access to the God of Jesus Christ. It is a matter, in the first place, of a historical putting of the question—hence one attendant upon a determined situation. And in the second place it is a matter of a dialectical relationship—of a wealth that produces poverty, with the result that you are either with the dominators or the dominated. Such a putting of the question is not the cancellation, but the framework, of the sense in which a personal asceticism of poverty may be cultivated—which, nevertheless, must finally be based upon the theologico-historical meaning of Jesus' poverty, and not on any presumed efficacious relationship with a historical Jesus who is now transcended by the Christ of the resurrection. For, though he be transcended, he is by no means replaced.

The gospel gives a series of reasons for this historical and concrete preference for poverty—or, if you prefer, for the poor—as the privileged locus of God's revelation. But I shall limit myself to some of the reasons cited by those best acquainted with the life of Jesus.

Luke comes right out and calls wealth "tainted" (Luke 16:9)—dishonest, or even better, unjust. And this is what occasioned the Pharisees' sneering and Jesus' protest: "You are the very ones who pass yourselves off as virtuous in people's sight, but God knows your hearts. For what is thought highly of by men is loathsome in the sight of God" (Luke 16:15). The meaning is clear, if only we attend to what is stated in the verse immediately preceding. The Pharisees laughed scornfully when they heard Jesus' teaching about wealth and poverty, and Luke gives the reason. We have already alluded to it. "The Pharisees . . . loved money." Therefore they are not just, however much they may present themselves as just before the people. For the wealth that is their love is an abomination before God. The text leaves no room for the facile evasion that only unjustly acquired wealth is reprehensible—no, wealth itself is qualified as unjust, and always in connection with the poverty that is its inevitable correlate.

The New Testament condemnation of wealth does not occur in a social context exclusively. Wealth is also condemned by reference to God. One cannot serve God and money, because no other lord can be set up alongside God (Luke 16:13, Matt. 6:24). Or, as Luke explains elsewhere (12:15–21), because it causes forgetfulness of God's sovereignty. In other words, of its own dynamism, wealth becomes an absolute value and necessarily leads to idolatry—an idolatry that often will not consist in denying God's existence and deifying wealth, but in interpreting God's being in such a way that God can be transformed into Lord of the rich—that is, God can be read in such a way as to render permissible the accumulation of wealth in this world.

It is unnecessary to conduct a historical investigation where the capitalistic interpretation of Christianity has led, both among Protestants and among Catholics. Max Weber's work can illustrate this point abundantly. If history does not sufficiently prove that it is an anti-Christian interpretation, Jesus' warning does: the word of God, fallen upon a heart delivered up to riches, can only suffocate. "The one who received the seed in thorns is the man who hears the word, but the worries of this world and the lure of riches choke the word and so he produces nothing" (Matt. 13:22). That is, the thorns of wealth may not prevent the word from germinating, but ultimately they choke it to death.

This intrinsic difficulty with wealth—that it prevents the word, once received, from bearing its Christian fruit—is perfectly well established in the gospel. Two series of texts demonstrate it clearly. One of them refers to the rich young man (Matt. 19:16–22, Mark 10:17–31, Luke 18:18–30). As we see, all three synoptics give him a great deal of space and importance.

The rich man's question concerns eternal life. Jesus' initial response alludes to the keeping of the commandments—among which "Thou shalt not steal" is included. The rich young man now insists that he already observes them all—but as he is convinced that he still does not possess eternal life within himself, the true life, he asks Jesus what else he lacks. Jesus' reply differs slightly in each of the synoptics. Matthew introduces it with "If you wish to be perfect," which has led to perverted interpretations in the form of complex detours defending the rich. Mark and Luke, on the contrary, simply resume the phrase of the man himself: "There is one thing you lack," Jesus admits (not in order to be perfect, but in order to obtain and possess eternal life). This something is clear and simple: to sell all his goods and give the proceeds to the poor in order then to follow Jesus—taking up his cross, Mark adds. Whereupon, as Mark tells us, the young man looked downcast, and "went away sad, for he was a man of great wealth."

This passage has been falsified in a good deal of ascetical and "spiritual reading." Eternal life is understood simply and solely as ultraterrestrial life— but then one is left with an interpretation precisely contrary to the actual meaning—that one can attain to eternal life by keeping the commandments, when it is clearly stated that something further is necessary in order to attain to eternal life. This objection is sidestepped by asserting that the latter is a question of perfection—which of course takes no account of the fact that the meaning of perfection is simply the totality of the possession of eternal life. No, we must find another interpretation.

It is a basic matter of being Christian—of following Christ. The mere keeping of the commandments does not constitute Christianity. One who merely keeps the commandments is not a Christian and does not possess eternal life. Christianity is not an ethical entity whose purpose is to assure the observance of laws. Christianity is a person following, in faith, the life of Christ, and as far as possible actually leading that life. One of the inescapable conditions of this following is the leaving of one's riches and giving them to the poor. Only thus can one follow Jesus—and in this consists the taking up of one's cross, whose meaning, as we shall later see, does not fail to have a zealotic nuance. Only those who are free of riches are in any condition to follow Jesus and continue his mission. The synoptics' final comment could not have been more explicit: ". . . for he was very rich" (Luke 18:23). Otherwise so well disposed, still this young man could not follow Jesus. His wealth did not keep him from hearing the call, but the word "fell among thorns" and was suffocated.

This key event in the life of Jesus is underscored by the words that the evangelists attribute to him. Those who do not renounce all of their goods cannot be his disciple. "It is easier for a camel to pass through the eye of a needle than for a rich man to enter the kingdom of heaven" (Matt. 19:24). "It is easier for a camel to pass through the eye of a needle than for a rich man to enter the kingdom of God" (Mark 10:25). "How hard it is for those who have riches to make their way into the kingdom of God! Yes, it is easier for a camel to pass through the eye of a needle than for a rich man to enter the kingdom of God" (Luke 18:24–25). The language is that of Semitic exaggeration, but it may not be watered down to the point where it has no meaning. The least it can mean is that between the possession of wealth and entry into the kingdom the distance and the contradiction are almost insuperable.

*Two Key Biblical Passages*

The same theme can be considered from the other end as well, from the viewpoint of poverty—or if one prefers, from the viewpoint of the poor.

Among the many passages that can be cited, from Jesus' choice of a lifestyle to his selection of his followers, I shall examine two of the most significant: Matthew's description of the last judgment and Luke's account of Jesus' first preaching.

The importance of the Matthean text derives from its context of the last judgment, the final judgment to be rendered upon human beings, and to a certain point, upon history. "When the Son of Man comes in his glory, escorted by all the angels, then he will take his seat on his throne of glory. All the nations will be assembled before him and he will separate men one from another" (Matt. 25:31–32). The passage is a familiar one, and two of its aspects, which are the key for our interpretation, bear emphasizing. First, the judgment is conducted according to an altogether material bill of particulars, with immediate reference needs—hunger, thirst, homelessness, want of clothing, illness, imprisonment. One's activity with regard to those in need is identified with one's activity with regard to the Son of Man. The least of all, just by being the least, are his sisters and brothers, and what is done to them is done to him. There is no excuse for falling into a false supernaturalism here. There is nothing in the catalogue of deeds to indicate a "religious" or cultural "supernatural." Nor is there the faintest suggestion that those on the right or the left should have been able to *see* Jesus in the objects of their good or evil deeds. It is not evident, at the moment of the opportunity itself, that the persons for or against whom these things are done conceal within themselves the Son of God. Those who accuse the political mission of the church of horizontalism ought to turn more frequently to this text on the last judgment and meditate the meaning of its words.

The other text, from Luke, refers to Jesus' first preaching, in Nazareth. The passage is important for its reference to Isaiah, because Jesus announces that he is connecting his mission with what he considers to be most fundamental about propheticism:

> The spirit of the Lord has been given to me,
> for he has anointed me.
> He has sent me to bring the good news to the poor,
> to proclaim liberty to captives
> and to the blind new sight,
> to set the downtrodden free,
> to proclaim the Lord's year of favor [cf. Isa. 61:1–2].
> . . . This text is being fulfilled today even as you listen
> [Luke 4:18–21].

The text Jesus has taken up to read is from Third Isaiah, and it speaks of the prophetical mission in a clear context of political mission, albeit transcended (Isa. 61:3–10, 62:1–12, 63:1–19). Hence, not only does Jesus place himself in the line of the prophets, but within the aspect of the prophetic line comporting political mission. In the very words Luke cites, the proclamation of the good news is made first of all to the poor and to prisoners, and what is announced is liberation. The meaning of this liberation demands extensive explanation. But even without it the passage is sufficient in itself to establish in what terms Jesus' preaching is expressed *initially,* and hence its interconnections with the *final* proclamation, the last judgment. Between this beginning and this end, Jesus taught a great deal. But it cannot be denied that these two series of texts are crucial for determining the mission of Jesus and the mission of the Christian.

It is along these same lines that the activity of Jesus in the satisfaction of material necessities will have to be situated. Whatever critical reading be made of the miracles, there can be no doubt that the primitive community saw, in the satisfaction of altogether concrete needs, the sign of the presence of the kingdom—to the point where the satisfaction of these necessities on occasion led the multitude to erroneous interpretations of the character of Jesus' propheticism. The passage in John immediately following the multiplication of the loaves is a good illustration. The action has been a "signing" one—but the sign is not rightly understood by the hearers. They take a first step, a correct one, when they say, based upon Jesus' words and deeds, "This really is the prophet who is to come into the world" (John 6:14). But then they at once take a turn that Jesus rejects, and one to which we shall have to attend apropos of the question of a political mission in the strict sense: "Jesus, who could see they were about to come and take him by force and make him king, escaped back to the hills by himself" (John 6:15).

Two basic aspects of Jesus' propheticism have now been identified: (1) his new concept of the proper relationship of the individual with God, and (2) his equally new concept of the dialectical interrelationship between wealth and poverty as a factor for shaping the kingdom—and therefore again of the due relationship of human beings with God. Both aspects, which are essential to Jesus' life and mission, bring him into conflict with the authorities. The exercise of a prophetic calling, as well in its religious as in its social dimension, interferes with the public and collective structure and by that very fact with the system of powers that shape society. From this viewpoint alone one can discern in Jesus' mission not only a public character, but perforce a political one.

To be sure, we are not here confronted with any political project or crusade *per se.* But neither are we able to find any retractation or revision of Jesus' mission in consideration of the political implications it is necessarily going to have. Indeed, as the gospels testify massively, we note an ever increasing struggle with those in power, as they feel themselves more and more threatened in that power and in the structure that supports it. Of course, we see that this is a struggle more in the area of social politics than governmental politics—a fact that will not lack its importance when one undertakes to determine the precise political character of Jesus' mission. And yet, true as this may be, in virtue of the very dynamics of the relationship between social politics and governmental politics, there will be no dearth of struggle in this second dimension as well, for it is both the foundation and expression of the first.

# NOTES

1. Abundant evidence of all that we have been saying will be found in Vogtle's article, "Exegetische Erwägungen über das Wissen und Selbstbewusstsein Jesu," *Gott in Welt* (Freiburg, 1964), pp. 608–67; Rahner's article, "Dogmatic Reflections on the Knowledge and Self-Consciousness of Christ" in volume 5 of his *Theological Investigations* (Baltimore: Helicon, 1966); the joint work of both theologians in "Jesus Christ" in *Sacramentum Mundi* (New York: Herder and Herder, 1968); the whole of *Concilium* 11, *Who Is Jesus of Nazareth?* (New York: Paulist, 1966), especially Engelbert Gutwenger's "The Problem of Christ's Knowledge," pp. 91–105; and Schnackenburg's work in the christological part of *Mysterium Salutis*.

2. See Joachim Jeremias, *Paroles de Jesús, le Sermon sur la Montaine, le Notre-Père* (Paris: Cerf, 1963); Eng. trans., *The Sermon on the Mount* (Philadelphia: Fortress, 1963).

3. See Dietrich Bonhoeffer, *Nachfolge* (Munich: Kaiser, 1937); Eng. trans., *The Cost of Discipleship* (New York: Macmillan, 2nd ed., 1967).

*Chapter 8*

# JESUS' ATTITUDE TOWARD POLITICS: SOME WORKING HYPOTHESES

## *Segundo Galilea*

The "politicization" of Christianity in Latin America, with the resulting complex interrelationships among faith, apostolate, and politics, has thrust the theological and practical questions that must be asked with respect to the tasks of liberation into the foreground of Christian thought. Then, in their turn, liberation theology and pastoral practice inspire the concrete forms of political commitment to which Christians and the Latin American hierarchy, each in their own fashion, are called—with a view to a liberating activity that will be genuinely efficacious.

Today it is no longer possible to avoid questions concerning the political involvement of the church. The discussion tends to center on the political commitment of the priest. The problem is as old as Christianity. And at bottom it is insoluble, for it is more a matter of pastoral wisdom than it is of dogma. The age-old relationship between church and politics is currently approached from various interdisciplinary angles—sociological, political, biblical, theological, pastoral, and cultural. In this spirit I should like to offer a contribution from a point of view that, although very particular, can be enlightening and fertile. Instead of taking a point of departure in the rational process of theology and the human sciences, I propose to approach the subject from the gospel—from the attitude of Christ himself toward the political contingencies of his time. For, apart from the inspirational character that his stance has for the church, it can serve as well as a basis for formulating certain working hypotheses for pastoral ministry.

## INCOMPLETE INTERPRETATIONS

*The "Naive Christ."* Before I attempt to offer a balanced interpretation of
Christ's attitude toward the politics of his time, there are certain incomplete
interpretations abroad in current hermeneutics that it will be in order briefly
to examine. A first incomplete picture of Christ's attitude toward the socio-
political problems of his time is that of a Christ who is marginalized in their
regard, who moves outside their ambit. According to this view, the meaning
of Christ's coming would be exclusively religious. His message is said to be a
religious one, not a social ideology. When he proclaimed that we were to
"give back to Caesar what belongs to Caesar and to God what belongs to
God" he was taking God's part, we are told, and was dissociating himself
from political authorities and their conflicts. In his preaching we find nothing
about politics, or so it is said.

In this view, the facts of Christ's life, especially his passion and death, take
place outside the historical and political framework of his time. This framework (with Pilate, Judas, the Sanhedrin, and so on) is a sort of puppet theater
supplied by the providential Father, as a backdrop for Christ's work of redemption. Strictly speaking, some other scenario, or other characters, could
have been chosen without any essential change.

*The "Revolutionary Christ."* Another interpretation, diametrically opposed to the preceding and currently in vogue in revolutionary circles in Latin
America, holds that Christ was basically a political revolutionary, who stood
up to the established system and collided with it. He came into confrontation
with the Roman imperial authority as well as with the dominant Jewish
classes, and his death, that of a revolutionary martyr, was the result of this
confrontation. Once he put the defense of justice and of the poor at the center
of his preaching, collision was inevitable.

This view of Christ yielded what I call a "spontaneous pseudochristo-
logy," based on Christ as model and image of the Latin American revolutionary who dies for the cause of the oppressed.

## ATTEMPT AT A SYNTHESIS

*Thesis 1: In virtue of the incarnation, and of the historical nature of his mis-
sion, Jesus was part of the society of Israel, with its political tensions and its
power conflicts. His trial and death are political events.*

When we speak of the "historical incarnation" of Christ, we are not only
asserting that God became a human being in a particular and identifiable
place and time; we are also asserting that Jesus became part of the historical,
religious, social, and political movements of his time, and that these movements constitute the framework and matrix of his activity.

Concretely, Jesus was a Jew who lived among the conflicts and aspirations of Palestine at that particular historical moment. Like the rest of the Jews, he was subject to the Romans. Like them, he shared their aspirations for liberation. Like them, he was subject to the pressure of the situations created by the political factions of the time, from the Herodians to the revolutionaries, or Zealots. Like them, he had to take a position vis-à-vis the established Roman power and vis-à-vis the abusive religious system of the priests and Pharisees. His trial before the Sanhedrin and Pilate took the historical form of the suppression of a subversive: "We found this man inciting our people to revolt, opposing payment of the tribute to Caesar, and claiming to be Christ, a king. . . . He is inflaming the people . . . " (Luke 23:2, 5). "Anyone who makes himself king is defying Caesar" (John 19:12).

All this clearly shows us that Jesus' behavior and preaching impinged upon the political questions of his time and came into conflict with the civil as well as the religious authorities:

> Then the chief priests and Pharisees called a meeting. "Here is this man working all these signs," they said, "and what action are we taking? If we let him go on in this way everybody will believe in him, and the Romans will come and destroy the Holy Place and our nation" [John 11:47–49].

Thus Jesus' death was a political event, with religious and political causes typical for a "colonial" country. It was a death brought about by religious authorities who were most influential in society and very careful to "be on good terms" with the system. To the extent that Jesus questioned this established religion, he also questioned its social power and its conformist meaning.

*Thesis 2: On the other hand, Jesus neither claimed to be nor behaved as a revolutionary or as a political leader. His message contains neither a program nor a strategy for political liberation. Jesus essentially proclaimed the kingdom of God as a religious and pastoral message.*

Paradoxically, in the exercise of his mission, as well as in the content of his preaching, Jesus was a religious leader and not a political official. Neither in his position vis-à-vis the established authority (Luke 22:17ff., 18:33–34, etc.), nor in the content of his preaching (the kingdom of God), nor in the orientation he gave his disciples (who established themselves in a religious group, or church) does there appear anything resembling an ideal for a temporal society or a program of political activity. His message contains no elements of strategy or activity vis-à-vis Roman imperialism—and so Jesus cannot be assimilated to any of the parties or political movements of his time. As to the Zealots, the most revolutionary group, the absence of any relationship with Jesus has been abundantly demonstrated.[1]

More positively, Jesus proclaimed the kingdom of God. That is, his message is essentially religious and pastoral. His proclamation revealed the true nature of God the Father, the true calling and destiny of human beings—and God's ultimate gift, offered to human beings in Christ: their liberation from sin and from all evil, and the promise of a new society, which would achieve its fullness in the eschatological kingdom ("new skies and a new earth"). The kingdom of God is proclaimed as a promise already being put into effect among human beings (Mark 1:14–15), along with a set of values whose synthesis is the Sermon on the Mount and whose center is the person of Jesus himself.

This proclamation is to be the object of the preaching and pastoral activity of the church for all time. The church follows in the Master's footsteps. It has no models, programs, or socio-political strategies to propose in its mission.

### Thesis 3: Nevertheless, in his religious and pastoral message, Jesus generated a dynamism of socio-political change, for his time and for all history to come.

Jesus' proclamation of the kingdom of God had consequences for politics and for social change, even revolutionary change, in his own time, as well as wherever the Christian message can become a leaven in society in the future.[2] The Christian message is not a social ideology, nor is it a revolutionary program. But by reason of its dynamic character and its call for the conversion of individuals and society, it acquires the nature of a principle of nonconformity and criticism vis-à-vis every society and every politics. The gospel itself, inasmuch as it contains a principle of freedom and reveals the true calling of the human being and of the world, offers values that can question systems, and consequently generate movements and conflicts of political liberation. In this sense, the gospel, and Christianity, are revolutionary, and the religious and pastoral message of Christ has proclaimed the values of justice and freedom that are at the basis of socio-political liberation movements.

In this same sense, Christ's activity, too, is political. For, in its consequences, it veers into the realm of political society and produces changes in political societies. It is the most meaningful example, the prototype, of faith and pastoral ministry that have the inherent tendency to spawn implications and consequences in the political domain. The proclamation of the kingdom constitutes the implantation in history, once and for all, of a principle of freedom and social critique, both as promise and as denunciation. As promise, it is the leaven of nonconformism. As denunciation, it demands the removal of everything in society that assaults the nature and destiny of the human being as revealed at the heart of the gospel. Jesus' message is political not per se, but through the mediation of pastoral and religious theory and action.

### Thesis 4: The political consequences of Jesus' message in the society of his time are due to the fact that that message relativized Roman totalitarianism and called the poor to the kingdom, to the universal consciousness that it

*created in the disciples, and to the proclamation of the specific values of the Beatitudes.*

In the concrete society in which Christ lived and taught, his message had consequences for politics and social change—even in his generation. This was due mainly to the following factors.

First, in the proclamation of the one true God and Jesus Christ, God's messenger, all idolatry is brought to an end. He relativizes, puts in their place, the values and persons that in his time take the place of that God. Among these are the emperor and his authority—the cornerstone of the mythic might that holds the Roman empire together. Christ destroys the ideological bases of its totalitarianism. In a parallel movement, he gives every human being a sense of freedom and equality vis-à-vis the lords of power, whom he places in dependence on the power of God (John 19:11–34).

Thus, Roman authoritarianism and totalitarianism are undermined not by a frontal assault, via the political route, but via the proclamation of the truth about God and humankind. Socially and politically this is highly subversive, in the short run and the long. Jesus goes beyond the ambitions of the Zealots, or of any revolutionary program or activity by destroying the very foundations of the imperial system.

Secondly, Jesus calls the poor to make up his kingdom. In fact he announces that one must become poor in order to enter it (Matt. 5:3; Luke 6:20, 16:19–26, 18:18–23, etc.). He gives them priority, he gives them the ultimate sense of their dignity. He calls them, he mobilizes them, to form his church.

Given the cultural context of his time, this mobilization of the poor could not help but have deep socio-political repercussions. It had the effect of setting in motion, of lending a mystique and a social power to, a group hitherto marginalized and without political significance. It introduced, in the empire and in the aristocratic society that the empire had generated, a majoritarian force, conscious of its dignity, independent of the system and established authorities, and desirous of reestablishing justice. This new force was to be decisive in the enfeeblement and eventual collapse of the empire, and this call issued to the poor of the kingdom would be at the root of all authentic revolutions, in the measure that they are carried out in the name of justice for the poor and oppressed—the lowly of the gospel.

Thirdly, as consummator of the proclamation of the prophets, Jesus proclaims his kingdom to be universal, bursting the frontiers of Jewish nationalism and of an exclusively Jewish salvation (Matt. 24:14, 21:43–46). Here he goes beyond the tribalism of the Pharisees and Zealots. He sends his disciples forth on a universal mission—one at the heart of the empire, yes, but beyond its frontiers as well, as a minority—the "remnant"—who bring hope to all the rest.[3]

In this form, Jesus' message makes the Christian poor into a universal force capable of calling the empire into question from within, from its centers of power, such as Rome itself. It debilitates the traditional religious system of the Jews, too, so nationalistic, sectarian, and turned in upon itself. Indeed, in bringing to fulfillment the prophecies of the universal mission of the "servant remnant" of the Jewish people, Jesus enfeebles the whole dominating religious system, for his criticism strikes at the very roots of the Jewish theocracy and its authorities. He powerfully injects his disciples, who were heirs to this decadent tradition, into every echelon of ancient Roman society. Herewith is the beginning of the conversion of the empire—the "multitude," who receive the influence of the "remnant"—and the beginning of the end for the political power of the Sanhedrin.

Fourthly, and most important of all, in his proclamation of the kingdom, formulated especially in the Sermon on the Mount and the Beatitudes, Jesus renews Israel's prophetic and moral consciousness. He reissues its call to equality, to a community of brothers and sisters. He preaches to his disciples a new orientation, a new vision of humankind, new values—values that contrast with the society of his time and with the values promoted by political power, for he preaches love of neighbor, poverty, humility, detachment from prestige and power, forgiveness, and the like. He preaches freedom and love as the human vocation and as the dynamism of all existence. To the extent that these values penetrate the heart of men and women and society, they pass a death sentence on every socio-political structure at variance with them—the Roman empire, to begin with—and they take root as the permanent seed of freedom.

Without offering a model for a better society, or any concrete program of liberation, Jesus creates a movement for freedom and community that we encounter at the origin of so many later social changes.

*Thesis 5: In his conflicts with the established powers of his time, Jesus assumed a pastoral and prophetical stance. This led him to renounce all use of temporal power and every form of violence.*

In his inevitable conflicts with the powers of religion and government, Jesus likewise assumed a religious and prophetic "style," consonant with his mission, his message, and his role as "Servant of Yahweh."[4]

This style is expressed particularly in two attitudes of renunciation: renunciation of political power and renunciation of violence. The style is surprising for its time, but it is altogether consonant with Jesus' option and mission:

> As the originator of a religious mission whose objective was to alter human beings and society at their very roots, it would have been easy for Jesus to set himself up as a temporal, political official. The temptation of political power, in the convulsed Palestine of his time, evidently lay in his path (Matt. 4:8–9), and he had to reject it both within himself (in the temptations on the mountain, during his forty-day fast) and in the pressure exerted on him by the crowds (John 6:15), or as he stood before the Romans (John 18:33–40). His liberty to criticize the religious

or political system of his time (Matt. 11:8, Luke 13:22–30, 11:37–54) is in inverse proportion to the radical quality of his renunciation of power. Like every renunciation made for the sake of the good news of the kingdom, Jesus' renunciation is creative. Jesus creates new forms of politico-social transformation. By proclaiming an ethic and a religion based not on the legalism of the Torah but on love and an imitation of the Father, Jesus is preparing the collapse of established religion in Israel. By proclaiming an equality and universal community of sisters and brothers and demythologizing any and every system or ideology of domination, Jesus is undermining the power of Roman imperialism— and the principle of all totalitarianism along with it, for he is establishing the great creative principle of every revolution whose aim is liberation. By calling the poor and the "little ones" to his kingdom and giving them the privileged places (Matt. 25:31–46, Luke 14:21–24), he is welding together and conscientizing a decisive instrument of pressure for the course of future history. His powerlessness—a powerlessness that is full of historic, transforming fecundity—has its complement in his renunciation of violence. His commandment of love, the central element of his preaching, excludes as a matter of principle all use of violence against another human being (Luke 6:35, 11:4). Jesus lived in accordance with the form of action he preached (John 18:11), finally demanding of his disciples that they forgive without condition, seeing that all are sinners before God and stand in absolute need of his forgiveness (Matt. 18:21–22, Luke 18:9–14, etc.).[5]

Paradoxically, Jesus' free decision to render himself helpless in the face of violence will lead him to become the sole possible center of the human community of brothers and sisters. Because of sin and the divisiveness resulting from sin, there is no historical form of justice and human community without an antecedent reconciliation and a mutual pardon. Jesus makes this principle a reality, and, in his helplessness, posits it as the basis of all society.

## PASTORAL CONCLUSIONS?

How far is it possible to extract, from Jesus' attitude toward politics, valid pastoral applications for today—seeing that, when all is said and done, his attitude is framed in such a concrete historical situation?

In the first place, it seems to me that Jesus maintains in this area certain attitudes that are typically "charismatic." That is, they are not normative for Christians. The renunciation of violence cannot be considered required of every Christian. Of course, there will always be Christians who will opt, systematically, for nonviolence. We have these Christians among us even today, and their witness is a most important one. Theirs is a charism in the church. The same will have to be said of the renunciation of political power: it is a form of poverty, which will be embraced by certain Christians who make an option for this form of impotence in order to take up the type of activity that Christ exercised, and the prophetic freedom that he enjoyed.

Jesus' renunciation of socio-political leadership has the same meaning. It is prophetic, not normative. This option is linked to a form of charism that is absolutely necessary in the church and elevates human beings and society by communicating to them potentially transforming values and inspirations. It is what we call today "a pastoral life with political consequences." Obviously, this form of activity in society on the part of Christians, complementing directly political activity, is in harmony with the various forms of the prophetic pastoral ministry and is as necessary for human liberation as action that is directly political.

Consequently, what Jesus' attitude toward politics offers us as a norm of Christian activity in the socio-political area is precisely the full "political" effectiveness, and social necessity, of men and women dedicated to the prophetic proclamation of the kingdom. What Jesus' attitude offers us in this area is a picture of the importance that such prophetic proclamation will always have, in Christianity in general, and in Latin America, steeped today in conflict and politicization, in particular. The more our society becomes politicized, the more need it has of political involvement on the part of Christians—but at the same time the more need it has of charism and propheticism in the ministerial aspect of the church. A total partisan "socio-politicization" of the apostolate would, in the long term, emasculate the fuller and more liberating content of the Christian message, and the presence of a form of Jesus' activity that is indispensable for the redemption of the poorest.

Along these same lines, one finds another permanent contribution of Jesus' political deportment. I refer to the power of a message that calls the poor to form the better part of his kingdom—in equality with all, and in a society of brothers and sisters—independently of any system or established authority. This alone, in any age, is the great program and great challenge of the pastoral theory and praxis of the church. This is what will be decisive for the future of Latin American Christianity.

Ultimately, it is a question of Christians' capacity to create, at this precise moment in the development and liberation of the poor, that movement for dignity, justice, and equality that Christ created in his time. The calling together of the poor that is proper to the Christian apostolate has to pass by way of history and by way of analyses and conflicts. And it issues in political dynamics. Calling the poor to form today the kingdom in Latin America translates into altogether concrete social aims and endeavors and is identified with very precise movements and longings, of urban and rural workers, Amerindians, and the other marginalized of Latin America. The proclamation of a society of equals, of sisters and brothers, "has a name" today. It corresponds to historical undertakings and precise political programs, whose ideals—a society in solidarity, a community of brothers and sisters without special privileges—are but the socio-political translation of the call to the poor to come share the kingdom. It is a call that ought to have been sounded valiantly down all the long corridors of history, and in Latin America has been sounded, to a degree, ever since Bartolomé de Las Casas.

This is the pastoral challenge to the church: to cry out, with "historical names," that the good news is proclaimed to the poor in our very day—the good news of the Beatitudes; and to denounce, also by name, whatever sets itself up as an obstacle to this good news "being fulfilled today" (Luke 4:18–21).

# NOTES

1. "The new interpretation of Jesus as a political and social revolutionary with connections with the Zealots is based on a one-sided interpretation which does violence to the sources" (M. Hengel, *War Jesus Revolucionär?* [Stuttgart: Calwer, 1970]; Eng. trans., *Was Jesus a Revolutionist?* [Philadelphia: Fortress, 1971].

2. By "politics" here I mean any kind of influence on or participation in the power or powers of social decision.

3. See Segundo Galilea, *Reflexiones sobre la evangelización* (Quito: IPLA, 1970), p. 135.

4. See Galilea, *¿A los pobres se les anuncia el evangelio?* (Bogotá: CELAM, 1972), pp. 59ff. (on powerlessness as poverty and as a prophetic attitude).

5. Ibid.

*Chapter 9*

# THE POLITICAL DIMENSION
# OF CHRIST THE LIBERATOR

## *J. Severino Croatto*

In considering the Christ of the gospels there are different aspects to be distinguished. The gospels offer us several distinct redactional perspectives—tantamount to many different "readings" of the Jesus-event. Ultimately these readings issue from particular stances assumed vis-à-vis the problematic of Jesus' mission—in other words, they are a function of particular stances taken by this or that evangelist with regard to the complexus of questions implied in the intention and vicissitudes of Jesus' total praxis. When it comes to a redactional thematic, everything turns on Jesus' deeds and words, and then what happens to him. A redactional thematic centers entirely upon the meaningful episodes of his life, and on the culmination of that life in the trial that leads to his death; and finally, on the resurrection as the key to the meaning of everything that has gone before.

Now, is the Christ of the gospels a Christ whose meaning we have "exhausted"? If, at bottom (or right from the start, for that matter), the praxis of the faith is a political praxis in the best sense, then does Christ not turn out to be an apolitical, apocalyptical, and hence utopian, spiritualist? Is he not, when all is said and done, a preacher, unaware of and far removed from the socio-economic reality in which his Palestinian compatriots are living at the moment? Is not his own message most open to an "ideologization" in the form of the "spiritual commitment" of the churches—an ideologization adroitly taken advantage of by the dominating classes and uncritically internalized by the dominated ones? Furthermore, what is the reading that we Christians make of Jesus' death at the hands of this so strange collaboration between Jews and Romans—dominated and dominators in concert?

The gospels seek the "meaning" of the disconcerting personage who was

Jesus of Nazareth. Below I shall attempt to place this same "meaning" in relief via a double, and simultaneous, route. That is, I shall take two points of departure at once: ourselves and the gospels. The outcome, the hermeneutic approximation that will now be at the disposal of our reading (and an approximation is all we can expect to have, unless we are willing to relapse into exegetical scientificism), will suddenly leave us with a strange question: Are we not going to have to go beyond the "meaning-closure" set by the gospels—decontextualize them in order to reexpress the reservoir of meaning of these same gospels?

This, in brief, is the objective of my reflections.

## JESUS AS THE ONE WHO REVEALS HUMAN VALUES

Jesus does not speak in order to carry out a mission of speaking. He speaks from within himself, from within his daily life. Hence the weight of his word. His word "conscientizes" at the very heart of an occurrence, or a deed, or a protest by the Pharisees. His word is contextual at every moment—not with the context of the evangelists, but with that of his own life-and-testimony. And so we should almost have to treat Jesus' deeds and words simultaneously. But we shall first detach his actions and attitudes, in order the better to understand, afterward, his word-in-the-event.

The sacred institution of the Sabbath offers Jesus a privileged situational framework for a discernment of values. He works and operates in a courageous and typical fashion in his day. To the "repose" of a false conscience he opposes the "work" of liberation, of a liberating praxis. The vocabulary of working, of performing, of operating, occurs with the greatest frequency in the Gospel of John. Jesus identifies himself with the Father, who is ever at work (John 5:17). He affirms the working of liberation on the occasion when the Jews criticize him for curing the cripple on the Sabbath at the pool of Bethzatha. He enters a "danger zone"—but he does so intentionally, for he seeks to unmask the perversion of the primary meaning of the institution of the Sabbath.

Let us note, right from the start, that those who are scandalized in him—in spite of his good works—are those who proclaim themselves guardians of the sacral institutions. In the example in John 5, Jesus' response is *theological*. He is the Father's equal, and the Father is above the Sabbath. ("My Father goes on working, and so do I"—John 5:17.) This offends the Jews even more. Now they are more alarmed, for this man professes equality with God (John 5:18). In the Gospel of Matthew, or the other synoptics, Jesus' replies are expressed on the level of *anthropology*—without, for all that, ceasing to be theological.

Jesus' activity on the Sabbath means he places himself in a provocative stance. And indeed this is clear from the Pharisees' alienation, their oppression of consciences, and their characteristic scandal when confronted with deeds of liberation. The "equivalents" of the Sabbath today are not to be sought precisely in the Sunday rest, which would be to attempt to conduct our investigation by way of external concordances. The transgression of the Sabbath rest is less offensive than certain other acts and attitudes that assault what is most jealously guarded of all—such as "authority" from God (a quality of the prevailing superstructure, with biblical foundation but subjected to an ideological tergiversation); its correlate, obedience on the part of those who have no voice; and the established "order," an order con-secrated, rendered sacred, through works of magic and an extraneous tradition. One could readily add to the list of Jesus' irritating and provoking attitudes, here concentrated in their own moment and in a Sabbath context.

Are there other concrete contexts of Jesus' liberating activity?

In striking fashion, Jesus seeks out the sick, the lowly, sinners, children, foreigners. What is special about these categories of persons, or common to them? They all "lack" something: health, opportunities in life, prestige before the "just" and the judges, capabilities, acceptance among the Jews. They are all marginalized. The concrete, social prejudice against them is the result of an interior prejudice against them and prejudicial judgment upon them. If they have values, they are not permitted to express them—the poor, because no one promotes them or does them justice, or because they are not permitted to promote themselves; and the others, because "religious" society scrupulously excludes them. And as crown and culmination of it all, they are all saddled with the guilt of being what they are. "Call a dog mangy and you have to kill it."

There is something grand, then, in Jesus' decision to go to those whom society and the synagogue marginalize. His option in their favor is the germ and seed of the gospel as the "good news" of liberation. With this option his trial begins. His trial is not held in the last week of his life; it merely culminates there.

Now let us go to the root of the situation we are describing, for it explains the resentment of the Pharisees and the authorities against Jesus, as well as Jesus' confrontation with them rather than with others. It is a matter of the "just"—those who know the will of God and are its faithful observers and who can therefore pass judgment on others. These three moments—knowledge, justice, and judgment—in that order, are correlatives. Each begets the next. But that is precisely their profound weakness. These "just," these manipulators of the divine "truth," do not acquire their security, their sureness, from a commitment to or involvement with the God-event in history, but from a "gnosis," from a knowledge of the law. Thus their whole praxis proceeds *from the law*, and not from love. Paul will put it in his own devastating language in his Letters to the Galatians and the Romans.

The Pharisees "excluded" persons from the kingdom by reason of their lack of *knowledge* of the law. A sinner was one who was ignorant of, and hence did not practice, the law. Illness was considered to be a consequence of sin, and hence related to the practice of the law. The Jews marginalized the sick. It is remarkable that the Old Testament legislation contains nothing in favor of the sick. In Leviticus they are "put to the test" all the more, with the demand that they expiate their "sin," as in the case of the leper, Leviticus 14:19ff., or the poor person, 14:21ff. (of whom less is required). If Christ accepts a connection between illness and sin (in John 9:3 he emphatically denies it!), in any case, far from rejecting the sick, he goes to them and cures them. This is a sign of the messianic age, as is pointed out in the gospels, in the history of the first Christians (Acts 3, 5:12, 15–16, 8:6–8, 9:33–42), and in the Pauline doctrine of the charism of healing.

Nor were children much favored by society. They have no voice, no "word," and no account is made of them. The Pharisees, however, had one reason more for excluding them: their *ignorance* of the law. Jesus, on the contrary, "lifts them up"—takes them into his arms—and blesses them, proclaiming their simplicity, which makes them "clear and pure" in God's sight. Foreigners, as well, are looked down upon (and the Samaritans are "hated"), because they do not know the God of Israel and because of the political consequences that derive from this circumstance. Even today religious circles in Israel oppose granting residence visas to non-Jews. The "Holy Land" is for a particular, chosen race. And the poor? The wise prescriptions of old that guaranteed them relative protection (see Deut. 15:7–11, and other passages that speak of "the poor, the orphan, and the widow," frequently adding the foreigner to the list) must not have been a prime concern in Jesus' time, seeing that he presents himself as the one who saves the poor and declares that this is precisely a "sign" that he has been sent by God. The scene in Matthew 11:1–6 is very suggestive: "The Good News is proclaimed to the poor; and happy is the man who does not lose faith in me" (Matt. 11:5).

How often in our society, and sometimes even in our churches, do those who concern themselves concretely with the poor meet with scandal or puzzlement or complications! Jesus begins his work by concerning himself *with the poor*. This is his *sign* of credibility. Let us keep in mind the rich prophetic vein in the series of symbols contained in Isaiah 11—king to come, Messiah, and so on. Other concerns, such as Israel's *political* dependence, tend to make us forget this aspect—one, however, that is linked to the whole Eastern tradition of a king's function.[1] Ironically, the "people of the earth"—originally, the lowly ones, the ones left behind on Palestinian soil by the Babylonian conquerors, who had carried the more qualified into exile (technicians, laborers, and the like, 2 Kings 24:14)—now were displaced persons themselves, at the hands of Jerusalem's "religious society." Uneducated with respect to the law, they seemed excluded from salvation.

Now it is in this situation that Jesus singles out the marginalized—those laboring under the double oppression of human selfishness in general and the "religious" structure in particular. He begins his liberation by assigning a value to their personhood. They are human beings too—only, they are oppressed. In the next section, below, we shall see that Jesus' word *interprets* his own deeds of liberation, denouncing the oppressor, and conscientizing the oppressed as they commence the ascent from the obscurity of "being less" to the "being more" of being "new persons." And further, it was the *deed* of Jesus to enter into solidarity with the poor, to become one of them. Only from a place among them could he carry out his work of liberation.

Jesus experienced what it was to be marginalized, to be denounced, to be accused, to be plotted against by the centers of power. He had no "structural" or institutional defense. His marginalization with respect to power coincided with his option for the marginalized on this same level. He always moved at the level of the foundation. There is a great difference between becoming rich and powerful in order to liberate the rich and powerful, and becoming poor and oppressed in order to liberate the poor and oppressed. The former attitude and behavior is self-contradictory and serves to consolidate the mechanisms of domination. The latter is liberating, because the poor and dominated are the oppressors' raison d'être. Could we imagine a Jesus installed in power as a high priest, a scribe, or a Pharisee, and preaching the liberation of the poor, of sinners, of foreigners, of the marginalized in general?

### JESUS' CONSCIENTIZING WORD

From his position in solidarity with the oppressed and by his conduct calculated to unveil personhood and its values, Jesus is enabled to perform a work of conscientization, through a word-of-interpretation. He clears the roadblocks of tradition, law, and other structures to let the *human being* emerge. The buried and the suffocated rise again and are reconstituted as new beings. On *this* level—in the encounter of human being with human being—oppressed and oppressors both find liberation. The latter, deprived of their correlative, are left to their alienation. It is only in this way that they can be liberated themselves.

Matthew 12 reports a sequence of deeds and words of Christ that are apposite to our reflection. When all is said and done, those who had the "light," those who did the judging, suddenly find themselves stripped naked before the truth, and judged by another Light (Matt. 12:31–37, 38–42). Let us see how Jesus extricates himself, in concrete episodes in which oppressors and oppressed meet each other in action.

The first case is that of the plucking of the ears of corn in the fields on the Sabbath (Matt. 12:1–8). What is important to the Pharisees is not the disciples' hunger, but that they observe tradition. And they point out to the "Master," their teacher, that in their opinion he should have kept that in account. Jesus responds with three appeals to the scriptures. After all, the Pharisees have opened the discussion by recalling a sacred law. He meets them on their own ground—but only in order to demonstrate to them the exclusivism and one-sidedness of their interpretation. *David* transgressed the law that reserved to the priests the eating of the shewbread, which was a kind of sacrifice. The *Levites* performed work on Sabbath days in the temple area, performing their functions, without being reproached for violating the Sabbath rest on that account. If they moved about in the vicinity of the temple on the Sabbath day, could the disciples not now do so in the vicinity of the *new* temple, which he is himself (Matt. 12:6)?

His response is as meaningful for us as it was unexpected by the Pharisees. Christ displaces the old and replaces it with himself; so then why discuss the old? The latter is typical of the person of structures, the person who sacralizes tradition. How many discussions, meetings, documents, and decisions we see in the churches that have no bearing on the reality of human persons, on the novelty of history, and, above all, on the life of the marginalized! Jesus, as a new event, empties the very meaning of the legalistic Pharisees' concerns. But he goes further still, with a third argument, drawn from the prophets, whereby he recalls to them what the *will of God* is: mercy, and not sacrifice (Matt. 12:7; cf. Amos 5:21, Hos. 6:6). Your neighbor, not your rites. In other words, the socio-political (one's task for others) instead of worship. The *human being* is more important than ritual "prescriptions." Simply because they did not understand this truth of God's, the Pharisees condemned the innocent (Matt. 12:7).

And indeed, for that matter, was it not *they* who were the sinners? Jesus, with his word, had set the whole set of problems on its head—and not with a subtle dialectic to silence the ingenuous, but by unmasking the false justice of the Pharisees, who were "left with the check" as the real sinners by *not knowing* the salvific will of God and condemning the innocent. This last denunciation by Jesus, leveled at no lesser personages than the "judges" of orthodoxy and orthopraxis, gives one much pause.

The second confrontation arises from the presence of a paralytic in the synagogue, once more on a Sabbath day (Matt. 12:9–14). This time the confrontation takes place *before* the cure—whereby is seen the bad will of those present, who come forward to remind Jesus of the prohibition of work on the seventh day. They ask him a question—but not in order to learn anything (for the Pharisees "know" the law), but to accuse him (12:10). For they know what Jesus will do. And indeed he is not deterred and heals the cripple (12:13). But the conscientizing response he gives to the intriguers stands in relief. He cites the analogy of a sheep fallen into a hole on the Sabbath. With all astuteness, he does not set up the analogy as the case of a third party. The Pharisees would have said that the interested party must fulfill the law and leave the sheep. He asks them what *they* would do, with a sheep of their *own*. The "now," in the sense of "well, then," of verse 12, indicates the Pharisees' acceptance of the argument insofar as the *sheep* is concerned. "Well, then," it must be evident that Jesus is allowed to heal on this day of rest. Jesus' word has all the more impact in that we are dealing with a *human being* here, not an animal.

What a profound truth it is, however, that one does not easily conscientize those "on top"! The Pharisees understood the truth but failed to "see" it. Therefore they plotted against Jesus in order to destroy him (12:14). His word had turned out to be "dangerous," so they conspired to liquidate him.

This is the risk run by so many (or the climax of their endeavor) who have done something for their neighbor, be it only something small. They are blacklisted by the reactionary groups in power. And persecution is to the death.

In the third scene (Matt. 12:22–30) we start from the other end, with the cure itself. This time it is the deaf and mute demoniac. Let us observe the double reaction to Christ's deed, which is later complemented and completed by his word. "Can this man be the Son of David?" (12:23). That is, the *crowds* are capable of wonder and of "interpreting" the event as a sign of a new presence of God, and they make a connection between the situation and their messianic hopes. The Pharisees, on the contrary, are alarmed by this profession of faith in God, placed by design in the foreground of the structure of the account. Of the three protagonists—Jesus, the people, and the Pharisees—the last stand apart and alone, against the other two. The deed was there. There was the evidence. But the Pharisees—the erstwhile intelligent ones, in the dark now—have need of an "explanation." The deed they reject cannot provide it, nor can the explanation given by the people be the right one. And so they have recourse to lying. They take it into their heads to announce that Jesus operates in the name of Beelzebul, the prince of devils (12:24).

At this juncture the conscientizing word of Jesus reenters the action, demonstrating the internal contradiction, the stupidity, of their argument (12:25–30). And in passing he instructs them that they are in the presence of a "sign of the times" (12:28) that they are unable to discern. They read the meaning of the events backward—and by way of crowning foolishness, in the full course of a "signing" they demand a "sign." The richness of this episode resides in this "hermeneutic" opposition between the people and the leaders. It would be naive of us to assert—as has been done so often in our day, though now much less than before—that the lowly *have the truth of themselves*, or that they arrive at it very easily. We know in how many ways persons are managed, manipulated, and led this way and that by false promises, by illusions of liberation. Rather, the masses are an ambiguous value in the calculation. They are open to the new, they have the capacity for conscientization and for taking account of what is for their good. But they are also vulnerable to mass hypnosis and attachment to falsified ideals, for lack of a critical consciousness of this positive basis of theirs.

For their part, the leaders, the powerful, are not always evil. Power can have a salvific function, and a leader or public figure can be enlightened. But this potentiality is frequently inverted into an antisalvific or oppressive power, by a fixation on truth already known but converted into the fundament of a particular status quo. And now the leader's power has been perverted. In the case before us, the crowds concretely assume a conscientized and critical attitude with regard to the meaning of the event. The Pharisees, by contrast, close themselves off against anything new, for it endangers their privileges as spiritual leaders of the people.

The gospels recount many conscientizing encounters of Jesus. But lest we extend ourselves too far, let us leave the synoptics now and examine two scenes from the fourth Gospel.

In the account of the Samaritan woman (John 4) we have an "encounter" that is superficial, at first, on her part, but is then deepened in truth as it becomes an authentic encounter between her and Jesus. We can reflect upon Jesus' pedagogy of liberation. The Jews "do not associate" with the Samaritans (John 4:9). They behave in accordance with generalized and traditional prejudices, without taking concrete values into account. Jesus initiates the dialogue, and he accepts her as a person. Her sins make no difference to him. All that follows starts from here. This is where "entry" is made; now the conversation can develop, and Jesus can require of her the whole truth—*her* truth (John 4:16–18). What is important is that Christ manages to have *her* "say her word" and that she ends by believing in him for having heard her as a person instead of prejudging her as a Samaritan and sinner.

In the discussions that ensue upon the healing of the person born blind (John 9), here too the one who encounters Jesus comes to "recognize" the Son of Man (John 9:35–37) from his own experience. By contrast, the Pharisees become confused and cavil like a cluster of busybodies: "This man cannot be from God: he does not keep the sabbath" (John 9:16—notice the type of argumentation!); or, at best, the man had not been blind at all (9:18); or "this man is a sinner" (9:24); or "we are disciples of Moses . . . as for this man, we don't know where he comes from" (9:28–29). All these explanations have a common denominator—"religious" prejudice against Jesus because he heals a sick person on the Sabbath day (9:14). Facts are secondary. Likewise, the blind person *has* to be a sinner, for he thinks differently from the leaders (9:34). Until this moment, Jesus has said nothing to them. Now, working with the symbolism of light in relation to the blind person who has been cured and who has believed, he asserts that he has come to the world for a *krisis*—a "discernment" that reverses positions:

> so that those without sight may see
> and those with sight turn blind [9:39].

The Pharisees catch the allusion ("We are not blind, surely?"—9:40), and Jesus subtly deflects the symbolism:

> Blind? If you were,
> you would not be guilty,
> but since you say, "We see,"
> your guilt remains [John 9:41].

In one way they are blind. The account itself demonstrates this. But as Pharisees, as "knowers" of God, they bear witness to their own condemnation. "Seeing" but unable to *see*, they have no way out. Their sin *remains*.

It is clear why Christ has not the slightest intention of changing them. From start to finish, what did he get from them? Is it perhaps possible to liberate oppressors (here, oppressors in the area of religion) from a point of departure *in themselves?* As a matter of principle, Jesus *is not about* to conscientize Israel's leaders, but denounces their sin against the light on the occasion of a deed performed among the marginalized. As a simple matter of fact he cannot do good to the lowly without vexing the exalted.

## THE BEATITUDES

The two lines of thought of the four Lucan Beatitudes (Luke 6:20-23)—amplified by Matthew (5:3-12) with a more spiritual interpretation and four other beatitudes of the same ethical tone—refer to the poor and the persecuted, whom Jesus proclaims "happy," or "fortunate." It is unlikely that the Beatitudes were proclaimed on the inauguration of his preaching. The maturity they presuppose in their auditors inclines one to think that their original context is rather that of the end of Jesus' life. In a certain fashion, they afford a glimpse of the experience of the primitive church of Jerusalem, poor and persecuted as it was to be.

The reason why Matthew situates them where we have them is in order to point up their programatic meaning. They are Jesus' *proclamation.* In other words, they constitute his essential message. The programatic declarations made by chiefs of state in their inaugural addresses are invested with special meaning by reason of the occasion on which they are made (except that they are not generally carried out). Their special value is in their orientation and the "possibilities" they open up, to be further elaborated by *other* statements and pronouncements. Every programatic discourse has to undergo interpretation. Otherwise it is nothing more than bad prophecy.

But if the Beatitudes are the *synthesis* of Jesus' preaching, they acquire a different importance altogether. They are the result of his experience (the allusion to persecution at the hands of the synagogue is an indication), especially of his experience of real involvement with the marginalized.

And now we come to the urgent question of our day. Do the Beatitudes have anything to do with the "liberation" of the marginalized persons to whom they are addressed? If the poor and the persecuted are "happy," or "fortunate," then why not let them continue that way? Thus it would appear that Jesus urges the resignation of the oppressed. Conclusion: the kingdom of heaven, of the skies—a future kingdom, of course—will be theirs. Copiously will they be compensated. Has this spiritualistic and eschatologistic interpretation not been the normal one in the churches?

The hellenization of the biblical message has, as it happens, caused us much ado about that "other world"—understood as the kingdom of the immortal and the disincarnate and as salvation from all the evils of *this* world. Things will be taken care of *later*, in a universe that has nothing to do with the present one. Here a Platonic and Plotinian immortalism joins the biblical apocalyptic in a single embrace. And this is the line that has prevailed in traditional Christianity, especially beginning with the Neoplatonic Saint Augustine. The dominant atmosphere in Jesus' time was indisputably apocalyptic. We need only recall the prolific literature in the genre. Thus we cannot escape a vision of cosmic reach as a focus for our analysis and grasp of the new set of challenges and problems introduced by Christ.

But two further factors must be kept in account:

1. First, the apocalyptic current of thought (which separates and distinguishes two worlds, and considers the second, the world of definitive salvation, to be the only one that is the exclusive work of God) is not the only biblical focus, especially in the New Testament. Antecedent to this soteriological focus we have the prophetic vision of history and of eschatology.[2] In the latter vision, our history has two moments—moments of the same history, not two separate worlds. And the new and definitive order is to be prepared by the people's response to the manifestation of God *in this history*.

Indeed, nothing in the gospels tells us that the "kingdom of heaven" is the spiritual and transcendent world, the one to be expected after death. It is well known how the Jews thought of the "kingdom" they looked for. It was primarily *earthly*, defined in specifics. It was a return to the law of Moses, but also to a political sovereignty *of Israel*. The Beatitudes have to be read in light of the messianic hopes inscribed in the heart of the prophets and explored by the thinking of the Jews. In the Old Testament there is a well-defined prophetic context in which, with the resumption of the theological conception of Yahweh as defender of the poor, this conception is carried to its furthermost limits in the description of the king to come as the establisher of *justice* and the liberator of the *oppressed* (Isa. 9:5-7, 11:1-9; Jer. 23:3-8; Ezek. 34:23-31). For example:

> [David's descendant] judges the wretched with integrity,
> and with equity gives a verdict for the poor of the land.
> His word is a rod that strikes the ruthless,
> his sentences bring death to the wicked [Isa. 11:4].

And so Jesus will "interpret" not only his calling, but his historical moment as well, as that of the realization of these hopes. "Happy are the poor," because *now*, with him, the liberation begins. If "theirs is the kingdom," and the "kingdom," as we have said, is not an ethereal and spiritual thing, then it will come only with a deep change in human beings, with the inauguration of justice at every level. The "*theirs* is the kingdom" means more than a simple reversal of the poles of oppression—the very expression is structurally and conceptually contradictory—but the total eradication of the bipolarity itself. When the oppressed take power there are no more oppressed, nor, therefore, any more oppressors.

2. Secondly, one can ask oneself why Jesus did not express himself more clearly with respect to this tenor of his proclamation to the poor and persecuted. Besides, Matthew's Gospel turns the message toward the spiritual and ethical.

The first Gospel is engaged precisely in a rereading. It rereads the words of Jesus from a point of departure in the situation in which *it* is being written—a situation characterized by opposition between Christians and Pharisees. We make our own rereading *from our viewpoint*, from a point of departure in our own real situation. We resume the nuclear sense of the gospel message and understand it from where we are, from a situation that causes its reserve of meaning to emerge.

The meaning of an expression is always "reduced" by the context in which it is spoken or written. But the "distance" of this context permits us to reopen it and broaden its original horizon of expression. This is what Matthew has done, in one direction, and it is what we can do ourselves in another—inasmuch as we are "situated" in another context-of-appropriation of the original meaning. As a result, the rereading will go beyond (or stop short of!) the meaning presented by the author of a text. Yet it does not change or obscure it. On the contrary, it is an act of exploration, and thus it is the sole manner in which it is possible to surpass the "history" of the meaning and fruitfully appropriate it. This is the path taken by the hermeneutic act, to which we shall return below.

## CHRIST'S LIBERATING DEATH

A great deal is written today about Jesus' trial and about the gospel accounts of his death and its "political" dimension.[3] Whence comes this new interest? The primary reason is that, in certain sectors, the praxis of the faith—which has always had, and always will have, political connotations—has become extremely sensitive to the social, the economic, and the political. This is due to its deeper incarnation in history. Secondly, the liberation processes—which have their leaders and their martyrs—raise the question of a contribution of Jesus to the revolution. That is, is the Christ-event "exhausted," or is it a reservoir of meaning for the deed of liberation to which, for example, our dominated Latin America aspires?

The gospels distinguish a Jewish moment and a Roman moment in Jesus' trial. The former is not purely religious, for the Sanhedrin enjoyed a political jurisdiction as well. Let us recall that the Roman procurator resided in Caesarea—doubtless a strategic location, but remote from the epicenter of Jewish institutional life, which was Jerusalem. Under cover of the religious, the Sanhedrin played a political role. It operated within a theocratic worldview. Ever since the restoration after the exile, it was the high priest who concentrated in his hands political power as well, its only limitation being the successive dominators of Palestine—here, the Romans.

### The Role of the Sanhedrin

The key to understanding the trial of Jesus is not Pilate, but the Sanhedrin. Throughout the gospels, there is nothing calculated to alarm the Romans, but much to agitate the Jews and to pave the way for the denouement with which we are all familiar. We must not read the account of the passion without situating it in the structure of the whole gospel. This is the least that can be demanded of an interpreter. We have seen that Jesus' deeds and word, orientated to the recovery of humankind and its natural values, aroused the fury of the power groups—high priests, elders, scribes, Pharisees—and motivated their decision to eliminate him. Jesus' praxis—action and theory together, in mutual interdependency—was unmasking the superstructural and ideological universe that the leaders of Israel controlled, and whose axis of viability was the law understood as "tradition." Hence Jesus' praxis was "critical," and troublesome, calling into question as it does the vicious circle and Achilles' heel of power—namely, authority.

The interference becomes explicit at the moment of transition from Jesus' public life to his falling into the hands of the leaders of Jerusalem (Mark 11:27-33, = Matt. 21:23-27, Luke 20:1-8). The chief priests, the scribes, and the ancients, or elders (none of the synoptics detail the religious factions—only the instances of power are of interest), ask him, "What authority have you for acting like this? Or who gave you authority to do these things?" (Mark 11:28; the parable of the homicidal vinedressers; the tribute to Caesar, the question of the Messiah as both David's son and lord, follow immediately). This gives us the picture of a Jesus who is perceived as the rival of the authority and distorted mission of the Jewish leaders, who now will seek to liquidate him, but who for the moment are restrained by fear of the *masses*—for they interpret Jesus as a new leader (Mark 11:18, 12:12, 14:1-2).

But the leaders finally attain their end, through the treason of Judas Iscariot (a *sicarius*, a dagger-wielding Zealot, disenchanted with Jesus?). There is no doubt, based on the convergence of all four evangelists on this point, that it is the *Jews* who proceed against Jesus (Mark 14:43, etc.), in the person of "the chief priests, the scribes, and the elders," the same ones who had been the antagonists in the episodes upon which we have commented above.[4] The imperial authority plays no part whatever.

Formal proceedings against Jesus are instituted later, before the Sanhedrin (Mark 14:53-59), where "proofs" are forged on the basis of which he is declared to be guilty of a capital offense. I shall not dwell here on the familiar. I wish only to call attention to the fact that Jesus is condemned as a *religious subversive*, on grounds of having threatened to destroy and rebuild the temple and, especially, that he claimed to be the Christ, the Son of God. And let us not forget what lay behind the overt, superficial bill of particulars in Jesus' indictment—all his deeds and words critical of the religious status quo, and of the authority of the leaders who are passing judgment upon him. Such activity is subversive of itself, for it corrodes the "power" of the prevailing religious structure and its leaders. But the height of indignation is displayed (Mark. 14:63) when the high priest rends his garments, upon Jesus' *Messianic profession* (Mark 14:61-62). Here the religious impinges upon the political. The Messiah was to be the savior of the Jews, but the leaders of

Israel could not bear that it be *this* person, who was so vexing—that it would be *he* who would put an end to their mandate and their power privileges.

Now we understand the paradox of what follows. How comes it that the Jewish authorities do not accept, or at least put to the test, a "Messiah," who could rescue Israel from foreign domination? Why do they not receive the clear testimony of the people (Mark 11:9–10)? Suddenly they find themselves collaborators of the forces of occupation. During this period they could not execute the death sentence—only the Romans enjoyed the *jus gladii*, or right to carry out capital punishment. And so the Jewish authorities hand Jesus over to Pilate (Mark 15:1). Now, before the procurator, the only accusation they bring will be a political one, involving subversion of the new order of domination.

And indeed the concept of a Messiah, owing to its religious/political ambivalence, lent itself to an attack upon Jesus on two fronts. In the religious sphere, he could be judged to be a blasphemer for having called himself the Christ, the Son of God. In the political sphere, to claim to be the Messiah involved a pretension to usurp the power reserved to the Romans. Hence it was not difficult to transfer the proceedings of the Sanhedrin to a Roman court. Pilate's question, "Are you the king of the Jews?" (Mark 15:2) demonstrates the Roman official's jurisprudential stance: this is a matter more of a pretender to the status of a liberator from the domination he represents and maintains. Mark is most general and indefinite about the charges against Jesus. They "handed him over to Pilate" (Mark 15:1); "the chief priests brought many accusations against him" (15:3; cf. 15:4); when asked, "What harm has he done?" (15:14) the reply is not to the point.

But Luke is explicit. "We found this man inciting our people to revolt, opposing payment of the tribute to Caesar, and claiming to be Christ, a king" (Luke 23:2); "he is inflaming the people with his teaching all over Judea; it has come all the way from Galilee, where he started, down to here" (23:5). In the episode concerning the tribute to Caesar, Luke, and Luke alone, states pointedly that they tried to take Jesus by surprise, looking for something that would "enable them to hand him over to the jurisdiction and authority of the governor" (20:20). They seek to build against him a case for a political crime: "You brought this man before me," Pilate reproved them, "as a political agitator" (23:14). What more could Pilate have desired to exercise his crushing authority?

All four evangelists note the power the Roman leader had to set Jesus free, but it is John who, after Luke, paints the best picture of Pilate's convictions and efforts in this concern. We know Pilate as someone weak, someone unjust in spite of everything, because he did finally sentence someone he knew was innocent. But this is the typical case of someone who is influenced by pressure, someone fearful of a noisy mob and its "powerful" little leaders (the Sanhedrin of the Jews). "If he were not a criminal, we should not be handing him over to you" (John 18:30); "if you set him free you are no friend of Caesar's" (John 19:12); "we have no king except Casear" (19:15); "they kept on shouting at the top of their voices'' (Luke 23:23); they "had persuaded the crowd to demand the release of Barabbas and the execution of Jesus" (Matt. 27:20). Pilate did what he could to defend Jesus, and at last passed sentence on him.

Here several observations are in order. First and foremost, is it true that Mark presents an original account and that Luke distorts the trial?[5] It would appear that Luke makes additions and completions, whereas Mark is synthetic. But when we read Mark's account of the trial before Pilate we have the sensation of contacting something hollow, abbreviated, as we have just noticed. What Luke notes appears more consonant with a political trial, with a sophisticated marriage of a *religious and political* trial, altogether understandable within the Jewish world of those times.

There has to be something very important in Pilate's nonalarm, in his serenity and tranquility in the presence of an accusation of sedition, subversion against Caesar, and pretension to the Jewish throne. His irony goes so far as to present Jesus to the Jews precisely as their "king" (John 19:14, 19–22). He must have had the perspicacity to take account of the real question. Jesus—in his eyes—must have been no "danger" to the Roman power. I think that to assert instead that the gospels did not wish to inculpate the Romans in the death of Christ and directed the guilt against the Jews, as a *captatio benevolentiae*, an attempt to render their Roman hearer benevolent, so that Christians could preach the gospel in the empire, is altogether gratuitous. On the contrary, as Walaskay notes, the case makes Roman justice, that classic instance of judicial severity and rectitude, look rather bad. Pilate's behavior is weak. In a *captatio benevolentiae* the evangelists would have attributed to him a more lucid judgment.[6] And for that matter, John is writing toward the end of the first century, when the imperial persecutions of the Christian communities are raging at their worst. It is the age of the Apocalypse, the Book of Revelation. No, the whole trial of Jesus has its epicenter in the diagnosis and opinions of the leading Jews of Jerusalem—the elders, the scribes, the priests, and the religious groups.

*Capitulation to Roman Hegemony*

Now we can return to the question, or paradox, that we raised earlier. Why is it that the Jewish authorities did not co-opt the new leader in order to assert their hope of liberation from the Romans? This is the real question. And it so happens that Jesus, on the one side, is hammering away at the symbolic universe that keeps those leaders in power—that is, the law, tradition, and the privilege of authority with which these are crowned and adorned. All these things have been conditioning a genuine oppression of consciences and human values. Jesus unmasks the oppressors and liberates the oppressed. On the other side, the hierarchs of Jerusalem "get on well" with the Romans. The Romans dominate Palestine, bleed it white with the heavy tributes they impose—but they do permit a certain internal autonomy with respect to government, which has its local theocratic chieftains. The latter *owe* their positions and titles to Caesar; hence they collaborate with Rome and betray the people. The presence of a "Messiah" complicated and compromised their status. And there was no better solution than to seek the assistance of Caesar against this impostor—this "subversive."

It is the classic picture of ecclesiastical power in symbiosis with civil or military power for the purpose of maintaining its superstructural privileges—to the prejudice of the genuine liberation of the people. Seen in its Latin American projection, Jesus' trial has a tragic profundity. It proclaims the betrayal by the churches of the hopes of a people that believes in new leaders, leaders who often indict these churches by their very presence. It proclaims—this time in the civil realm—the treason of the national middle classes who ally with the imperial oppressor against a people struggling to gain independence. There are groups of persons who are sold—that is, bought by those in power who use their power to perform acts of betrayal. "The chief priests and elders, however, had persuaded the crowd to demand the release of Barabbas and the execution of Jesus" (Matt. 27:20).

### The Liberation Inspired by Jesus: Political Because Radically Human

With these questions clarified, we can return to the question with which we began. Does the life and death of Jesus have a political dimension? His attitudes and behavior, and his word—as I have emphasized, and now I emphasize it again—head straight for the heart of human beings, to become incarnate there, to uncover anew the values of human beings, to enable their "being more," to conscientize them, by denouncing their oppressors. Jesus' option for the marginalized was "interpreted" by the people, but it generated an unexpected alarm in the religious leaders. Suddenly his life had acquired a political tone. Suddenly their "authority" was at stake. Jesus was a new leader—and unmistakably one under another sign. When he set about liberation, he pulled the rug from under the oppressors' feet. Now they had to defend their status and their privileges.

No wonder, then, that a faith praxis orientated to the liberation of others meets head on with "powers" and thereby acquires a political cast, which explains the "spiritual" interpretation of the faith given by those who hold religious "power." Religious power, when perverted, is the typical symbol of oppression. Its arms are spiritual. That is, it achieves its aims by ideologizing. But "when the chips are down" it has recourse to material force (not necessarily civil power), as in Jesus' trial and elsewhere—as well as to intrigue, censorship, and a thousand and one other recourses.

But our other question remains. Was Jesus a revolutionary? What did he teach for the liberation of the Jews from their subjection to Rome? If not even his death is to be defined as that of a political revolutionary, in spite of the best efforts of the Sanhedrin to perpetrate such a fraud—then what remains of his death, or his life, that could serve as a model for a political faith-praxis? If Jesus admitted one must pay Caesar his tribute, then, it would seem, he does not hold out much hope for us in our situation of dependence.

Many today, in order to extricate themselves from this quandary and discover a "political Christ," cherish the idea of Jesus' membership in the Zealot group. The Zealots were guerrillas, revolutionaries who attacked the Roman presence directly and violently. Oscar Cullman's statement of the question, expounded by others as well, is classic.[7] To tell the truth, there is not much to be said in favor of a pro-Zealot Christ. Those who seek to identify this Zealot Christ fail to take into account what an ill service they do the cause of liberation. The Zealots were reactionaries. They were of the "extreme right." They strove for the expulsion of the Romans from Palestinian soil, but their purpose was not human salvation—not an integral development of human beings in all their aspects and potentialities. Their purpose was the reestablishment of the law and the resurrection of lost religious and political institutions. The Zealots had no way out of their "vicious circle of legalism."[8] Christ, on the other hand, could not struggle or suffer for the law. Rather, he suffered the power of the law as a structure of death. The longing for a Zealot Christ is a quest for a religious nationalism, a "fascist" Christ. It is one thing to seek to recover one's own religious and cultural values. It is something else altogether to seek to recover an oppressive legal system, which, as Christ shows us, is what the law is in its interpretation and application in his times. And Christ came to save humankind, not the law.

It seems to me that the question of Christ as "liberator" has to be approached differently. By Christ as liberator, of course, I do not mean a Christ who is *only* an eschatological liberator, nor a liberator in some purely spiritual or mystical conception of liberation. Committed, involved Christians—committed to and involved with *real human beings*—will continue asking themselves about the political, socio-economic, and cultural consequences of Jesus' religious message, rather than about ambiguous themes such as the "reconciliation of all things in Christ" (which is ambiguous not because of its theological profundity, but because of its ideological use in the churches, and, along with the churches, by dominators).

Reconciliation seems to be the preferred theme in these, Latin America's dark hours. It is being mauled and manipulated and voided of its challenging and revolutionary content. It has cold water thrown on it, it is slanted, until it becomes a sort of individualistic settling of accounts with God—and thereby it misses the *real* conditions of struggle and conflict that total reconciliation presupposes. After the epistemological breach that has been made in our circle of philosophical abstractions by the social sciences, reaching all the way to a reinterpretation of theological language itself, we cannot afford to be so naive in our Christian commitment. Otherwise, "others" will be called to carry out our aborted mission.

But it is just as superficial to go to the opposite extreme and be moonstruck with the Zealots—political revolutionaries, yes, but who pursue the full reinstatement of the ancient and the "sacred." Then what would we be left with?

Christ's message does not appear on the scene as a program. Still less is it a strategy for political liberation. Jesus was a religious leader. The Zealots were religious too, but they were religious revolutionaries who sought to recover tradition by blood and the sword, driving out pagan dominators by means subversive of the prevailing political and religious order. They strove to undermine and destroy the "grand accord" between the current Jewish authorities and the foreign overlords. By contrast, Jesus did nothing we know of to liberate the Jews from the Roman yoke. It appears that he made no political and nationalist commitment like that of the Zealots. When all things are put in perspective, it is precisely here that we see his lucidity and his greatness. Had he been a revolutionary leader on the *surface* of the revolution, he would have been doing *the Jews* a favor—but his activity would have been exhausted on this political, racial, and geographical level. Let us keep in mind that the exodus had been a liberation symbol for centuries, yes—but for the people *of Israel*. Only with Christ did that symbol take on the universality it has today. There are, therefore, other elements that enter into consideration.

Jesus' message attains its political dimension—a universal political dimension, in favor of all peoples and persons—more by way of what it does for the milieu and foundation of a radical liberation, a "liberation of the opposite sign." Here we must proceed methodologically. On the one hand, we must hunt out the "implications" in Jesus' deeds and message. On the other, we have to submit these implications to a hermeneutical examination, in order to provide ourselves with a critical lamp by whose light we may approach the text of the gospels as we have them today and examine what they have to say about Jesus. Let us now proceed with these two steps.

1. What are the implications of the Christ-event for liberation? If Christ had been a political revolutionary "of the first instance"—that is, a revolutionary struggling on the surface of revolution, whether after the manner of the Zealots, or (as a possibility) bypassing the *religio*-nationalist mode—then his activity would have been exhausted on the merely political level. Indeed it would have encountered its closure-of-meaning on the *Jewish* horizon, and its whole radicality would have been absorbed in this. *At that time* his deeds would have failed to spark a theology of liberation for *other* races or peoples.

I emphasize "at that time," in order to distinguish the situation of Jesus from that of the exodus and from our own. I distinguish it from the exodus situation, inasmuch as Jesus' act is not a simple repetition of the exodus. It is a *new* event, and as such can engender an original complexus of symbols and an unprecedented historical consciousness. I distinguish Jesus' situation from our own, inasmuch as a scientific and critical analysis of reality (which is a modern procedure) *does* permit the contemporary believer to discern a kerygmatic and theological meaning in a revolutionary *political* action. And this observation brings us at once to the following point.

*At that time*, the religious conceptions of the Jews, centered as they were in the cult of the law and on the ideology of election, would have caused each of these two possible readings of the revolutionary event to vanish like a puff of smoke. To be sure, the "tactics" argument is invalid—the notion that Jesus did not organize the people against the Romans because he would surely have failed, considering the invaders' enormous apparatus of repression. This would be an encomium of Jesus' political lucidity, but that is all it would be. And furthermore it is pointless to demand this of him, for his message (in its practices and in its teaching) was inserted into a *religious* plane—though opposed to that of all the religious groups, including that of the Zealots.

On the other hand, let us take into consideration that the interplay of contradictions forthcoming from the various manipulative practices and attitudes of Jesus' milieu were not susceptible of reconciliation. The Zealots opposed the Romans radically. But the Sadducees—and here is the first and principal contradiction—did not experience imperial oppression, for it was to the representatives of this oppression that they owed their office and their "authority" over an oppressed people. Given this state of affairs, one feels Jesus to be closer to the Zealots than to the other groups called "religious," but in actuality traitors to the people. But, had the main contradiction, as seen by the Zealots—namely, the contradiction between the Romans and the Jews—been resolved, then a new central contradiction would have emerged—the one that hovered in the background: the contradiction between a law that oppresses and a people oppressed by Jewish structures and traditions. For these structures and traditions would then have taken on their proper ideological and juridical force, and nothing would have been done in favor of *humankind*. Jesus must therefore move in another direction.

In the first place, his practices favor not the law but the human being. What is important is not the salvation of the Jews so that they can freely practice the law, but liberation from *all structures of death* and the recovery of the human being. Jesus initiated a new liberation process by enlightening the consciousness of the human being oppressed by religious ideology. In the second place, he establishes a new praxis, which moves along the line of service to and love for others. Such praxis necessarily triggers an alarm for power factors, which are the key in any situation of oppression or domination. Love of neighbor becomes practical politics. The first instance of this is Jesus himself. Having initiated and proclaimed a praxis of conscientization and salvation *of the human being*, he brought down on his head all the wrath of the Jewish authorities, rather than that of the Romans, and perhaps incurred the spite of the Zealots as well. Jesus' activity had a political content. It opposed the structures of domination of the moment.

Let us recall once again that the Sanhedrin was not only a religious authority, but a civil authority as well. It was made up of high priests, elders, and scribes, mostly Pharisees. The Sanhedrin began Jesus' trial, then delivered him to Pilate, demanding of Pilate that he carry out its death sentence.[9] Jesus appears to its members as subversive of the "order" they maintain, a religiopolitical and theocratic order. He was unmasking an authority that was ideologized, that was an oppressor of consciences, that was compromised with whatever regimen happened to be holding sway, and, by that very fact, was incapable of generating any liberation project, political or spiritual.

Jesus initiates his program of liberation by *redeeming human beings*, rescuing them from the structural power of the law, from the "traditions," and from the marginalizing prejudices of institution, sect, race, and religion. He denounces the legalistic "justice" of the Pharisees (especially in Matthew, and in the theological elaboration of Paul), and the perverted and alienating "authority" of the Sadducees. It will be "authority," evidently, and not the Pharisees, that will later contrive the trial and execution of the new leader of the Palestinian people.

As a leader, Jesus generates a new symbolic order, which culminates in the political. The *poor*—the epicenter of his deeds and declarations—constitute a new force, as they are gradually conscientized. It is they who will be the foundation of the primitive church, as well as a decisive factor in the enfeeblement of the Roman empire. *Equality* among all human beings, acted out in the deeds of Jesus and converted into theological discourse by Paul, will effect a break with the socio-economic system of the ancient world. The slaves of the empire—the poor, called now to liberation—will be the revolutionary ferment of the first centuries of Christianity. The cult of the god-emperor is being eroded, beginning at its base—the masses of slaves—and demythologized at all levels. It is deprived of its oppressor function, which had been maintained by means of a mythic ideology.

The *anthropological*, not Jewish nationalist, direction of Jesus' praxis universalizes that praxis. In union with the other elements indicated, it can generate liberation processes in every human being in every nation or human group. Everything is synthesized in this capacity of Christ's practices and word to liberate the *human being*, from every alienating and oppressing system, religious or political. Jesus' praxis is *prophetical*—denouncing oppressive evil and proclaiming the liberation of the oppressed—but with a necessary reference to politics. Any praxis orientated to human liberation confronts, takes a "frontal" stance toward, the superstructures of power. Vain, then, are all the attempts that are made to maintain a merely or predominantly "spiritual mission" of churches and Christians. If that had been the way it was to be, Jesus would not have finished the way he did.

2. The history of Christianity serves us notice that the gospel kerygma is ambiguous. We have a certain nostalgia for many aspects of a return to the theocratic, a turning back to the pseudo-spiritual, to the old collaboration with dominating empires. In Latin America, the churches do not accompany liberation processes to the same degree that ecclesial pronouncements have gone—Medellín, San Miguel, and so on.[10] The reason is that their theology lacks a *hermeneutics* of the gospel. To what extent does the gospel "suffice" as an index for contemporary Christian praxis?

There is, in the symbolic order that Christ generated and that we have been examining, an interpretative key of our faith that can make a contribution to the liberation of our peoples. But there is also something "unsaid" in the gospel: the political, socio-economic, and cultural dimension of the task of Christianity and the churches. In the first place, the *reality* we are living is different from that of the Jews of Palestine in Jesus' time. Furthermore, our capacities for "reading" that reality are different, and they arouse another type of *conscientization.*

The arrival of the social sciences on the theological scene cannot supplant the gospel. They operate on a different level. But they can help to discover in the gospel a reservoir of meaning that opens up only from a point of departure in our own situation. Here there appears the "unsaid" in what the biblical kerygma *says.* The meaning of Christ's praxis is codified in a *text.* This text, both as linguistic structure and as message, lies open to interpretation. This interpretation is not something *added* to the original meaning. It is this *same* meaning, now read in a richer and more inclusive dimension. Now Jesus' trial sheds a new light, because the light of a new reality is shed on *it.*[11] These are terms in which we might express the task lying before biblical hermeneutics today with regard to the political dimension of Christ the Liberator.[12]

# NOTES

1. See my article, "La función del poder: ¿salvífica u 'opresora'?" *Revista Bíblica* 34 (1972): 99–106.
2. For the distinction between prophetical and apocalyptical eschatology, see "Hermenéutica de las representaciones escatológicas," *Stromata* 26 (1970): 59–75.
3. See the well-known works of O. Cullmann, P. Winter, S.G.F. Brandon, and J. Blinzler, and especially *Judaism* 20 (1971), no. 1, which is devoted to Jesus' trial.
4. Matthew normally omits the scribes, and Luke replaces them with "the officers of the guard" (Luke 22:4, 52), i.e., the Jewish temple police. John 18:3, 12 mentions a Roman "cohort" and even a "captain," but "sent by the chief priests and the Pharisees," i.e., by Jewish authority (John 18:3).
5. See P. W. Walaskay, "The Trial and Death of Jesus in the Gospel of Luke," *Journal of Biblical Literature* 94 (1975): 81–93. According to Walaskay, Luke distorts the religious *and Roman* trial, presenting Pilate as favorable to Jesus even though he condemns him, this being an attempt on the part of the evangelist to curry Roman favor in behalf of the early Christians.
6. Ibid., pp. 84ff.
7. Oscar Cullmann, *Estudios de teología bíblica* (Madrid: Studium, 1973), pp. 77ff.
8. Jürgen Moltmann, *Der gekreuzigte Gott* (Munich: Kaiser, 1973); Eng. trans., *The Crucified God* (New York: Harper & Row, 1974), p. 142.
9. See M. Avanzo, "El arresto, el juicio y la condena de Jesús: Historia y presente," *Revista Bíblica* 35 (1973): 131–50, esp. 137ff. Avanzo explains the false perspective that includes the Pharisees in Jesus' trial. John 18:3 would be an anachronism, according to Avanzo (but we might ask whether, instead, it is a rereading).
10. See H. Assmann, "Medellín: la desilusión que nos hizo madurar," *Cristianismo y Sociedad* 12 (1974): 137–43.
11. Avanzo, "El arresto," pp. 131ff., 150.

12. I have attempted to bring the hermeneutic method to bear upon this matter, along with the new contributions of Paul Ricoeur, H.G. Gadamer, and others, in "Las estructuras de poder en la Biblia: la recontextualización hermenéutica," *Revista Bíblica* 37 (1975). In English, see J. S. Croatto, *Exodus: A Hermeneutics of Freedom* (Maryknoll, N.Y.: Orbis, 1981).

# PART FOUR

*Theological and Pastoral Reflections*

*Chapter 10*

# THE ACTUATION OF THE POWER OF CHRIST IN HISTORY: NOTES ON THE DISCERNMENT OF CHRISTOLOGICAL CONTRADICTIONS

## *Hugo Assmann*

> *"I shall want to know not what these self-important people have to say, but what they can do, since the kingdom of God is not just words, it is power" [1 Cor. 4:19–20].*

For several years now, we have been hearing about a "christological vacuum" in Latin American theology. "Avant-garde theology," we are told (euphemistic for "revolutionary" theology), has no christology. The "theology of liberation" stands accused of "prescinding from Christ."

At the basis of this just charge—and it is just—is another problem, however, and a deeper one. Namely, it would seem that the viewpoints that are at the source of the objection are in themselves irreconcilably divergent. In the case of a first group, the objection seems to issue from a fruitless search for an unassailable and self-consistent doctrinal christological corpus that would prescind from any historical mediation aimed at finding a Latin American relevancy for this christology. Here our answer would be a counterobjection. One might well point out to the objectants that, in prescinding from the historical moment, they renounce any intention of speaking meaningfully of Christ and are thus involved in an actual sabotage of christology in the name of christology. Of course, this is nothing new: in the Bible itself, and much more so down through the history of Christianity, we find sabotage of the gospel in the name of the gospel.

In the case of a second group of objectants, however, the accusation of a christological void arises, on the contrary, precisely from the fundamental coincidence of their position with the primary intention of a theology of liberation: to develop, from a point of departure in the practice of a Christian faith that takes a determinate position on the side of the oppressed, a theological language in which the oppressed can express themselves. To demand more and better christology from this point of view, then, does not mean departing from, but entering still more deeply into, the focus of the objection leveled by the first group. Ignorance of this fundamental distinction with regard to a christological vacuum leads to quite serious consequences. It leads to a breach in the solidarity that is essential to the struggle for liberation. It plays into the hands of the enemy.

One could easily multiply symptomatic examples of this contradiction within the cry for a Latin American christology. Let us take the case of Leonardo Boff's *Jesus Christ Liberator*.[1] For some of the bishops, Boff's work is "reductionist"—Christ is said to be reduced to a historical liberator in the social and political area. For others—Spanish-American critics—his book is simply a good synthesis of some vague European abstractions in exegesis and theology without benefit of any attempt to apply them to current problems in Latin America. With respect to this latter objection, it will be useful to point out its unspoken implication. The objectants seem to question the possibility of resolving the conflict in christologies by means of a simple recourse to "better" exegesis in order to arrive at an objective purification of christological doctrine.

And I must say I tend to agree—not only because the exegetical panorama is itself too contradictory to admit easily of an exegetically unassailable synthesis of the message of christology. Also, and especially, there is the clear sociological datum that biblical scholars and theologians have no effective control (though they do have influence) over contradictory christologies. These continue to be preached and published in all their extreme variety. It is difficult to imagine a completely effective purifying influence by "modern exegesis" on the contradictory images of Christ in Latin America, even in the vain presupposition that this exegesis would lead us anywhere beyond the liberal, intrasystemic Christ. Of course, this does not mean that the important contribution that biblical scholars could offer is to be neglected.

Let us put it this way: there is something too ingenuous in the intention of those who think that they can fill in the Latin American christological lacuna with a powerful "biblical portrait of Christ"—which might be, for example, an ingenious mixture of Marxism and existentialism, as in José P. Miranda's *Being and the Messiah*[2] or a violent contraposition of the christology of Mark and Matthew, as in Joan Leita's *El Antievangelio*.[3] Church institutions will continue to say that it pertains to them, not to exegetes or theologians, to give the authoritative answers to questions of doctrine. And all the while, in the dialectic of social reality, the actually received and cultivated images of Christ will continue to influence Christian practice, and they will do so not only through the mediation of explicit theologies, but also, and powerfully, via those that are subliminal and latent.

## CONFLICT OF CHRISTOLOGIES, CONFLICT OF SOCIO-POLITICAL FACTORS

From what has been said so far, we are now in a position to draw our first conclusion: that the conflict of christologies cannot be analyzed or resolved apart from the dialectic of socio-political conflicts, which has ever been what actually conditioned them historically in the first place. Any other manner of approaching the problem is vitiated by its idealism.

Once we accept the fact that the conflict of christologies is conditioned by the historical contradictions of our societies, we begin to understand something that has been very hard to accept for those who have faith: that the conflict of christologies holds no promise of finding a solution in the immediate future, for there is no prospect for an immediate solution for the grave social contradictions in our "Christian" America. In order to word our affirmation in this way, of course, we have to grant that there exists a historical "Christian" milieu, in the sociological sense of the word, which has a historically conditioning effect in Latin America. Any attempt to imagine a process of liberation of our peoples without taking this historical milieu into account would run the risk of overlooking the motives of social consciousness, which have such a powerful effect on social processes. It is notorious that the forces of reaction would never think of committing a like error. The "metaphysical left," however, with its idealistic ideological radicalism, commits it regularly.

In other words, the outlook for the near future in Latin America is that the "Christs" on both sides will go right on being what they are, the revolutionary ones and the reactionary ones—with the aggravating circumstance that the latter will be the more "authorized" concepts of Christ, because it is the reactionary side that fights for continuity. This means that revolutionary Christians will have the task of maintaining the tension. Their "own" Christ will not be the only one to be invoked in the social dialectic, hence it would be rather vain to attempt to "monopolize" the image of Christ and make him a pure Christ the Liberator. No, Christ the Liberator will go right on being the "lesser" Christ, the one less "authorized" by official church institutions, however evident it may be that this image is more authentically based on the Bible. Christ the Liberator will continue to be an image of Christ opposed to the Christs of the middle classes. There will continue to be something of the heretical in him, given the biblical sources and the historical Christian testimony that support this image. Official denunciations will not be wanting. In many ecclesiastical circles the right to denounce "unauthorized teaching" begins much earlier than with the image of Christ the Liberator; it begins with the "liberal" Christ of the predominant current in modern biblical exegesis.

Then let us face this fact: faith in a Christ the Liberator, whose liberating power is vitally involved in class struggles and "takes sides" with the oppressed, inevitably collides with all the Christs of the oppressor classes. And these have them in abundance, for they fabricate them according to the needs of the moment.

Which Christs are currently invoked in Latin America? An exhaustive list is not possible here—we could not even cite all the principal ones, much less all the peripheral, secondary ones, which, within basic parameters, still cover a broad and diversified gamut in our peoples' "Christian" piety. Here I wish simply to call attention to certain dialectical fragments of the conflict of christologies.

Ever since the military coup in Chile, pronouncements of church and state alike have reflected a strong recrudescence of christologies that, during the Allende period, many would have thought illegitimate. Basically they are two: (1) the "Third Christ," the All-Reconciler, for whom there are neither victors nor vanquished, only one great family of brothers and sisters gliding serenely above all the social conflicts; and (2) the "Christ of the Coup," who underlies the invocation of a "defense of Christian values" as justification for the coup. Variations on these two are enlightening enough for a sociologist, but troublesome for a theologian or biblical scholar who counts on the possibility of making history advance by a simple purification of ideas. An examination of certain texts—for example, the statement by Bishop González of Temuco—demonstrates the difficulty of trying to "balance" a Christ who is "somewhat" the Third Christ and "just a bit" the Christ of the Coup. The least change of emphasis can profoundly alter the ideological sign—as witness the "discreet distance" of the Cardinal and Bishop Ariztía, on one side, and the "frank attachment" of Bishop Tagle of Valparaíso on the other.

As for the "christologies of the left," to whatever extent there were such—or still are, fragmentarily—some observations are in order. First, they do not generally exhibit the character of a new doctrinal corpus—rounded out, complete. Even their own claim to anything like the comprehensiveness of a system is quite modest in comparison with the claim of those who speak in the name of "the" Christ of the churches of the right. Rather, they are christologies of a "Christ too"—that is, they say, "This, too, is Christ." They have no pretensions to exclusivity. They are too conscious of the "other" christologies. It is the ideological hue of these christologies, and not so much their image of Christ in itself, that rounds out the picture and lends them the cast of a complete system of thought. (To the extent that the "Christ-image of the left" acquires class-consciousness traits, however, its antithetical character is reinforced, and it approaches exclusivity as its natural limit.) To boot, there is a certain Christ of the "broad leftist front" that is quite tolerant, and not particularly sectarian. A basic trait of the Christ-image invoked on the left is its Easter character—Christ's promise of life. It is interesting to notice the Easter content of the christological metaphors applied to freedom fighters who have died in the struggle. "Che lives!" or "Luciano lives!" or "Camilo?

Here!'' This note of paschal promise is present even in explicitly sacrificial metaphors, as in the chant of the children about "Che" in the "Year of the Heroic Guerrilla" as featured on German television: he died for all the children of the world.

Generally speaking, the christologies of the left like to do what Engels, Kautsky, Lunacharsky, and many another Marxists did, and make a great leap over the "distorted Christs" of the history of Christianity (a procedure that, be it remarked in passing, is neither very historical nor very materialistic) to a supposed "original Christ of primitive Christianity," who comes to meet the leapers as a "natural ally" so effortlessly that they do not see the hard task they have of clearing the way for him. A theology of Christ the Liberator should take more account of the Christs that have influenced history, rather than seeking to mediate, and thereby obstructing, access to the "Christ of the gospel." For the Christ of the gospel, as we have seen, has already passed through the medium of the kerygma.

With regard to the many "Christs of the people," or of the "baptized masses" in Latin America, many curious things are happening. In the 1970 elections in Chile, which Allende won, some 70 percent of the Pentecostalists voted for him. An authoritative spokesperson for the Pentecostal Church assured me that at least part of the explanation lay in the anti-Catholic attitude, and consequent anti-Christian Democrat attitude, of many Pentecostalists. An anti-Frei Christ? Here we must call attention to a more generic characteristic of the "popular Christs." Their power, and their pretensions to power, always in keeping with popular piety, are rather modest. They are Christs to which all power and dominion are *not* attributed. Christ here is more of a specialist, with very specific powers and prerogatives; the remaining "areas" are ceded to particular saints or to the Blessed Virgin.

This is most clearly demonstrated in the popular devotions of Brazil. The masses have no knowledge of Christ as Alpha and Omega, the Beginning and End of all. One may well wonder what dialectical role might be assigned to the Brazilian devotional Christs—which seem to be but "one more saint" in each case. Their usefulness for messianic ideologies that attempt to integrate a social mission seems quite limited.

At times one discerns a certain "ideological respect" for Christ, which actually prevents him from being assigned any "functions"—which it seems "better" to assign to the Blessed Virgin, for instance to "Our Lady the Generalisima of the Chilean Armed Forces" (Our Lady of Mount Carmel). Hence, incidentally, the tremendous symbolic power of the oath "In the name of Christ" taken by new cadets of the Chilean Military Academy since the coup.

Synthesizing, we can assert that the utilization of the Blessed Virgin has been earthier, and more explicit, in the recitation of the rosary against the "communist threat," as is done by "Tradición, Familia, Propiedad," "Fiducia," and other archconservative groups, in processions in Brazil and Bolivia, and so on. The Christ of the right cannot "lend his countenance" to this movement or that at the drop of a hat. His mission is exercised in the background.

For the sociologist, and even for the political scientist, this view of the range of christologies in conflict seems ridiculous or absurd only in the imprecision of my general, superficial observations. For the scientist, christological symbols, myths, and metaphors come forth naturally, as part of the conflict of ideologies—and to the extent that they are concretized in institutions, movements, or attitudes in social and political reality today, obviously admit of being assigned their relevancy as "power elements" in the context of collective consciousness.

The historian, the ethnologist, the anthropologist, the social psychologist, along with their analogues in the other social sciences, can perfectly well be interested in this approach to the theme, each one from their particular angle on reality. Even literary criticism can take an interest in the detection of deep levels of christologic metaphor at work—for example, in Gabriel García Márquez's short story, "El ahogado más hermoso del mundo" ["the world's most handsome drowning victim"], which recounts the sudden appearance on the shore of a fishing village of a large-framed, handsome dead man. No one can explain where the "imported dead man" comes from, or why he is here, but he arouses the people's spirit of devotion, in the women especially, and he is buried like a treasure, and inspires strange, rare moments of restfulness and peace.

But is this any perspective for a theologian? Is this enough for the person of faith, the person who believes in Christ? As we have seen, the revolutionary Christian and the "theologian of liberation" have no way of eluding the conflict of christological ideologies, nor any reason for attempting to do so, for its dialectic is altogether real. Accordingly, there is neither motive nor opportunity for leaving out of account the "real influence" or "dynamics of historical power" that is expressed through these christological ideologies. Leaving them out of consideration would do away with the possibility of a rational explanation of one's attachment to Christ and one's faith in his power.

## CRITERIA FOR AN OPTION

Precisely because our faith in Christ is at stake, revolutionary Christianity and the revolutionary theologian cannot afford to limit themselves to simply noting the "influences" that express themselves christologically. Their option for Christ, in faith, compels them to an effort of discernment. If it is true that there are "Christs in conflict," then faith in Christ forces the Christian to make an option for one of them—a vital and living option, one that is capable of being translated into action. This very possibly means an option that will eliminate contrary options, among the "other" Christs.

Where are the criteria of the option to be sought? As we have seen, the conflict of christologies admits of no easy solution through recourse to better biblical information. Such information can be of enormous help. In fact, to my way of thinking it is absolutely indispensable. But it would be naive to look upon it as sufficient, in view of the official interdicts that would soon appear. On the other hand it will help to keep in mind that for revolutionary Christianity and the "theologian of liberation," attachment to the "official" Christs of the churches is a dead-end street. Why? Primarily because these same Christs, over and above the disadvantage of their plural number and contradictory characteristics, are captives of authority and law, and largely intrasystemic.

Of course it will not do to exaggerate this handicap either: the christological doctrine of the churches, however much one may wish to keep it in subjection and under official control, still has "redeeming aspects"—essential elements that have a way of escaping complete captivity. Church christology contains elements that elude the churches. And it is precisely these elements that, in spite of all resistance that may arise, will be the point of departure, ready for use when the time comes, to dynamize little bits of liberating christology within the very bosom of the churches.

To put it another way, the christologies of the churches continue to constitute, despite all, a limited potential for alliance with a christology of liberation. This is valid on the doctrinal plane, to begin with. But it is valid above all by reason of the fact that revolutionary Christianity cannot permit itself to antagonize the adherents of church christologies when, for social and class reasons, it is seeking potential allies in the liberation process. Of course, matters are different in the case of those who use the name of Christianity to prop up their systems of oppression and domination. Their christologies are to be discredited and unmasked in terms of their conflictive contrast with other christologies.

But if recourse to the "fonts," for clarification of the "true" image of Christ, will not suffice, where *are* the criteria to be sought for a Christian's option for one image or another? There are, in addition to consultation of the biblical fonts, certain other criteria. I like to call them "criteria of approach," for they, too, fall short of being decisive or sufficient. I have gathered a few examples from the evolution of christology over the last decades.

## From Christ "in Himself" to Christ in Christians

The traditional Catholic treatise in christology, in the period preceding Vatican Council II, was principally apologetic (in problems concerning the "historical Jesus") and philosophical (with regard to the human and divine "self" of Christ). In a word, it was concerned essentially with a Jesus of yore—with Christ as Son of God in a kind of philosophical defense of the Council of Chalcedon. The burning theological questions—the incarnation, the contemporaneity of the historical Christ today, the paschal mystery in our current human history, and so on—were treated only tangentially. As compared with the classic tractates, the axis of the christological thematic has shifted considerably in recent years. From "Christ" it has moved to "total Christ." From Christ "in himself" it has moved to the Christ in Christians—and, very gradually and timidly, to Christ as active power today across the breadth of human history.

As can be seen from this rapid sketch of the evolution of christology on the historical plane, this theology was moving closer and closer to the *dilemma* implied in the affirmation of the power of Christ as an acting force in all history—hence also in our contemporary history of conflict. Which dilemma, concretely? The one that takes shape as the central challenge for the "theology of hope" and for "political theology": to speak of the power of Christ as a historical force means either to posit the concrete political relevancy of this historical force, or to declare once and for all that the power of Christ is purely posthistorical and eschatological.

As we know, there are still those who opt for pure eschatology in today's Christian panorama. But the theologians to whom I refer have the merit of having opted decidedly for the active contemporaneity of the power of Christ and the might of his resurrection. They have decided upon one of the horns of the dilemma, rejecting a purely individualistic, "intimist," salvationism. What is new in this? Is this not the most traditional affirmation the church could make with respect to the power of Christ? Yes, indeed it is—at least at the level of words. But, as Saint Paul insists, "the kingdom of God is not just words" (1 Cor. 4:20). The theologies of which I am speaking claim to take this Pauline "leap to deeds" seriously—a "leap" that goes all the way to the power residing in the reality of socio-political facts.

## The Locus of Christ's Power

Once they have come to this crucial point—the power of Christ acting politically today—the "political theologians" made one more giant step. They began to dismantle the alibis with which the churches keep the power of Christ "politically innocent"—the ideological subterfuges, which are susceptible of analysis in function of their politics. But *abyssus abyssum invocat*—abyss calls to abyss—and one dilemma conjures up another. To unmask the alibis of the indetermination of Christ's power means much more commitment and involvement than the simple, equally indeterminate, generic affirmation that this power is "currently present and acting in our history." It means we have to determine, even though not in exclusive terms, just *where* this power of Christ is acting in conflictive human history.

This new dilemma—that of locating at least the central focus of the activity of Christ in history—means plainly and simply this: determining where—with whom and against whom—Christ's power is taking sides. To my way of thinking it is at precisely this point that European "political theology" has begun to grow afraid of its own courage and has passed to vague niceties that fail to find their way to expression even in the scientific theological language and concepts already available (if imperfect) with respect to the conflictive gambits of power in history. They simply have not dared to continue their analysis of the historical mediations of the role of power.

## Taking Sides

It was at this point that Latin American theology dared to take a few timid steps of its own. Without nourishing any illusions of being able adequately to "locate" the activity of the current historical power of Christ, it nonetheless began to insert into the process of theological reflection certain instruments of analysis permitting a closer approach to a determination of Christ's "taking sides." What resulted from this "leap" was something approximating the first sketches of a Christ the Liberator at the heart of the only history we have, a history marked by contradictions and conflict.

The activation of his power necessarily comports a definite meaning and direction: on the side of the oppressed, against the oppressors. Now it is no longer a matter of the Great Reconciler, hovering far above all the conflicts of the here and now—however clearly the final intent of his acting power be the comradely reconciliation of human beings in the present life, at the heart of our earthly history. Nor is it a matter of a sectarian, partisan Christ, or still less of a fanatical promotor of one single system and tactics. Indeed Christ's power is not exercised apart from the history of concrete human beings. It has no "history of its own" in this sense. Rather it is a power that participates in history in and through human beings.

## Liberation Christology

Incipient liberation christology has said nothing to date that the churches themselves do not support, or have not supported—powerfully, at times. Only, it has said it under the opposing ideological sign. The "heresy" is not in any exaggerated concretion and localization of the power of Christ. On this point the intent of determination has remained sufficiently discreet, and even broadly open. Christ's power is not snatched at and captured as a legitimating element, firm and definitive, in any narrowly partisan historical movement. The challenging image of Christ the Liberator is ever in the fore, it points ever out ahead of us, for we encounter it only on the frontiers of the future. Its challenge to the liberation of the oppressed implies an ongoing revolution, yes, but a realistic, not an idealistic one. Then where is the scandal? In the scandalized. And in the audacious intent of a christology of liberation to oppose their vested ideological position with a clear, if at times unconscious, political option of its own.

No one can fail to see that a christology of liberation is a seedbed of new dilemmas. The scientific instruments for "reading reality" are still highly imperfect. This has to be said, against every type of systematized, schematized Marxism—and indeed for the benefit of Marxism if you will. But these instruments of analysis—and this has to be said too, without, however, falling into a scientific positivism—are no longer at point zero. To have to make a choice among so many available scientific instruments itself constitutes a dilemma. By this very fact, the choice implies an ethical step. And whatever involves ethics involves the possibility not only of error, but of blame.

Thus the new dilemmas of a christology of the liberating power of Christ in our history are of multiple origin. Human history doubtless contains many facets that our vain science will never manage scientifically to "verify." But surely this is no dispensation from the obligation to make use of whatever degrees of verifiability are available and agreed upon.

One generally speaks of the mechanisms of conflictive power in human history in terms of economics, politics, and society—in a word, in historical terms. But there are blanks, surprises, and a good many nebulous areas. Can it therefore be claimed that the historical dialectic of the liberating power of Christ, in its contemporary phase or moment, partakes of the nature of the "economic object," the "political object," and so on? For a Christian, this is a real dilemma in many respects—by reason of the determinative nature of that mysterious and somewhat vague "ultimate instance" attributed by Marxism to the economic sphere, or, more broadly, to the material structure of society.

A certain renascence of "historicism" in certain Marxist currents is opening the way for a re-evaluation of the primacy of politics. On this terrain, perhaps, Christians could feel more in their element, as Christian faith in humankind, and human freedom, gradually grows and spreads. But in our aversion for "economistic materialism" (and nothing is more "economistic" than capitalism), we are often tempted to fall into a certain kind of voluntaristic "spontaneism." Perhaps the following parallelism will help to show how certain particularly nondialectical classic christological schemata will, according to the needs of the moment, fit into either a sort of determinism of the "objective datum," or into a decidedly anarchical voluntarism:

Objective redemption: power of Christ,
                    objective conditions

Subjective redemption: justification by faith,
                    subjective conditions

The theology of liberation seeks to maintain (admittedly, with a considerable degree of fragility) a dialectical tension between the two essential elements of its methodology: recourse to the "mediations of analysis" and the primacy of a "critically examined praxis." By this very fact, the notion of "power" with which it operates can never be a "pure substantive" power, a power held or acquired. It must always be a "verbal" power as well—the exercise, or praxis, of power. Consequently the notion of "Christ's power" may never be reduced to a preexisting force, as an objective quality in history, for it must inescapably pass by way of our praxis. But our historical praxis develops amid conflict and, inasmuch as it must take the direction of a liberating dialectic, can have no definitive point of crystalization. After all, it moves dialectically, in the midst of conflict. A deeper appreciation of this characteristic of praxis—its liberty as something "unpredeterminable"—could lead us a step closer to the prohibition of the creation of definitive images of the power of Christ in history.

The old christological faith speaks too "substantively" of Christ and his Easter actualization in history. All these substantives, which have promised to become verbs in a praxis of liberation, have practically always remained adverbial. But Christ did not impinge on history merely tangentially. And his power—precisely because it was not susceptible of "substantivization," or reduction to constructs—ended up identified with the powers that be, with power in the substantive, power established. Thus it had lost its active dynamic as an ongoing counterpower—a power that critically differentiates itself, opposes, and counterposes. And it finally became the auxiliary power of the "powers and dominations." This is what occurs when one speaks of power without inquiring into the channels of its efficacity. For the ones who are efficacious in the area of domination are the ones who appropriate it.

Presumably apolitical christologies—theologies of a Christ who "has" power, but who does not exercise it, who never "takes sides"—are simply forms of hiding the fact that one has already taken sides. Political christologies are efforts at unmasking apolitical Christs and revealing their true face.

Presumably apolitical christologies are but theological (or rather ecclesiastical) Yalta Agreements. They are an accord struck regarding "zones of influence," in the deep, political sense. They always end in "peaceful coexistence"—two histories, two worlds, two separate tasks. Divide and conquer.

Will anyone deny us the right to ask with whom the accord has been struck?

The dolorous Christs of Latin America, whose central image is ever the cross, are Christs of impotence—an impotence interiorized by the oppressed. Defeat, sacrifice, pain, cross. Impotence, powerlessness, is accepted "undigested," recognized in advance and submitted to. Defeat is not perceived as a temporary reversal to be overcome in struggle. It appears as an inevitable necessity, as a condition of the privilege of living. The impossibility of real, effective power is posited as a necessary condition for the continuation of a life idealized as a promise of power that can never be kept.

A blind trap, a perfect alibi. But for what perfect crimes, and whose?—we may be permitted to ask.

On the other hand, the rare glorious Christs of Latin America—seated on thrones and wearing royal crowns like kings of Spain—are not *other* Christs, they are the *same* Christs, the same sorrowful Christs, their necessary counterparts. They are their other face—the one the dominator sees.

Thus there is no way to separate cross and resurrection without falling among Christs that alienate, Christs that estrange. Christs of established power (who have no need to struggle, because they already dominate), and Christs of established impotence (who are too dominated to be able to struggle) are the two faces of oppressor christologies.

And yet, to affirm in faith the actuating presence of the power of Christ means to struggle in history where defeat is but preparing the way for victory, to struggle in the ongoing process of liberation, in the presence of the ongoing dialectic of cross and resurrection today.

# NOTES

1. Maryknoll, N.Y., Orbis, 1978.
2. Maryknoll, N.Y., Orbis, 1977.
3. Barcelona, Laia, 1973.

*Chapter 11*

# HOW SHOULD WE SPEAK
# OF CHRIST TODAY?

## *Raúl Vidales*

One of the key tasks of the church in Latin America today is a reformulation of the great themes of the faith. The nucleus of this set of problems is, without a doubt, christology. The problem is a complex one, and I believe we should approach it from the very start with the modesty and sensitivity one feels when touched to the quick of one's own spiritual experience.

What is certain is that Christ has become a "sign of contradiction" in the midst of a continent in contradiction. Christ has always been, in himself, an enigma, and one that is difficult to solve. Announced as a sign "for the fall and for the rising of many" (Luke 2:34), Christ appeared "contextualized" in such a peculiar world. Our modern problems of colonialism, imperialism, racism, and the like, had sunk their tentacles into Israel, too, an oppressed land, convulsed by numberless divisions and internal struggles. It is in this milieu that Jesus proclaims his message—whose most profound, original, and mysterious dynamism is realized in the dialectical contradiction of dividing in order to unify, leaving in order to possess, dying in order to gain life.

When he finally comes to be executed he is a political revolutionary to those in government, an enlightened idealist for the devout, an ultraconservative in the view of revolutionaries—and for the people a prophet, or a messiah, or a liberator, who ended frustrated and frustrating. Jesus left no one indifferent. He touched each one to such depths that he provoked the most radical polarizations and options. He awakened hope in all. But when any particular group sought to subject him to its programs, he suddenly could not be found. Many hoped he would found a political party of the poor (he

137

had declared them "blessed"), by which he would occasion the downfall of the rich and powerful. He fails to do so, and disappoints many. And in spite of this, no one has bestowed political power upon the poor as Jesus has. Christ is the sign of contradiction who remains a sign of contradiction, and who even to our own day launches movements, stirs up contradiction in the face of inhuman conditions, and then provokes very concrete changes.

What is surprising is that this contradiction springs up as it were on the edge of Christ's intentionality. What is decisive in his message is not the arousal of noble sentiments and honorable thoughts, but a driving process that brings a human being toward a new mode of activity, springing from an interior renewal. The human being renewed by Jesus necessarily does "new things."

Jesus takes his place in the history of the process of becoming in a double projection—a historical one and a metahistorical one. And these two projections are not merely juxtaposed, parallel, or somehow intimately "united." They are two vectors of a single force that drives men and women and historical processes. Thus, although the ideal of the new human being is verified only in the small, incomplete conquests of the everyday, these same achievements necessarily embody our permanent pro-vocation, our calling forth, toward the future consummation.[1]

Let us put it this way: if Christ turns out to be "conflictive"—an occasion of conflict—for Christians committed to liberation processes in Latin America, this before all else is because he continues among us as a "sign of contradiction."

The new experience of one's first faith, and thereupon the total fullness of the liberation commitment, are the basic loci that have provoked and called forth the genesis and evolution of the theological task of liberation. A new way of understanding, accepting, and actualizing the gospel message gradually emerges. This attitude toward the message is called faith. And little by little this faith shows itself to be a liberation praxis. Thereupon it begins to constitute the daily matrix of an ongoing critical reflection—called theology—that has both its point of departure and its proper object in that liberation praxis. And the whole reciprocal process tends to carry its subject more and more within the interior of political commitment.

Consequently, confronted with the problem of how to speak of Christ today, we cannot get on with a solution except via this same route. We are not interested in formulating a scientific philosophical doctrine apropos of Christ. But this does not mean that our approximations are going to wander off capriciously, deprived of all methodological precision. Our intention is different because our *need* is different. Our viewpoint is an experience of conflict, the situation of persons who experience a very concrete need, a neediness, to believe in Christ anew. I say "anew," not because they ever stopped believing in him, but because they experience faith as an ongoing incitement, orientated toward the *diakonia* of concrete times in history— which at the moment are especially dense, hostile, and unsure.

The question, How should we speak of Christ today? is, before all else, this other question: How is Christ actually believed and proclaimed by committed Christians? But to be able to observe this experience from within and make a first approximation of an answer to our question we have to place ourselves within a situation comporting the possibility of encountering the paths of a joint endeavor. So huge a task demands an elementary schematization, which at the same time reflects a methodology:

1. the perspective of faith
2. the perspective of theology
3. the perspective of evangelization

## THE PERSPECTIVE OF FAITH:
## CHRISTIAN EXPERIENCE

The nuclear event for Christians involved with liberation is basically this: a new experience of Christ. Their new way of being believers in Jesus Christ necessarily involves a new manner of understanding, accepting, and actualizing his message. The original, primordial adventure is an unprecedented christological experience. The field remains open for a more exhaustive investigation, by way of christology, a science that has gained its current explication via the route Christians have taken from the age of the "Christian mentality," through that of the "distinction between the sacred and the secular," then "development," revolutionary radicalization, and finally liberation. The paths upon which I shall concentrate in the following paragraphs are situated within these last two steps.

### Encounter with Christ in History

At the moment when Latin America was radicalizing politically, the crisis undergone by Christians wore an ecclesiological face. The church began to appear not only powerless and irrelevant, but openly suspect of complicity with powers that maintained an established order that was inhumane because it involved the enslavement of whole peoples. The resulting drastic tension between rejecting and belonging had a deep effect on the early movements, and the rifts have perhaps not healed. Various "immediatist" measures were undertaken to resolve the tension, both by way of concrete conciliatory strategies and certain doctrinal subterfuges.

Little by little, the accusations made against the church in the name of Christ himself began to explicate and delimit the concrete shape of a deeper christological problem. In the midst of the revolutionary struggle, Christians were experiencing ever more intensely an irreversible thrust toward radicality, toward a greater depth in the posing of the pertinent questions, and toward a more refined scientific critical approach. The pioneers in the affair were absolutely helpless and abandoned, for they were on terrain where the problematic of the faith seemed utterly abandoned itself, in the almost total

absence of any assistance from traditional quarters. The image of Christ began to seem violent and rebellious, or fugitive and hard to find. Many began
to feel that, in the midst of revolution, they found no inspiration or orientation in the gospel. Others did not believe they could find anything to imitate
of Jesus in this area of endeavor. The attitude of Christ himself in the face of
the political problems of his time left them with the feeling of a certain "ab-
senteeism," in a neither pro nor contra "borderland"—that is, an apparently
conciliatory program of peaceful coexistence. What seemed really to be
needed was for him to have carried them to full radicality and thus rid them of
the ambiguity with which they were imbued. One wanted to see in Jesus a
more absolute posture against the exploiters and for the people. The image of
the militant revolutionary, or of the charismatic political figure, would have
suffered great violence had it been accommodated to that image of Christ—
and vice versa.

To make matters still more complex, there was another problem in the
search for a relevant christology: the image of a reactionary Christ, the Christ
of the "rear guard," the traditional Christ of "Christian Western
civilization"—an unbiblical, unhistorical, idealized image of Christ. This
was an authoritarian formulation of a christology long since superseded—an
image of Christ that was replete with lofty attributes, titles, and privileges,
and yet an image that was opaque, naive, and impotent, incapable of setting
souls on fire.

And so the movement led to the challenging search for a new face of Christ.
But now a surprise was in store. "The crowds were appalled on seeing him—
so disfigured did he look that he seemed no longer human" (Isa. 52:14)—the
twisted face of a whole continent, revealing traits, lines, and reliefs hitherto
unsuspected. Now the faces of Christ sometimes have a name, and a familiar
set of attributes, culminating in a heroic death—a death for others, somehow
summed up in the crucifixion. Sometimes, however, he is anonymous—
average, faceless. He is the rural poor of the interior of Brazil, he is the
marginalized ones of the shantytowns that Lima calls *barriadas*, "districts,"
Santiago *callampas*, "mushroom cities," Buenos Aires *villas miseria*, and
Montevideo *cantegriles*. It is not so much the church, it is Latin America that
is setting afoot this new movement toward Christ.[2]

This experience, however embryonic, represents not only a break, but a
radical and definitive launch into the adventure of a new christology. For this
new stance and attitude led to the discovery of new places and milieus of
encounter with Christ—in the world of the other, of the poor, the oppressed,
who exist as a despoiled social class—the world of revolutionary options and
liberation processes. And this experience of Christ, in turn, is extremely demanding in terms of concrete and effective realization of filiation and fellowship.

The encounter with Christ in history passes by way of the oppressed, and
there is no detour. This is why the basic nature of the new spiritual experience
is a continuous movement of conversion. But to be converted to Christ means

to be converted to one's sisters and brothers, and to be converted to them means to make concrete options with them in their struggles. To believe in Christ poor is to live the faith as an act of political charity, reaching through to the poor of this world. This faith becomes an act of solidarity with them, of protest against the poverty they live in, of identification with the interests of the oppressed classes, and of the forthright denunciation of the exploitation that victimizes them. Hence, in spite of the incipient and ambiguous character of these first steps, they take on a radical importance, and are, in their own right, linked to any ulterior theological development.

The discovery of the world of the other, of the poor, has necessarily entailed a new understanding and grasp of the political, a new way of understanding and making a commitment to poverty. But this ultimately means a new experience of the Spirit, and it is within this new Christian experience that the gestation of a new christological development is rooted, as Gustavo Gutiérrez has put it:

It is only through concrete deeds of love and solidarity that our encounter with the poor person, with the exploited human being, will be effective—and in that person our encounter with Christ, and through them with Christ (for "you did it to me"—Matt. 25:40) will be valid as well. Our denial of love and solidarity will be a rejection of Christ ("you neglected to do it to me"—Matt. 25:45). The poor person, the other, becomes the revealer of the Utterly Other. Life in this involvment is a life in the presence of the Lord at the heart of political activity, with all its conflict, and with all its demand for scientific reasoning. It is the life of—to paraphrase a well-known expression—contemplatives in political action.[3]

### Political Charity

Little by little, the path has been cleared of debris. Or, at least, one has learned to take a few more confident steps along it. The discovery of a qualitatively new world, in need of radical changes, has gradually led this spiritual experience to something qualitatively new, to actual liberating praxis. An acute scientific analysis and interpretation of the reality of Latin America has come to demand a new service to the faith, a task that can be carried out only from a point of departure in historical praxis, animated by hope in the Lord of history in whom everything was made and everything is saved. The image of Christ as *liberator* is a trait that emerges in powerful accents, for it is he alone who is capable of making us the free gift of total liberation. Believing in Christ is an act absolutely and utterly reserved to the interior of a person, for Christ reveals himself as an ongoing challenge from within realities and processes, from within the heart and cry of everyone oppressed, from within the multitudes and the crowds, from within the structuration of an unjust order. Believing in Jesus necessarily turns out to be "political charity," a liberation praxis. The bestowal of the gift of his word of freedom thrusts the one who receives it toward its verification in concrete reality, though no historical concretion can exhaust it. Seeing history as a process in which Christ's liberation is under way broadens one's perspective and accords to political commitment all due honor and meaning. Only from a position of revolutionary involvement can one proclaim Christ's free and liberating gift of love—a love that goes to the very root of all exploitation and injustice: the dissolution of filiation and fellowship.

Thus it is that the personal experience of Christ is the ultimate and definitive criterion of discernment transcending all others. And thus also—because Christians know that the total liberation they hope for is Christ's free gift— the new Christian experience develops in an atmosphere of gratuity that spontaneously becomes a *call to prayer*. Faith is ever irreducible to systems, whether of reality or of thought. But at the same time it demands formulation in language and works. This mutual implication, which is constitutive of Christianity, is verified, of course, in the case under consideration. Nevertheless, there is a moment in faith that perdures as a moment of acceptance, of gratitude, of attachment, and of profession before the mysterious Other who forms part of this faith. It is this aspect of dialogue, this I-Thou of faith, present in the most elemental faith, that is at the basis of the prayer of committed Christians. Because, on the other hand, faith is collective—is a We-Thou relationship, inasmuch as it unites independent freedoms in love and commitment—Christian prayer that would not bespeak an essential relationship with concrete historical commitments would appear to be vitiated in its very roots.[4]

This is the explanation why committed Christians now experience much more lucidly that they are collaborating with the Lord in redemptive tasks within the transforming evolution of their political options.

## THE PERSPECTIVE OF THEOLOGY

Christological faith has always been a painful part of the history of Christianity. Thus it was in the first centuries—and not only because Christians underwent martyrdom at the hands of a polytheistic Greco-Roman society for their alleged atheism ("We are called 'atheists,' " said Justin, " 'those who have no gods.' Surely we confess our atheism—for we surely have not these so-called gods")—but also because of the difficulties that appear in the first christological controversies.[5] The anguish appears indeed in an Arius, an Appollinarius, or a Nestorius, but it appears no less at Ephesus and Chalcedon. The affirmation of the two natures was not an ontological speculation, but the response of Christian freedom in the face of the agony of a period of transition. Our forebears in a christological faith are only confirming the words of Paul:

And so . . . here are we preaching a crucified Christ; to the Jews an obstacle that they cannot get over, to the pagans madness [1 Cor. 1:23].

This same painful scrutiny has been repeated in our own day. The road has been complex and exhausting from the first scientific studies on the life of Jesus by the rationalist, or liberal, school. Beginning with the first writings of D. F. Strauss and of Renan, the movement continued without interruption until, in our century, it yielded up its central conclusion: critical studies of the gospels lead not to the Jesus of history, but to the oral tradition about Jesus. W. Wrede (1901) and K. L. Schmidt (1919) are among the forerunners of the renowned *Formgeschichte* school, the methodology of a "history of forms," which attempts to reach the primitive tradition with respect to Jesus via an analysis of the literary and preliterary forms this tradition takes.[6]

And yet, neither the liberal school nor *Formgeschichte* succeeded in placing the problem in its proper context. For both, mystical experience never transcends the mundane phenomenon proper to the life of *homo religiosus*. The mystical Christ here is not the Utterly Other, the Word of God.[7]

The problem later came to be posed on three closely related, but by no means identical, levels: that of the historical Jesus, that of the idealized Jesus, and that of the Jesus of faith. This putting of the problem is dialectical, inasmuch as its nucleus will consist in the synthetic relationship of the third level to the other two. That is, we could ask the question in this way: How is the historico-idealized Christ to be related to the Christ of faith? Now the human sciences will be called into play, along with theology, and their interaction should yield a tentatively conclusive response.

It is not my intention to discuss the problem, but merely to situate the conclusion of these theological currents. At the same time this will serve as a vehicle for my own methodological stance. The Christ of history, says E. Käsemann among others, is the Christ of faith, and the road to him is the *kerygma*.[8]

Now, from the perspective of the theology of liberation, certain new situating elements have to be posited. A christology based in the theological perspective of liberation has its point of departure in a double frontal pole—the word, and the praxis of liberation, both converging dialectically in the concrete historical process. But in order validly to realize this contribution of our dialectic, the theology of liberation must entertain a methodological rehearsal of the faith journey itself in its second moment: that of the *kenosis*, "evacuation," or "self-emptying." And indeed it is only from a theological perspective that incorporates the laws of the incarnation and resurrection as something intrinsic to its work dynamic that a vital and popular christology can be developed. For this is precisely the contact point at which the danger, and the challenge, presents itself:

In the hiatus between a vague and undifferentiated christology of a suprainstitutional mold, *ad usum omnium*, and a christology that is functionalized ideologically for a determinate situation, there is a legitimate need for a christology capable of historical mediation—one that will be meaningful for the basic questions of a historical situation.[9]

But we are still the beginning of a christology of liberation. Our efforts are still sporadic and scattered, and do not always evince a single perspective.

Furthermore, the reason why Christian experience collides with the image of a traditional Christ is that the theological task runs up against a theology that has long left in abeyance any consideration of theological problems in their historical meaning and projection. Here, as in other areas of theology, we can find the culprit in an elitist christology, a christology belonging to the apex of a pyramid, worked out far from daily tasks and struggles, far from the priority requirements and challenges of specific contexts and connections.

The problematic thickens when we consider how nimbly the theological *logos* has been sequestered and manipulated by the dominating classes of our traditional Christian Western civilization. For it is precisely in our civilization that persons who succeed in manipulating the idea of God will possess a powerful advantage in their efforts to maintain a given social order—the one that suits their interests:

> This recurs in the history of religions with great frequency, at times indeed in a cyclic rhythm bespeaking some kind of normality. "God" is a prodigious name, and anyone who succeeds in manipulating the notion of God will indubitably enjoy excellent chances of manipulating the masses for whom God is so important.[10]

Theology would just be reduced to the innocuous—to neutrality and indifference. The manipulation referred to can occur only when theology is an abstract, idealistic activity, prevented from approaching the terrain where historical battles are joined. The phenomenon is a familiar one, and has already been abundantly examined and deplored—but then theology withdraws to the domains of domestic privacy, and just as definitely abandons the frontiers where the fate of human processes is decided, venturing at most to inject remote and peripheral considerations. The result is that theology not only turns out to be an elitist product itself, but is converted into a factor that actually helps maintain the elite in power. It draws orthodoxy onto its own terrain and manipulates the parameters of dogma and heresy with uncontested sovereignty.[11]

There are certain theological advances that we can point to, breakthroughs and prospects that have come out of the legacy of Christian experience.

## Silence and Prayer

A christology that has liberation for its perspective will take its point of departure in the experience of Christ. But one encounters the Word, the Utterly Other, only if he is received and professed in the realm beyond all language, the realm of silence. Hence any theological consideration of Christ begins necessarily in silence. But this silence has nothing in common with the contemplation proper to a tragic Greek ethos of old, nor with the silence of the pietists, nor even with the mystagogical wordlessness that is only the chatter of the mind with itself. Christ is the Word silently pronounced in flesh, history, and destiny. He is in himself the Word, yes—but historicized. For this reason Christ, at the same time as he is received within the depths of all that is human, demands to be "proclaimed," to be historically verified and actuated.

To pray is at once to be silent and to cry out—before Christ and his word and before human beings and their history. And because the primordial christological act is the experience of Christ in the midst of a political, politicized existence that is both generative of, and itself characterized by, conflict, Christ can at no moment be reduced to a scientific object to which we apply an instrument of analysis. Such an attitude and procedure would lead us precisely toward a dynamic of "distancing," to an objectivization of Christ, and an alienation from him. What is crucial is to maintain the ongoing transition from being "wise concerning Christ" to "believing in Christ" in our everyday existence.

But if the human response cannot be adequately contained in any language, if all discourse is finally imperfect, then true faith will not be one that produces words, but one that produces works. Thus the works themselves become paradigmatic language of faith at the same time as they become its historical content and truth. Efficacious charity, which consists in works, is the fruit of the Spirit. Hence the authentic Christian language is spoken in works, which here means that it is spoken in a "liberation praxis." For the radical experience of Christ is to be sought amid silence and deeds, where the seed of christology itself lies germinating.

## Openness to Christ, Openness to Others

Encounter with Christ leads to an active openness in favor of others— many others. The sequence is not chronological, with a before and an after, but dialectical, in the form of an "interpresence." The concrete person of the poor, actually encountered as a social class exploited and in conflict, is the privileged place where Christ reveals the mystery of his own person. Faith in Christ comes into being by way of the cause of the poor—and this dynamism "localizes" on the deepest level of evangelical conversion. Filiation and fellowship are the touchstones of its authenticity, and at the same time they turn out to be concrete struggles. Thereby they constitute the next two themes of the christology of liberation:

> To make an option for the poor, for the exploited classes, to identify with their lot, and share their fate, is to wish to make this history that of a community of brothers and sisters. There is no other way to receive the free gift of filiation. It is an option for Christ's cross, in the hope of his resurrection.[12]

This option implies the experience in one's own flesh of the tragedy of hope, the experience of struggles, repression, and death itself—which are not the customary categories of a theologian's analyses. An option for the "real people"—not the "official people," made up of "myopic minorities and egotistical oligarchies," as F. Bourricaud put it—is an option to enter into the experience of a "latent rebellion," into the revolutionary subconscious of the multitudes. The logic of the creative act, which ultimately is the logic of liberty, imposes upon the Christian the task of discovering a "common freedom" gained in a common struggle. "There are no typically revolutionary situations," said Sartre, "there are only *terrors*." And this is what translates, for the Christian, into the living experience of *kenosis* as the price of "new personhood according to Christ."

Further, the Word discloses to human beings what they are for God—and then what God, as manifested in Christ as their neighbor, is for them. Thus it is the ceaseless confrontation with the "Absolute that is God" that leads necessarily to the "absolute that is one's neighbor."

## The Christ Encountered

Just as Christ is encountered as the Utterly Other, so also is he discovered in his historical singularity. And in our present case, his coming upon the scene in a particular tradition and culture, as a human being really belonging to that tradition and culture—that is, in his actual concrete, not an ideal, humanity—comes to constitute an essential element of God's revelation. For it is in this dynamism and structuration of forces and realities that the mission of Jesus is situated. He like no one else has realized his historical destiny as a "contextualized" being. The concrete problematic of the Jewish longings for liberation, the oppression and imperialism on the part of the Romans, the internal domination groups ("Herodian" groups), racial discrimination, ideological and class struggle, slavery, and so on and so on, necessarily shape Christ's physiognomy and message.

But besides, we know that Christianity does not live on just a memory. It celebrates and proclaims a *presence*. And Christ, sown in history and in the cosmos, drives Christians to interpret the world and history not only from a past that projects forward into today and tomorrow, and not only from a future already in process of accomplishment, but also from the weight of the present, where the human being appears as Christ's greatest sacrament.[13]

It is here that liberation christology emphasizes not only the personage and attributes of the Christ of Nazareth, but the traits of the "Christ of mystery," who waxes in rhythm with history and human beings because he is within them. And he pushes out against their frontiers and limits until he breaks free in liberation. Which is the Christ the masses believe in? Which is the Christ of the oppressed?

Obviously, only those grassroots theologians, who are undergoing a *kenosis* consisting of their own approach to the masses, can have the sensitivity required for this experience.

It is not often that the theologian sees the world the way that others see it. There in the world is the miserable one in misery—the misery of a whole lifetime. This is life penetrated as it were by death, by death everywhere, by the aftertaste of agony souring the whole of life. Who but the one committed to the grass roots, the base, can detect the efflorescence in the everyday of the collective consciousness of such a long history of misery, bent toward and impregnated by an end and purpose not its own, breaking its moorings and sweeping away from its secular enchantment, from its passivity of the past? This is the launch pier, this is where the vessel breaks away from a history of discouragement, where it is impossible to continue to live when death and the vacuousness of life become so familiar now, fill one with the total shock of their truth. It is here that the new task of christology arises—a christology that will be incapable of formulation as a dogmatic truth, because in a dogmatic truth the oppressed are never more than a human hypothesis.

## The Political Dimension

These elements lead us to the central point of the theological task of liberation christology: the political dimension of Jesus and his message.

There is no doubt that what stands out in the clearest delineations is the figure of Christ the Liberator. It is he who can bestow the free gift of radical liberation. And it is Christ's free and liberating love that lends breadth, depth, and transcendence to the liberation commitment. With his activity and his message, he unveils the meaning of the struggles of history. He calls continuously for an ongoing conversion, change, and revolutionary transformation in human beings and their societies. It is he who delivers human beings from an oppressed consciousness and bestows upon them the necessary elements for a new, critical consciousness. He reveals a new dimension of social and structural sin and lends impetus to new forms of struggle against this perduring antithesis of the universal community of sisters and brothers.

This is how he provokes and occasions the generation of revolutionary processes and movements for liberation, and this is why these processes and movements will always attain their plenitude only in himself. In just this way, Christ is the only bearer, in its fullness, of the physiognomy and comportment of the "new human being," made free by the mystery of his saving deed.

The political dimension of Christ's message appears not so much as a strategy or set of tactics, but as a subversive dynamism, for the short term as well as for the long, for both the proclamation and the activation of the truth about God, about the human being, and about that human being's history and reality:

> If you will make my word your home
> you will indeed be my disciples,
> you will learn the truth,
> and the truth will make you free [John 8:31–32].

Jesus is a liberator when he calls the poor to form his kingdom and be its privileged members. The "personhood" that Christ bestows upon the voiceless is neither prestige, nor power, nor security. It is rather the basis of all movements of authentic liberation. The universality of the kingdom proclaimed by Jesus converts Christianity and Christians into critical antagonists of all totalitarian and absolutist systems, not only economic and political, but religious as well. Just so, in proclaiming the comportment and physiognomy of the "new person," Jesus brings human beings a new prophetic consciousness. Without offering concrete models for a better society, he sows the seeds of a dynamism of the freedom, truth, and fellowship that are at the root of all ameliorative social changes.

A political reading of the life of Jesus is inevitable and absolutely necessary. Just as the originality of Christ's message would surely be mutilated if we claimed to be able to reduce him to a revolutionary, and his message to a political proclamation, so it would surely be an equal betrayal to wish to deny him any and all political pertinence.

All reductionism is to be avoided. We have to be careful to remember that although being a "revolutionary" fails to exhaust the personhood of Christ (as is the case with all his attributes), his being a revolutionary is nevertheless a trait that must be approached with seriousness—not only in the sense of keeping the figure of Christ from all reductionism, but also in the sense of a positive consideration of those contours of Christ's physiognomy and comportment by which he is indeed genuinely assimilated to the nature of a revolutionary. Although I recognize the everpresent temptation to reductionism and ideologization, it is also necessary to approach the image of Christ as a "protestor," a "subverter of the economic and political order," a "political liberator." Indeed, these are the traits that are the most fascinating for the so-called implicit Christians of today, or at least for those men and women who, though outside the visible boundaries of the churches, are committed to liberation and feel somehow near to Christ and Christians, as witness Roger Garaudy:

> You concealers of the great hope of which Constantine robbed us, give it back! His life and death are ours too! They belong to all of us for whom they have meaning—to all of us who have learned from him that the human being has been created a creator.[14]

## The Hermeneutical Problem

Every science is determined by its fundamental principles, and its truth derives from the guarantee afforded it by its fonts. Thus, traditional dogmatic theology is based upon exegesis and seeks to build upon it by every means available to its proper methodology. This is where, within the evolution of both disciplines, the attitude of the dogmatic theologian has fallen behind. The dogmatist has sought to make of theology the norm and directive of exegesis, in the sense of authoritatively requiring that whatever is "explicitly" believed be found in some manner, at least implicitly, in scripture. And on the other hand, the exegete has acted as if the work of exegesis could be a self-sufficient, autonomous undertaking. This is why there are few principles of systematic theology that the exegete will embrace more earnestly than that of the need for a serious integration of new projects within contemporary theology.[15]

For its part, however rudimentarily, the theology of liberation is beginning to break new trails in theologico-biblical hermeneutics. It is in the area of christology that this need is most sharply felt. Not only are we beginning to build a political christology, but we are engaged in a political "rereading of the gospel message" as well, as an integral part of the theological task. Hence, on this terrain, our formulations will necessarily appear more venturesome and more vulnerable to reaction. But I hasten to point out that the theological perspective of liberation has need of a different hermeneutical key—or else of a hermeneutics that will be able to receive and accept "other texts" and dynamically follow the course of a forward-moving truth that goes on building up historically.

The theology of liberation has need of a hermeneutics that will listen not only to the voice of the sciences that help it to better understand the biblical world, but also, and with greater urgency, to the language of the people, the culture of oppression, the geography of hunger in the politicized totality of Latin America, and the structures of an unjust social order in need of the message of freedom *now*.

To be sure, it is not, as we have noted, a matter of promoting novel paradogmatic fundamentalisms, or mechanistic processes of inconsistent and uncritical transposition, comparison, accommodation, or parallelism. It is a matter of constructing and applying a hermeneutical process that will be able to establish the dialectical interrelationship, between the historical event of Jesus and his word, and the historical experience today in which the commitment of faith is required now here, and now suddenly there.

A theology that only interprets God's salvific deed will not suffice. We must have a theology that also carries its task forward to the field of efficacious collaboration with praxis. *This* is the proper task of that common endeavor of theologian and exegete for which we hear such an urgent call.

One hears of an "existential hermeneutics," a "revolutionary" hermeneutics, and a "political" hermeneutics. Looking at the matter from our specific viewpoint we might speak of a "hermeneutics of liberation," whose task would be to examine the perspective of a transformation of concrete realities, within the area of its competency and efficacity, and within the purview of a methodology that would enable an advance through the concrete and immediately verifiable truth of historical factuality toward the full truth of the future. Just as the theology of liberation has laid claim to the "critical function" of theology, so its hermeneutics would have the task of keeping theology correctly positioned on the everchanging front of the inhu-

mane situations most deserving of critique and denunciation—as well as the
task of maintaining its critical stance vis-à-vis itself and its hermeneutics. The
task of a hermeneutics that has access to the Word of freedom is to make
possible not merely the search for truth, but the struggle for truth that makes
men and women free.[16]

In this perspective, and analyzing the biblical texts from this point of view,
with the aid of the critical method, we shall surely encounter the "language of
the apostolate," as Jürgen Moltmann assures us. But:

> We shall not be able to read the Bible as the "charter of our religion" or
> tradition. It must rather be understood as the creative witness to our call
> and commission in the world.[17]

Hence Christian hermeneutics cannot concern itself exclusively with proclamation and language—"for they themselves are uttered in the broader political and social forum of public life."[18] This is a perspective that removes, to
a large extent, the danger of an interpretative formalism that seeks uni-
laterally and retrospectively to attain to a comprehension of the past under
the conditions of the present. A sustained understanding of the temporal, incarnate, and present dimension of the kerygma, while also grasping its
metahistorical, transtemporal, and future dimension, in their mutual dynamic relationship, is the challenge to the new hermeneutics. "This
noncontemporaneous contemporaneity is the backbone of the gospel, and it
is deeply inserted in history." It is not only a matter of understanding hermeneutics as "the art of interpreting the written expression of life" (Wilhelm
Dilthey), but as that of interpreting all the historical expressions of life in a
political context. For this is the source of the method by which faith is
brought to realization—the community of liberated life, under the changing
conditions of the malaise of the present.

Doubtless this new hermeneutical effort will tend to assign special values to
elements that, in other perspectives, have been relegated to the background:
historical and anthropological aspects proper to Latin America, and Latin
American philosophical, socio-economic, and political peculiarities. For we
are more critical than dogmatic, more "globalizing" and "process-oriented"
than formalistic, more social than personalist, more popular than elitist,
more defined and concrete, looking more to the future than to the past, and,
finally, we give orthopraxis the primacy over orthodoxy.[19]

It is also in this context that the profiling of themes in the theology of
liberation is to be elabotated—that is, as so many different criteria and parameters of interpretation at the service of hermeneutical endeavor.

## A Nascent Ecclesiology

A new ecclesiology can arise only from a new christology—not in chronological, but dialectical sequence.

Just as we observe that, in an incipient fashion at least, a new way of being believers in Jesus Christ is taking shape in Latin America, we can also perceive the gradual germination of a new image of the church in Latin America.

All things considered, the ecclesiological terrain is at present one of the most difficult and delicate. Probably no other is so highly charged with emotionalism. How, then, can one hope to cultivate a new ecclesiology, when the experience of a new, qualitatively renewed believing community is itself so extremely problematic? And how, too, can one hope to gain the necessary theoretical "distancing" in the presence of almost irremediable antagonistic ideological passions? When all is said and done, is theology, in its ecclesiologies, condemned to a discourse of self-repetition, addressed only to itself and to the interests that manipulate it, and thus to being a theology of the church for the initiated, the educated, and the doctors of theology? Are believers condemned to accept a second-rate ecclesiology?

The effort to get on with new work in this area has in fact been frequently characterized by too prompt a recourse to purely biblical considerations of the church, with their subsequent application to the present day by way of comparison or contrast. In their eagerness, our ecclesiologists have overlooked or undervalued the historical distance between the present situation and the nonrepeatable moment of the biblical witness. But a biblical theology should not blindly presuppose a nonproblematic state of the question as to the content and intentions of the biblical witness to the church, or presuppose that any problem will arise only afterward, in the application of this content and these intentions to the church of today.

Others have become entangled in a seemingly revolutionary, a speciously renovative praxis divorced from any theology in the form of critical consciousness. But when one declines the effort of methodical criticism, one runs the risk of a praxis that will be sporadic, approximate, repetitive, and, in the end, not very efficacious. An uncritical practice of this nature could lead to the adoption of a symbolically—that is, apparently—new ecclesiastical reality, without re-creating it actually—with the result that it will be absorbed, or eliminated, or taken advantage of anew by the system of dominating ideas, which it will not have succeeded in changing.

Not far removed from this option is a certain direct confrontation, frequently polemical, with the institution and its theology. To be sure, a critical function pertains to the raison d'être of Christian theology and praxis. But in this instance it ought to review and revise the strategy of its de facto effectiveness.

Facing this problematic, and diametrically opposed to it, is the stance assumed by another theology of the church which we cannot afford to ignore. This position consists in a blanket legitimation and defense of the dominant ecclesiastical conceptions. For this radicalized fundamentalism and positivism, crises and challenges are only incentives to resistance, and to the strident call for orthodoxy and acquiescent loyalty. J. B. Metz has said of it:

This tendency to an ecclesiological fundamentalism is full of problems—especially the blindness it fosters to the specifically ecclesiastical issues of the stagnation and alienation of the masses. It impedes changes that are urgent.[20]

The focal point of a new ecclesiology in Latin America appears more and more clearly as the *kenosis* of Christ. The key to a new ecclesiology will be the *kenosis* of the church. Given its own source and place of birth at the heart of an oppressed people, liberation theology cannot but accord such a *kenosis* a privileged position within its own perspective. This is the church that the oppressed, the poor, actually live—with neither power nor prestige, neither voice nor a hearing. And yet it is this *powerless* church that manifests the *force of the Spirit*. I sincerely believe that the deepest conflicts that today afflict the majority of our established churches are owing in large part to the total absence of a *kenosis*. A critical church can arise only from a poor church. Only from a church that lives through the dialectical experience of the incarnation and resurrection can there emerge a truthful testimony, kerygma, and prophecy. It is only in its message of freedom that the church is rich. In every other area, the church is a mendicant, a beggar, accepting the formative gift that leads it to its part in the reconstruction of the world.

It is not difficult to detect the infiltration of a Calvinistic ascetical theory in what Max Weber called the "spirit of capitalism." Citing Richard Baxter, Weber wrote:

If God shows you a way in which you may lawfully get more than in another way (without wrong to your soul or to any other), if you refuse this, and choose the less gainful way, you cross one of the ends of your calling, and you refuse to be God's steward, and to accept his gifts and use them for him when he requireth it: you may labor to be rich for God, though not for the flesh and sin.[21]

This Calvinist ascetical theory, penetrated by the "spirit of capitalism," considers poverty an illness. Of course, if one has the illness then one should do something about it. In the Lutheran profession of faith cited at the Council of Trent we read: "The one who is poor by his condition should bear it, but if he glories in continuing to be poor, it would be the same as if he gloried in being a chronic invalid, or in having a bad reputation." Be that as it may, Protestantism has generally been logical and consistent. (As time goes on there are more and more exceptions, and more significant ones.) But our churches (religious institutions, congregations, and so on) continue living a life of wealth, in peaceful coexistence with poverty, as if evangelical poverty, the poverty of the gospel, had ceased to be a critical standard.

We need a church that is poor. We need a church that does not claim to hold the key to political, social, cultural, economic, or even ethical problems. We need a church of *kenosis*, a church emptied of self, a church reduced to and embracing "nothingness." We need a church completely free of a superiority complex. We need a church that will seriously try to eliminate, within itself, the alienation and class struggle that are antagonistic to Christian filiation and fellowship. In sum, we need a church whose strength is not measured by the number of doctrines believed or ritual prayers recited or diplomatic relations maintained or apostolic works financed or political parties controlled much less by stock quotations that show mounting capital investment.

This would be the church born "from below," the one to fulfill the sense of the conciliar formulation on the church as the "spouse of the Word incarnate," or that of the "church of the poor" so repeatedly proclaimed in Latin America.[22]

## THE PERSPECTIVE OF EVANGELIZATION

On a third level, the pastoral problem arises. It is not only methodologically and praxeologically that this is the major problem. How should we proclaim Christ *here and now*? Without denying the complexity of the series of problems that revolve around this initial, thematic query, for my purposes in this chapter I can only point out some directions for reflection—keeping in mind that they are in some way moments of activity already undertaken by many groups.

The question, "How should we speak of Christ today from the point of view of pastoral theory and praxis?" must be studied from the following angles: praxis as witness, kerygma as praxis, and the praxis of prophecy.

Here we have three moments, interrelated dialectically, of the single activity of proclaiming the foundational Word, Christ. Accordingly, we must avoid, as suspect of atomization, any partitioning of this Christian task. It is only out of considerations of space and time that I do not accord the whole of it a detailed treatment in these pages.

### *Praxis as Witness*

At this point as well we must begin with the new experience of a liberating evangelization such as that being worked out in the various committed Christian communities in Latin America.

A liberating evangelism must take its place within the single process of the unitary historical becoming, in and through which human beings liberate themselves and are liberated. This task of evangelization embraces not only the economico-political dimension of human beings, but the total human being, in multidimensionality, maintaining at every moment the autonomy and originality of the "new person according to Christ." These three parameters—the economico-political as a determinant, human totality, and Christian originality—are irreducible one to another, but are intimately interrelated.

The *content* of the primordial evangelical proclamation is the radical event in which the Christian is encountered by an ongoing revelation, a liberation obtaining and verified at the heart of history. Recognition of this requires the vision of faith.

The primordial evangelical proclamation also comports the gladness of *self-discovery*, of the experience of oneself, of the experience of oneself as loved by God (filiation), and of working for love and its verification among others (fellowship).

This proclamation (the gospel message) is made from a point of departure *in basic solidarity with* the exploited classes, and hence necessarily has a political dimension—not something adventitious, or added by us who make the proclamation, but an intrinsic dimension of the Father's love for all human beings.

This evangelizing proclamation *contributes*, as something typically its own, a political and class influence, direct and critical, upon the liberation process all-inclusive.

This liberating conscientization is essentially *involved* with the conflictual character of history, and reveals dimensions of fullness there that only its message can bring to realization.

This liberating proclamation of evangelization has its *locus of realization* in the option for the poor. Any proclamation is made from a concrete locus and situation. In this case that locus and situation is the context of the exploited classes. The universality of the gospel message is maintained from this basis. No one is excluded from the message. Quite the contrary. But inasmuch as the very essence of the message demands a radical definition and position taking, a liberating evangelization is carried into effect from a point of departure in this option.

## Kerygma as Praxis

We also have need of a restructuring of the question of mission. We must recover a respect, a modesty, and a sensitivity with regard to the gospel message. We must once more demand of ourselves a process of *kenosis* and purification with regard to ourselves and our concrete commitment.

It is not we who are the basic "preachers" or proclaimers of Jesus Christ. Not at all. It is Christ himself who speaks of himself, it is his Spirit who speaks. It is Christ who works and reveals himself through a "total language," working and speaking from an involvement in history and from an interiority to every human being as well as to the internal dynamisms of a society. Hence, radically speaking, the most profound evangelizing activity takes place in a certain form of silence as well—the silence of an attitude and comportment that is totally praxeological, where it is possible to hear the voices and detect the activity that are the work of Christ. Christ's work is the bringing together, and the growth and increase, of both things and human beings. From that perspective mission can be seen as "service," a commitment and a shared responsibility.

The apostle becomes a companion on the pilgrimage and helps the "evangelized" to hear, receive, and perceive voices, to identify signs, and to do justice to all their demands. Mission becomes critical and democratic. What is essential to mission is not preaching but fact, presence, dynamism.

A service of evangelization from the polarity of an unhistorical reading of the gospel message is, hence, unthinkable. The message has to be read from the concrete verification and the specific *diakonia* that are demanded by Christ present in every human being and culture.

The Latin American theology of liberation also exercises a mediatory function between the concrete experience of faith and its critical return upon the reality from which it has taken its origin. Thus it can be said to be a kerygmatic theology with a Latin American specificity.

Christ is the nucleus of the Christian kerygma. Hence the Christian kerygma has maintained, as an essential characteristic, not only the *logos* but also the *pneuma* and the *dynamis* of the *logos*. Paul said that in the word (*logos*) he spoke, the gospel (*kerygma*) he proclaimed, it was not human wisdom that persuaded his hearers, but the workings of the spirit and power (*pneumatos kai dynameos;*) (1 Cor. 2:4).

The Christian kerygma can be actualized only as a historical dynamism. This is why, when the original content of the kerygma is withdrawn and manipulated in the service of the dominating classes, evangelization itself becomes impotent, is deprived of its *dynamis*.

Traditionally, the orthodoxy of the Christian message has been reduced to its theoretical formulations or oral proclamation. It is more urgent than ever at the present moment to avoid reducing orthodoxy to a "correct" thinking or speaking. Rather we must strive to recover its fuller meaning as "correct doing." But in speaking of "doing," or praxis, we must not polarize it as a diametrical contrary of theory, as if the two were distinct realities, mutually repugnant, or in need of parallel juxtaposition. As K.Cosik has phrased it:

In a world of pseudo concretion there lurks a chiaroscuro of truth and deceit. It specializes in the *double entendre*. A phenomenon indicates an essence and at the same time obscures it. The essence is manifested in the phenomenon, but only in inadequate form, partially, and at times only from certain sides and certain aspects. The phenomenon refers the observer to something distinct from itself and subsists only thanks to its contrary. The essence is not immediately given; it is "mediatized" by the phenomenon and accordingly manifests itself in something distinct from itself. . . . Its manifestation in the phenomenon reveals its motility and demonstrates that the essence is not inert or passive.[23]

It is the totalizing or "englobing" conception of praxis that constitutes its dialectical character—and its one possibility of success. Hence, praxis transcends empiricism, voluntarism, and oversimplification.

Consequently, the proclamation of the Christian message must not be viewed as an isolated or purely pragmatic act. Rather it is one phase of the total activity of the historical projection of Christianity.

## The Praxis of Prophecy

The orthopraxis of a committed faith consists in a propheticism in words and works, options, and processes. And the prime instance of this propheticism is an evangelizing activity which begins with an option for the exploited classes and from real and effective solidarity with them:

> This proclamation of the gospel, summoning us together into *ekklesia*, takes place from within an option of real and active solidarity with the interests and struggles of the poor, the exploited classes. The effort to situate oneself in this locus means a profound breach with the manner of living, thinking, and communicating the faith in the church of today. It demands a conversion to another world, a new way of understanding the faith—and it leads to a reformulation of the gospel message.[24]

The proclamation goes altogether beyond the bounds of what has traditionally been presented as "preaching" and surfaces as something much closer to the primordial Word—hence as something more historical, multiform, and multidimensional. To speak of Jesus Christ is to fill the proclamations of salvation with historical content, to bring to accomplishment, under new concrete forms, Christian love and a Christian community of sisters and brothers.

Receiving and accepting the Word becomes an imperative of converting that Word into an immense, ongoing cry of freedom in the midst of the battlefield. It is in the "nonverification of the kerygma" that the great heresies of Christianity today are to be found.

Therefore to speak of a "liberating evangelization" means that the men and women to whom the message is adddressed, and among whom it strives to become reality, will be men and women shaped and determined by the structuration of a society that stigmatizes them as exploited and oppressed. And what is more, the only limits to our proclamation of the gospel today are the limits of Latin America itself. For Latin America is the concrete horizon on which we can search out the conflicts that will be the price of this gospel:

> Are we confronted with a political reductionism of the gospel here? Yes, we are—in the case of those who utilize the gospel and place it at the service of the mighty. But no, we are not, in the case of those who start out from its gratuitous and liberating message in order precisely to denounce this utilization. Yes, this is evangelical reductionism for those who place the gospel and themselves in the hands of the great ones of this world, but not for those who identify with the poor Christ and go in search of solidarity with the dispossessed of Latin America. Yes, this is reductionism, if we keep the gospel prisoner of an ideology in the service of the capitalist system; but not if we have been set free by the gospel ourselves and now strive in our turn to free it from that captivity. Yes,

for those who seek to neutralize Christ's liberation by reducing it to a "religious" plane, where it has nothing directly to do with the concrete world of human beings, we are faced with reductionism; but not in the case of those who believe that Christ's salvation is so total and radical that nothing can escape it. For these latter, the gospel is liberating because it is the proclamation of total liberation in Christ, a liberation that includes a transformation of the concrete historical and political conditions that men and women live in. But this is grasped in all its depth only when one knows that this liberation leads this same history out beyond itself, to a fullness that transcends the scope of all human doing or telling.[25]

Just as Christ's liberation is necessarily realized by way of socio-political mediations—without being exhausted by them—so also the message of evangelization. In a historical, totalizing, structural, and "process" perspective, evangelization inevitably goes the way of the process of conscientization and politicization, without being exhausted by or imprisoned in it.

A great deal of energy is expended in distinguishing between ("distancing") evangelization and conscientization; or, in the first instance, distinguishing between political conscientization and Christian conscientization, distinguishing evangelization from politicization. Although in the least pernicious case both terms of the distinction abide overtly intact, even here a latent, embryonic dualism is by no means absent. In a new perspective, these distinctions would be otiose. The problematic would be moved to the field of a politicization of the message. It is often forgotten that the relationship of the Christian kerygma to human beings is an essential of that kerygma, and hence that it must run its risks. It is the law of incarnation. For when all is said and done, what counts is the rescue and redemption of the human being. To speak of Christ, then, is to take up the challenge of a message that passes by way of its necessary political and politicizing mediations.

The primordial concrete historical project of the Latin American evangelizing task is an "ideological unfreezing." That is, its prophetic task must take the direction of an assault on the roles, mechanisms, and internal dynamisms constituting the battlefield where men and women are placed "in a changing situation"—where the kerygma is being privatized and manipulated. The propheticism of evangelization is situated within the process by which oppressed consciousnesses begin to stop "being for others" and start "being for themselves," as a demand made by their own liberation. Then evangelization becomes the incentive that provokes reactions of visceral consciousness.

Consequently, we should keep alert for the most concrete channels of efficacy taken by love in the transformation of history. This means that, although the new human being is not the quasi-spontaneous product of a structural change, nevertheless this structural change (an ideological change, in the present case) is the necessary condition for the "birth" of the new human being. This is why—and it bears reemphasis—that hollowest of terms, "witness,'' takes its new place at the heart of the liberation process as a concept charged with meaning.

As concrete praxis, the Christian kerygma must regard with special esteem those values that the human community is de facto living. The message is actualized and lived in different manners at different times, without comporting the exclusion or denial of other elements that this particular time and manner of living happens not to emphasize. The reencounter with Christ, under new forms and in different loci—the poor, filiation and fellowship, Christians as persons of reconciliation, *kenosis*, and so on—should be the relevant themes within the total purview of liberation and the revolutionary commitment.

## CONCLUSION

For me the question, ''How should we speak of Christ today?'' is a total question, and its answers will be totalizing answers. To ask this question implies a new manner of seeking Christ, a new way of allowing ourselves to be drawn by him. It implies a new form of accepting him and reflecting upon him, and a new mode of actualizing his message. But in this perspective, faith, theology, witness, kerygma, and prophecy are but diverse phases and moments of a single total historical and dialectical task, not isolated undertakings at variance among themselves.

To ask this question means to maintain the sensitivity needed to detect the respiration of the ''christic fact'' beneath the surface—beneath the surface not only of each human being and each separate human force and thrust, but above all in each collective occurrence, however that occurrence may fall short of exhausting its secret christic nature.

To be able to speak of Jesus Christ means continually to return to the springs that surge with his presence. It means to abide in the pressures of the existential, of that which *is*, as our proper ''circumstance.''

In the current conjunction of Latin American processes it is imperative that we sharpen our consciousness and be on our guard against frustration. Hence to speak of Christ means to be confronting the challenges of history with the hope that sees, in every breath and every challenge, the very act of creation. It means never to lose, not for a single moment, sensitivity to persons and to history.

Finally, we must be modest. We must be on our guard against all vanity and precipitation, and serve the people with our whole heart. We must not cut ourselves off from the masses for a single moment. Our point of departure must be in every case the interests of the people, and not the interests of given individuals or a privileged group. And we must identify our commitment to the people as the expression of fidelity to Christ and his word.

Wherever there is struggle, there are sacrifices to be made, and persecution is an everyday affair. But for those whose commitment is to the people in faith, and solidarity with the great masses in their suffering, in faith, to be daily dying is an honorable thing.

How should we speak of Christ today? By daily submitting to the *kenosis* of a people toiling along the path to liberation, we shall encounter ever new elements of the response.

# NOTES

1. See Eduard Schweizer, "Le Christ, signe de contradiction," *Communion* 26 (1972): 14–22. See also *Selecciones de Teología* 45 (1973): 27–30.

2. See Héctor Borrat, "Para una cristología de vanguardia," *Víspera* 17 (1970).

3. "Praxis de liberación y fe cristiana," an extract from *Signos de liberación* (Lima: CEP, 1973), p. 24; included in *The Power of the Poor in History* (Maryknoll, N.Y.: Orbis, 1983), p. 52.

4. This theme has been touched upon in various contexts by Segundo Galilea in his "Contemplación y compromiso," in *Contemplación y apostolado, Mensaje*, 1972, and Colección IPLA, no. 17 (Bogotá: CELAM-IPLA, 1973). In English see Galilea's *Following Jesus* (Maryknoll, N.Y.: Orbis, 1981). See also "Liberation as an Encounter with Politics and Contemplation," in *The Mystical and Political Dimension of the Christian Faith*, ed. Claude Geffré and Gustavo Gutiérrez, Concilium 96 (New York: Herder and Herder, 1974), pp. 19–33.

5. See J.M. González Ruiz, *Dio e gratuito, ma non superfluo* (Milan: Jaca, 1969; Madrid: Marova, 1970), pp. 22–35.

6. "*Formgeschichte* is a system that attempts to explain the origin of the gospels, and to determine their degree of historicity, via the analysis of forms, or literary genres, and their evolution, as the reflection and fruit of their social and religious milieu. It came from Germany, through the works of K. S. Schmidt (1919), M. Dibelius (1919), and R. Bultmann (1921), who speaks of the history of the primitive, or synoptic, tradition, and has as his forerunner Hermann Gunkel, who applied analogous criteria to the Old Testament and suggested them for the New" (*Diccionario de Teología Bíblica* [Madrid, 1960]). See Xavier Léon-Dufour, *Vocabulaire de Théologie Biblique* (Paris: Cerf, 1962); Eng. trans., *Dictionary of Biblical Theology* (New York: Crossroads/Seabury, 1973).

7. See Rudolf Bultmann, *Faith and Understanding* (New York: Harper & Row, 1969).

8. Ernst Käsemann, "Das Problem des historischen Jesus," *Exegetische Versuche und Besinnungen*, vol. 2 (Göttingen, 1954); Xavier Léon-Dufour, *Les Evangiles et l'histoire de Jesús* (Paris: Seuil, 1963).

9. Hugo Assmann, *Opresión-Liberación, desafío a los cristianos* (Montevideo: Tierra Nueva, 1971), p. 139.

10. González Ruiz, *Dios está en la base* (Barcelona: Estela, 1970), p. 15. See also Leonardo Boff, *Jesus Christ Liberator* (Maryknoll: Orbis, 1978); Martin Hengel, *War Jesus Revolutionär?* (Stuttgart: Calwer, 1970), Eng. trans., *W_s Jesus a Revolutionist?* (Philadelphia: Fortress, 1971); Segundo Galilea, "Jesús y la liberación de su pueblo," *Mensaje*, 1973.

11. See IDOC, *Processo alla religione*, Documenti nuovi (Milan: Mondadori,

1968); Peter Berger, *A Rumor of Angels: Modern Society and the Rediscovery of the Supernatural* (New York: Doubleday, 1969); Karl Rahner, "Ideology and Christianity," *The Church and the World*, Concilium 6 (New York: Paulist, 1965), pp. 42–62.

12. Gutiérrez, "Praxis"; *The Power of the Poor*, p. 52.

13. See Boff, *Jesus Christ Liberator*, pp. 217–19.

14. *Le Monde*, (Paris), Dec. 25, 1969, p. 7.

15. Concilium 70 takes up the problem explicitly: *Theology, Exegesis, and Proclamation*, ed. Roland Murphy (New York: Herder and Herder, 1971). See especially Gerhard Voss, "The Relationship between Exegesis and Dogmatic Theology," pp. 20–29; Gotthold Hasenhutl, "Dialogue between the Dogmatic Theologian and the Exegete," pp. 39–46; Meinhard Limbeck, "The Exegete's Answer," pp. 47–55.

16. See Jürgen Moltmann, "Toward a Political Hermeneutic of the Gospel." This was a talk given at Vanderbilt Divinity School on February 2, 1968, and then at the Claremont College of Theology in the same month. It was originally published in *Union Seminary Quarterly Review* (Summer 1969): 303–23; and in a slightly different form in his *Religion, Revolution, and the Future* (New York: Scribner's, 1969), and then for Latin America in *Cristianismo y Sociedad* 8 (1970): 23–42. See also Boff, *Jesus Christ Liberator*, pp. 51–62.

17. Moltmann, "Toward a Political Hermeneutic," See also Hans Schmidt, "Politics and Christology: Historical Background" in *Faith and the World of Politics*, ed. Johannes B. Metz, Concilium 36 (New York: Paulist Press, 1968), pp. 72–84.

18. Moltmann, "Toward a Political Hermeneutic."

19. "The question of the primacy of orthodoxy over heresy is in the same class as the problem of the chicken and the egg. The history of the Roman Church shows that successive dogmas have been, paradoxically, reactions to their nonrecognition; they came into existence at the same time as their negations. Once adopted, of course, a dogma allows us to define a heresy by reference to itself, but in the actual course of events it is a well-known rule that a dogma appears because an anti-dogma has already begun to take shape" (Leszek Kolakowski, *Chrétiens sans Eglise: La conscience religieuse et le lien confessionel au XVII siècle* [Paris, 1969], p. 69); Eng. trans. as cited in "Leszek Kolakowski's 'Churchless Christians,' " *The Concrete Christian Life*, ed. Christian Duquoc, Concilium 69 (New York: Herder and Herder, 1971). Concilium 69 has J. Beaude's comment: "In this vein, orthodoxy is the ideology of the organizing stratum of the institution; and, when opposed or deviant ideologies arise, is formulated to confront them. . . .

"Orthodoxy hardly ever expresses itself positively; creeds are always short—and their definitions, on the whole, sufficiently vague to obtain a fairly broad consensus. On the other hand, anathemas abound. At least this is certainly true of the Catholic Church, the acts of whose magisterium would provide material for a huge catalogue of heresies, alongside a quite slim collection of truths to be believed.

"Orthodoxy does not so much define itself in the face of heresies and in opposition to them as sketch the changing shape of its adversary in order to keep it at bay. This is why it is difficult to see what orthodoxy looks like; one can only trace its outline by marking off what lies beyond it, what it has categorically excluded as outside it" (Beaude, "Leszek Kolakowski's 'Churchless Christians,' " p. 95). See Karl Rahner, "Orthodoxy and Freedom in Theology" in *Perspectives of a Political Ecclesiology*, ed. Johannes B. Metz, Concilium 66 (New York: Herder and Herder, 1971), pp. 90–104.

20. Cf. the Editorial in Concilium 66, pp. 7-12. See also González Ruiz, *Dios está en la base*.

21. Max Weber, *The Protestant Ethic and the Spirit of Capitalism* (New York: Scribner's, 1930), p. 162.

22. After the Medellín meeting, with its fundamental documentation, numerous other documents in this vein have followed and have been published all over Latin America. They exist in several compilations, including *Signos de renovación* (Lima: Comisión Episcopal de Acción Social, 1969); *Iglesia Latinoamericana, ¿protesta o profecía?* (Avellaneda, Argentina: Búsqueda, 1969). See R. Vidales, *La Iglesia Latinoamericana y la política después de Medellín* (Bogotá: Indo-American Press Service, 1972). *Signos de liberación* (Lima: CEP, 1973) is another collection.

23. Cited in González Ruiz, *Dios está en la base*, p. 35.

24. Gutiérrez, "Praxis," p. 35; *The Power of the Poor*, p. 67.

25. Ibid.; *The Power of the Poor*, pp. 68-69.

*Chapter 12*

# CHRISTOLOGY IN LATIN AMERICA

## *Lamberto Schuurman*

Obviously, a christology cannot be constructed in the silence of an ivory tower. A christology needs the experience of a community, which discovers, in its historical evolution, the relevance of Jesus of Nazareth. As always, reflection comes later.[1] The objective of my brief investigation will be a modest one—simply to try to indicate certain considerations to be kept in mind. The vital discoveries that have already been made in certain Christian communities of Latin America are of great value and should be pointed out.[2]

On the other hand, theological reflection as it is being developed in Latin America can ill afford to overlook some of the interesting elements in European, and other, christological thinking. This is not to suggest imitation, but simply a reminder not to neglect an excellent aid for our dedication to the construction of a relevant christology for here and now. For it is in conversation with, but not in dependence upon, what is thought in other contexts that one attains ever greater clarity with respect to one's own context.

I propose to proceed as follows. First I shall give a summary of certain significant changes in christological reflection today. Then I shall suggest two concrete models for our own christology. Finally, I shall endeavor to apply these changes and these models to the context of our own Latin American task.

### NEW DIRECTIONS IN CHRISTOLOGY TODAY

One of the most meaningful facets of the modern christological task is the growing influence and importance of the Old Testament. One could assert without fear of contradiction that a hellenized Christian interpretation of the Old Testament is being gradually abandoned in favor of what might be called a judaization of the Christian tradition. Hendrikus Berkhof speaks of a christology "from behind," suggesting that the only possible real approximation to the Christ of the New Testament comes from placing oneself within the horizon of Jewish expectations and longings.[3] It would not be an exaggeration to say that the New Testament is being read more and more from the standpoint of the Old Testament. And thereby falls a centuries-old tradition in which it was rather the Old Testament that was read from a point of departure in a hellenistic understanding of the New Testament.

I think that this is ultimately the reason why we note an ever increasing consciousness of the validity of the old *munus triplex*. It turns out to be an excellent path to a grasp of the historical Jesus, his program, and his word.[4] Of course, we are not dealing with a simple repetition of what one can find in the thinking of Calvin; rather it is a matter of trying to rescue his model from the purview of a soteriological narrowness in the quantitative sense.[5] The result is most useful. One need only observe the dialectic of prophet and king so ably presented by Ricoeur.[6] In other words, we need the Old Testament in order to appreciate that this Jesus of Nazareth has his history, his projected undertaking, and his plan. Cross and resurrection lose their meaning unless they are related to this concrete history of the man Jesus.

## *"High" and "Low" Christology*

Another way of saying the same thing is in terms of "high" and "low" christologies.[7] We may take it that "low christology," meaning a christology "from beneath," as it were, refers to a presentation of the person and work of Jesus from a point of departure in a serious concentration on his personal history. In other words, a "low" christology is closely connected with what exegetes call the search for the historical Jesus. After the long silence occasioned by Bultmann, a new stage of concern with this concrete Jesus was initiated by Käsemann and Bornkamm. Both considered that, by way of a meticulous analysis of the sources, it was possible after all to arrive at fairly concrete ideas concerning the historical praxis of Jesus.[8] The conclusion, on the level of systematic reflection, should be that it is possible to break a path to the titles expressing Jesus' exaltation only through the mediation of clear ideas with respect to his de facto history.

"High" christology, by contrast, would be fated to issue in a historical vacuum, because its disconnection from the concrete history of Jesus ends up in abstract speculations.[9] We can find a good example of what "low" christology can yield in the studies of Etienne Trocmé.[10] Cross and resurrection are not facts that have value in themselves. They are qualifications and "valorizations" of the concrete praxis of Jesus of Nazareth. But one can legitimately synthesize these concerns by means of a consideration offered by Berkhof.[11] He calls our attention to the fact that the greater number of christologies developed by Christianity center on the concept of the *Logos*. Now, the *Logos* being the Second Person of the Trinity, "logological" christological reflection will be principally concerned with correctly establishing the relationship between the divine and human natures in the person of Jesus. Berkhof laments that these "logological" christologies appear in place of, and by way of substitution for, a "pneumatic" christology, which he considers to have been more fruitful and promising. It is evident that the very early replacement of the pneumatic by the logological in christology is closely connected with the acute hellenization of primitive Christianity.

In this setting of the problem, the basic question will be the relationship between christology and pneumatology. More precisely, does Jesus send the Spirit, or does the Spirit send Jesus? Berkhof contends that the New Testament presents both currents of thought, but that unfortunately theological reflection quickly lost the interpretative viewpoint that gives a certain primacy and priority to the pneumatological. In Berkhof's thinking, the expression "Spirit of Yahweh" means Yahweh-in-action. In the Old Testament, this action of Yahweh is the effort to search out a faithful ally, a human being who would, in a faithful and consistent way, fulfill the role of a human being: to be Yahweh's authentic representative on earth, and to exercise a perfect stewardship with respect to both neighbor and nature.[12]

In the successive stages of this history—in the world of Genesis 1-11 and then in the history of the people of Israel—Yahweh is disappointed. What Yahweh hopes for is not forthcoming. At the decisive moment, the faithful ally, who will represent Yahweh before human beings and human beings before Yahweh, fails to materialize. Undaunted, however, the Spirit (Yahweh-in-action) continues to search and to create—and the definitive result of this history of frustrated initiatives is the history of Jesus of Nazareth. This ally maintains, and bears up under, the tension of the two moments indicated (the two-way representation or mediation), and receives, accordingly, in the resurrection a universal approbation of his program.

It is easy to grasp that a christology with this focus can do justice both to the categories of the Old Testament and to a serious study of the concrete program of Jesus.

### *"Implicit" and "Explicit" Christology*

Likewise the work of Kurt Lüthi begins with the question of how systematic theology should handle the results of recent exegesis. Especially, how should it handle the conclusions of that exegesis, which, through the methods of the history of forms, redactions, and traditions, is in a position to tell us so much more about Jesus?[13] Lüthi likes to speak of the "implicit christology" in the gospels. The gospels do not transmit historical information. They themselves are an interpretation of the life of Jesus. They do not offer us historical immediacy. Nevertheless it is possible to enter into contact with the predominant facets of Jesus' life; but not everything the New Testament has to say consists of explicit christology.

It seems to me that what Lüthi manages to do here is to bring explicit christology into confrontation with the concrete history presupposed in that implicit Christology. Otherwise, explicit christology loses its historical dimension and goes up in smoke. Lüthi takes the example of the title *Kyrios*. What does it mean? Lüthi recommends an analysis of the concept of *exousia*—the tremendous freedom and liberty that Jesus exercises before all authorities. Now, this *exousia* manifests itself first and foremost in the communion that Jesus seeks to maintain with the marginalized of his society, with those who are discriminated against. If this concrete content of *exousia* is lost, the title *Kyrios* is very easily converted into something so general and universal that it is no longer possible to hear the undertones of its reference to this historical particularity.

"Implicit christology" in this form is brought into play by Lüthi as a check and control with respect to the affirmations of "explicit christology." A very interesting example is to be found in what he observes regarding justification. Evidently, and especially among Lüthi's colleagues, a predominant element of an explicit christology is the soteriological role of Jesus Christ, or a theology of the blood of the Lamb. Lüthi holds that the affirmations of this theology need to be reformulated with the aid of material from implicit christology. The divine *pro nobis*, as manifested in Jesus' ultimate deed, creates an operational coincidence between God's rights and the justification of humankind. This latter dimension, in ethical terms, will consist in creating space for those who have no rights.

It is also worth noting that Lüthi considers that systematic theology cannot afford to limit itself to the repetition of titles employed by tradition. It will have to create new titles, expressing the meaning and importance of Jesus for believers in a new situation. In saying this Lüthi sums up what many theologians see as a task of great importance: the rearticulation, or adequate translation, of what is transmitted by tradition.[14]

It seems to me that, whatever the other reasons may be for carrying out such a search, an important one is to be found in the growing consensus that the New Testament itself embodies a number of christologies. It is precisely the various social and economic contexts that oblige us to situate terminologically the common conviction as to the one and only Messiah. In like manner, contemporary christologies must be worked out *in loco*. European theology, at times with tremendous paternalistic generosity, does indeed grant this right to its periphery, convinced that we ought to have the right because exegesis itself has concluded to it.

### *"Ontological" and "Functional" Language*

Still another way to approach the same theme would be to introduce the categories of "ontological" and "functional." Without entering into a discussion of whether the very use of the terms indicates a dependence upon Comte, we can say that "ontological" refers to a very particular manner, almost an atmosphere, of thinking. With ontology we are in a climate of

Neoplatonism, and we realize that christological titles represent first of all an effort to solve the problem of being and individuation. "Functional," on the other hand, refers rather to the historical, to the question of relevancy. Its dimensions are marked out by the question, "Is it helpful? What is it good for? What purpose does it serve?" In Lüthi's terms, one could say that an explicit christology tends to an ontological language, whereas an implicit christology inclines to a functional language. In both cases, what is decisive is the relationship of a given christology to the historical.

It cannot be denied that it is the ontological language that has long predominated. Clearly, this is due for the most part to the hegemony exercised by Neoplatonic philosophy and its claim to constitute an adequate vocabulary for the articulation of theological affirmations.[15] It is not easy to say whether the whole tradition, over all these centuries, has been a distortion of the gospel. The well-known fact that Hebrew has no way of making ontological statements is evidence by itself of the enormous changes certain Hebrew concepts must have undergone in their transition to a Hellenistic milieu. On the other hand, thinking historically also means taking account of the horizon of understanding of one's forebears.

Be all this as it may, it appears that what is needed at present is a functional-historical language in theology as well. In the first place, this is the direction taken by our contemporaries. But it is also what is required in order to be able to pay our debt to the Judeo-Christian tradition. To put it another way, it is evident that Christianity has not succeeded in taking the necessary step from an ontological to a functional vocabulary. It is precisely on this point that the suspicions of Ricoeur find their justification.[16] Christianity is of no use either for solving the problems of society or for achieving the authentic integration of the individual person. Hence a new tack is called for. The new approach will consist in an option for a functional language. Later will be soon enough to see how this opens out upon the ontological.

What is interesting about this approach as far as christology is concerned will be that it is precisely in this way that an "implicit" christology can be developed. For example, Jesus' resurrection should not be interpreted first and foremost as the healing of human finitude, and therefore the cure for our ontic deficit. Rather it should be interpreted first of all as the universal approbation of the historical Jesus' functional program. Viewed in this way the resurrection will not invite us to a metaphysical contemplation but to discipleship, to getting the program of the historical Jesus underway in new situations.

Like observations could be made with regard to the cross and the ascension—to cite moments that have always so lent themselves to an ontologizing interpretation.

The problem remains of whether the ontological has any permanent and independent validity. "Jesus is the Son of Yahweh." Is this an ontological proposition, with a permanent validity? We are taken a bit by surprise when we note that there also exists a more functional interpretation of the category of "son." In the Old Testament, used of a king, or of the people as a whole, it expresses two things: a situation of total dependence and obedience, and at the same time a degree of intimacy with Yahweh altogether beyond the ordinary. In this sense, the category and title are perfectly applicable to Jesus. His commitment is total and his relationship unique: he calls Yahweh *Abba*. But if we speak of Jesus in this way are we not falling into some form of adoptionism? Cannot the ontological interpretation be explained as monophysitism?

It appears that we need a vocabulary that will not only express divine sonship as a projection with which Jesus identifies and which in no way can be expressed in a static ontic form, but which will also be a terminology in which divine sonship attains to a certain "institutionalization"—a terminology through which it manages to be converted into substance. Viewed in this way, both adoptionism and monophysitism will be seen as dogmatisms that fail to recognize the necessity of honoring both process and result.

## An Abstract Christ

Much of what I am saying can be found in an excellent article by Jon Sobrino.[17] According to Sobrino, an abstract Christ is always a Christ who can be manipulated, and this is why the theology of liberation is rehabilitating the figure of the historical Jesus. Chalcedon, he thinks, is beset with an ineluctable difficulty: "divinity" and "humanity" say what Jesus is without permitting Jesus to say how the concepts of divinity or humanity should be understood.[18] In other words, divinity and humanity are concepts that should "concretize" in the particularity of Jesus' history. Unless one takes into consideration the particularity of the historical Jesus—that is, the history of Jesus—any general or ontological notions offer an excellent method of separating the lion of Juda from his claws. This, according to Sobrino, is what is happening in three current christologies: doctrinal christology, resurrection christology, and existentialist christology. In all three cases, Jesus is not permitted to define what is said about him from the viewpoint of his historical functionality, his functional history.

I believe that Sobrino is introducing a very important element here.[19] The absence of an adequate christological epistemology not only obscures the true sense of the mission and history of Jesus, but also tenders a most welcome succor to certain determinate ideological interests. The two drawbacks go together. Viewed in this way a so-called independent exegesis is unmasked as an organ in the service of the status quo.

I believe Sobrino strengthens what has been emphasized above in his examination of the language of the concept of "God." "God" is not a category of ours to be applied to Yahweh. It is Yahweh's own proper identity, as Yahweh communicates self-revelation in works of liberation. Hence it is this identity that is to qualify the content of the word "God," and not the other way around. Here Sobrino takes the results of the *locus de deo* dispute and brings them to bear on christology.[20] His debt to the theology of liberation is in the concept of the "manipulability" of extremely abstract and universal, or historically unmediated, titles.

By way of synthesis, may I suggest that the change of atmosphere characterizing current christological discussion takes place on various levels that partially coincide and that therefore should be approached as a whole. I emphasize the importance of the rediscovery of the Old Testament. At the same time, I see that a new reflection upon the relationship between christology and pneumatology makes a meaningful contribution to an effort to reinvolve ourselves with the concrete program of Jesus' history. And it is here that the distinction between what is implicit in the gospels and explicit in christological titles can also be appreciated. The latter must always remain under the control of the former.

As to the language we need, we are discovering the growing credibility of a functional-historical vocabulary—not in order to do away with all ontological validity, but in order to establish a methodological order. For in the final analysis, a preference for abstract titles is an attitude deserving of suspicion, because it serves the interests of the system.

Again, I must emphasize the importance of the simultaneity of the two paths we are charting. It will not do much good to fall in love with the Old Testament if the Old Testament does not bring us to a necessary attitude of suspicion with respect to the contribution an abstract christological discourse makes to the continuance of prevailing political systems. On the other hand, vain will be our toil if we attempt to build a christology in the absence of serious exegetical work bearing first and foremost upon the hermeneutical importance of the Old Testament. In my opinion, any separation of these two efforts is condemned to failure. And I do not make this assertion for purely tactical reasons.

In any case it should not come as a surprise that suspicions concerning the manipulability of abstract titles are aroused in a theologian such as Albert Nolan, whose life and work is in South Africa. At the very least, this suggests that one's *Sitz im Leben*—one's geographical and historical context—is important in the theologian as well.

Without a doubt a very important element in the process of the abstract generalization of Jesus' importance consists precisely in the absolutization of one's own horizon. Who will have an interest in such a process but the one who has the most to lose? This is why the problem is most acute where the future is seen as a demand for change. Hence, are we not to be a little suspicious of the striking generosity with which the theology of the great nations today encourages the development of new images of Jesus in the former colonies? Can it not be, speaking *a priori*, that this is an effort to relegate novelty to the outlying districts, and thus maintain the imminent danger of a false pluralism whose only end is the consolidation of power and wealth in its present distribution—that is, within the prevailing system? The following pages will have the task of detailing this suspicion to some extent. My hypothesis is that it is not a good definition of particularity to assign it a merely partial, geographically limited, meaning. Surely the particularity of the history of Jesus—the particularity of the historical Jesus—is not to be understood in this way.

## TWO CONCRETE MODELS FOR CHRISTOLOGY

Keeping all the above observations in mind, I now wish to present two concrete models within the frame of reference just outlined—that is, two models that decisively embrace the methodological preferences I have indicated. We meet the first in the systematic theology of Berkhof. I think Berkhof's thought is a good example of what might be called ecumenical Protestant theology. His thought is situated within a clearly Europocentric perspective. Then I shall turn to Nolan, a South African theologian whose work has its point of departure in the painful experience of white racism in his country. Nolan himself is white, but I think that, like Gutiérrez and Assmann, he becomes the voice of those sentenced to silence.

These two models will serve to illustrate what it is that we find if we accord the primacy to an "implicit" (or Old Testament, or pneumatological, or functional) christology.

### The Berkhof Model

Berkhof observes that theological tradition has sought a relationship with the kerygmatic structure of the letters of the New Testament rather than with the narrative structure of the gospels.[21] He denies that this entails a dilemma, granted that the epistles presuppose a knowledge of the historical life of Jesus. If this concrete life of Jesus is not taken seriously, cross and resurrection are sailing in the clouds. Berkhof would consider them a sterile abstraction in this case. He adds that in spite of the evident advantages of the *munus triplex* model, it can be transcended via a historically consistent christological composition—by a properly christological model in which Jesus is seen as the fulfillment of Yahweh's quest for the good and faithful ally.

As for the inventory of predominant traits of the faithful ally as "Son" in the functional sense, Berkhof arrives at the following conclusions.

1. Jesus loves the Father. The intimate relationship between Jesus and his Father made the failure of Jesus' mission impossible, as is seen in the account of the temptations. The source of the energy characterizing the life of Jesus is to be found in Jesus' relationship with his Father through prayer. On the one side, this relationship is characterized by its unicity—by Jesus as the *sui generis* object of the *Pneuma*. On the other, it tends to communicate itself to other human beings—Jesus wishes all to participate in the same relationship of familiarity.

2. This radical, reciprocated love for the Father manifests itself in a no less

radical obedience to the Father. Jesus' food is to do the Father's will—not in an attitude and praxis of servility, but as a manifestation of the strength of his own will.

3. Jesus represents God to human beings. He places himself in perfect solidarity with the Father, and hence his words and works can be characterized as an analogue of the works of Yahweh.

4. This presence of Yahweh in the person of Jesus contains as its first element the striking of a pact or alliance—a covenant. This pact is one in which human beings are not ruled by competitive schema where God is concerned, but are totally governed by God's love and inspired to reflect this love by continuing it in their works. The *propositum,* or object, of the covenant, is rooted in daily life.

5. Jesus himself is this same order become a person. He responds to Yahweh's object and purpose totally, and he translates this response throughout his program. Yahweh has set out for an alienated world, one that is particularly characterized by two groups of persons, the guilty and the unhappy. To the guilty Jesus addresses a message of unconditional forgiveness. To the unhappy, he bears tidings of mercy. This word of mercy is expressed principally in the healings. Both elements of the good news, the forgiveness and the mercy, prompt the promotion of men and women to true humanity, and this promotion is made in accordance with the grace of Yahweh. Here Berkhof cites Luke 4:18, which is the passage from Isaiah (61:1-2) read and commented upon by Jesus in the synagogue on the occasion of the inauguration of his ministry.

6. This activity and praxis of Jesus is marked by the *freedom* with which he addresses his call to men and women, and which forms his own proper lifestyle. He does not defend things as they are. Rather, he assumes a fresh attitude—free of presuppositions—regarding the temple and worship, the synagogue and the law, the day of rest and public authority, his "fathers" and his "brothers," property and money, a large following and the coercive power of the state. All these things are secondary and relative. And so his attitude and activity are felt as a threat to the established order. Jesus' total disregard of external pressures arises from the exclusive priority he accords to the Father and the Father's regime of mercy.

7. This freedom of Jesus regards even the nonhuman part of creation—what we call "nature." For Jesus, nature contained chaotic and dangerous elements, represented by the demons. He considered himself lord and master of this part of creation and made use of his freedom to achieve the triumph of the signs of the kingdom of peace on these very deep levels of reality as well. Berkhof cites Mark 1:13: "He was with the wild beasts." Here we recall that, in an earlier book, Berkhof holds a third relationship to be constitutive of the biblical anthropology, besides that with Yahweh and one's neighbor—namely, an attitude and behavior of respect and dominion regarding nature. He sees in Jesus, as the faithful ally, the optimal realization of the three relationships in which human beings find themselves as their permanent situation.

Berkhof observes that traditional dogmatics compresses all these moments into what it calls Jesus' "impeccability." But Berkhof regards "impeccability" to be a posterior conclusion, which cannot be applied to the life of Jesus, exposed as it was to all manner of contrary pressures and forces. Consequently, instead of "impeccable," Berkhof prefers "humanistic"—possessing the fullness of being human, the total structure of all three relationships, the best of all qualities (liberty and freedom), and complete maturity (the status of ally and instrument of Yahweh).

In one way, in the plenitude of Jesus' being human we stand accused of our alienations. But at the same time, Jesus' being a human being also constitutes our invitation to incorporate ourselves with this way of fulfilling our human existence, and thereby becomes a promise in which Yahweh offers us something far beyond what we can imagine (Eph. 3:20-21).

These are the seven elements in which Berkhof synthesizes his functional reading of the gospels. His references to the exegetical literature serve to document the criteria by which he seeks to arrive at his conclusions.

*The Nolan Model*

Now let us turn our attention to another work—Albert Nolan's *Jesus before Christianity*.[22] The book is divided into four parts: "Catastrophe," "Praxis," "The Good News," and "Confrontation." In part 1 the author indicates his point of departure for his reading of the gospels: the sense of frustration and desperation that afflicts so many when they come to realize that the international system that governs local situations is based on injustice and violence. These problems, Nolan observes, are not difficult in themselves. They are open to solution. All that is required is for the rich to transform this order of injustice by committing themselves to a drastic redistribution of their goods. The problem lies not in the situation, but in the lack of good will. One need only journey in the Third World to realize that the preponderance of military governments there is not an accident. It is the only basis on which the system can continue. The problems of population, hygiene, inflation, violence, the extremes of poverty and wealth, left to themselves, will build up more and more pressure and finally erupt in total catastrophe.

What Nolan finds interesting in the historical life of Jesus is that he lived in a similar age. In his cultural situation, as well, there were signs of frustration and desperation—on a smaller scale than today. Jesus too lived at a time when many thought the end of history was rapidly nearing. In the midst of this apocalyptic situation, Jesus indicates a way out, a solution. And he makes of this solution the nucleus of his message. Nolan calls attention to what so many generations of New Testament scholars have found to be such a problem—what Jesus thought about the end of the world. For Nolan, this is precisely what becomes so interesting for us today. Consequently Nolan seeks to read the gospels from this viewpoint—the international frustration caused by our unjust international system. A rereading of the gospels reveals that John the Baptist as well as Jesus prophesied the approaching end of the world and the destruction of Jerusalem by means of the Roman armies—and that these prophecies are not *vaticinia ex eventu,* but genuinely prophetic proclamations of the impending end. (Nolan refers to the studies by Dodd and Lloyd Gaston.)[23] Faced with this national catastrophe, Jesus formulates his message. This is the analogy between his situation and ours.

Part 2 develops the themes of the poor and the oppressed, and then healing and forgiveness. The poor are the oppressed. Their most outstanding characteristic is marginalization. They have no role to play and are in complete dependence on the favors of others. Nolan emphasizes how the poor suffered from the notion that their condition was a consequence of faults committed by themselves or by their forebears. They lived in a climate of fatalism and resignation. They had no civil rights. They participated in no religious or political movements, which were all reserved to members of the middle class. It is with these persons that Jesus identified, and he did so in spite of the fact that he belonged to the middle class himself (although that of Galilee, which was looked down upon by the elite of Jerusalem). The identification was his own option.

The motive of his option was his compassion, in the powerful sense of the verb *splagchnizomai,* "a feeling that goes all the way to one's intestines." This compassion is shown in Jesus' many cures. In spite of the embellishment evident in many of the gospel accounts of Jesus' healings, it is difficult to deny that he worked "miracles." What is characteristic of Jesus is that he insists upon an attitude of faith on the part of the sick and the possessed. The cures are to be interpreted as a consequence of an attitude of faith and confidence that is diametrically contrary to the atmosphere of fatalism and resignation typical of the situation of the poor. This faith is the proper response to a God who takes such an eager initiative in the liberation of a people from alienation. Nolan also underscores the relationship between illness and forgiveness. Just as illness, according to the rabbinical theology, was a consequence of sin, so the healing must be understood as a consequence of forgiveness.

In part 3 Nolan describes the good news as liberation. But this liberation takes place within the frame of reference of the gospel of the kingdom. The kingdom is obviously a politically structured society of human beings here on earth. Nolan documents this assertion by noting the great frequency with which the kingdom is compared with a house, a city, or a community. This kingdom is characterized by its renunciation of the quest for wealth. The rich have great difficulty in entering the kingdom, for the characteristic attitude of the kingdom must be the will to share.

The real miracle of the multiplication of the loaves consisted in the fact that the hungry shared what they had with others. This is not an idealization of poverty, but rather derives from a conviction that there should be no poor and that the only way to make this possible is to form a community that shares its goods, as in Acts 2-4. The kingdom also pulverizes the value of social status and prestige—which is why Jesus prefers children, who had no status in society. This is not to say that the kingdom will be only for the representatives of a particular social class, but only that those who base their lives on prestige will have to be converted. In the same fashion Nolan calls our attention to Jesus' radically new attitude toward another group without status—women.

More positively, the kingdom is built on solidarity. But this solidarity bears no likeness to that of certain groups that perverted the concept, such as families with their *jus talionis*. The solidarity of the kingdom transcends groups and particular group interests. And obviously it is not a question of a vague, abstract philanthropy. Loving everybody means loving nobody, Nolan says. The point of departure of the kingdom is identification with the marginalized, and their liberation, and this is the particularity from whose viewpoint the concept of solidarity will have to be defined.

The same can be said with regard to the relationship between the kingdom and power. Once the kingdom is a political reality, *ipso facto* it will have power. But the kingdom will not be a situation in which oppressed and oppressors have switched places. The power of the kingdom is the power of service and freedom. Once again these concepts must be concretized, through an identification with the oppressed.

Part 4 of Nolan's book is devoted to the theme of "confrontation." He rejects the touted dilemma that consists in either identifying Jesus as a guerrilla or depriving him of all political activity. Nolan considers such interpretations anachronistic, having little to do with the moment in which Jesus is living. But the assertion that Jesus did not belong to the Zealots does not mean he had nothing to do with politics. Precisely part of the Jewish legacy is that the "religious" embraces all areas of life. Hence the very concept of a kingdom of God presupposes a relevancy to the political—and for Jesus personally, of course, this means the dependence of Israel upon the Romans.

Jesus is presented as the liberator of Israel most emphatically in Proto-Luke. What is unique about all this, however, is that Jesus actualizes this liberation in a form not foreseen by the majority of his contemporaries. He insists that Israel change its attitude. All the Zealots aspired to was a change of governments. Jesus demands total change. Citing Segundo's well-known article, Nolan observes that the most brutal exploitation came not so much from the Romans, but from the representatives of the middle class of Israel itself. The root of the exploitation was sunk deep in a theology that presented Yahweh as the one who welded together the establishment, the vested interests of the few. Jesus is not "against" the politics of the Zealots any more than he is "against" the politics of the Pharisees. What he is "against" is the theological and religious foundation of Israel's oppression.

The second confrontation is with the business establishment. Nolan agrees with Trocmé that the episode of the purification of the temple (which both writers place neither at the beginning of Jesus' life nor at the end) is the direct cause of the decision of the authorities to eliminate him. From this moment on, Jesus is obliged to lead a quasi-clandestine life. The purification had nothing to do with ritual matters, but rather should be seen as a direct assault on the abuses of money and commerce.

Jesus' fate is decided by these two confrontations. Inasmuch as Jesus has offered a way out of the destruction of the nation and Jerusalem, calling upon everyone to take on the responsibility of the building of a new society based on identification with those who have no defense and determined by a climate of love and justice—Jesus' condemnation by the authorities becomes their self-condemnation. Once Jesus is executed, there is no longer any avoiding the catastrophe.

Just so, says Nolan at the end of his book, our own world is headed for destruction if we do not heed Jesus' word. The principal responsibility is in the hands of those who hold power and possess goods. If they are unwilling to share, this world has no future, and what happened to Jerusalem will happen to us. For true Christians, says Nolan, it is far from hopeless to insist on this change of attitude. For their confidence is like that of Jesus: in spite of all opposition, the kingdom will come. And this is a confidence that does not fail even at the prospect of suffering as the only way to be faithful to the messianic word.

Having given a resumé of the studies by Berkhof and Nolan, I should like to make some comments. Formally speaking, there is considerable identity between the two authors' lists of characteristics of the historical life of Jesus. Jesus has a liberty, a freedom, that is contagious. And he sets his sights on those who suffer from sin and infirmity, he preaches the kingdom, and he is characterized by a most intimate relationship with the Father.

Nevertheless, there exists one rather important difference—an eloquent one. Nolan makes far more use of the categories of sociology and political science than Berkhof does in analyzing Jesus' context and comparing it with our situation today. To a certain extent, it would seem that Berkhof's Jesus acts in a historical vacuum. It almost seems unnecessary to make an analysis of the forces and counterforces of the society into which Jesus enters. Jesus' approach and likeness to his contemporaries is mainly a matter of anthropological constants. The anthropological factor needs no sociological elucidation in order to be able to explain why there obtain such and such tensions among various groups. To take an example, both authors speak of the many sick persons around Jesus. Berkhof gives no specific historical explanation. Nolan does. He argues that the circumstances of dependence and marginalization inclined the oppressed to psychosomatic illness. Their mental illnesses reflected not only their physical conditions but their psychological conditions as well. A situation of total dependency creates a climate favorable to the development of all manner of illnesses manifesting the alienation in which human beings find themselves caught.

Thus Nolan is unwilling to speak of Jesus and *illness* as such—the illnesses of all times and places—but only of Jesus and the *illnesses* of his milieu. It is via an analysis of the collective neurosis of Jesus' time that one may grasp something of the nature of these illnesses and Jesus' reaction to them. Jesus' relationship with illnesses cannot be simply and rigidly applied to other ages. One must undertake a detailed investigation of what is occurring in a given concrete context in order to be able to articulate the relevancy of Jesus' message for different situations.

It seems to me that Sobrino has some very incisive observations to make here. It is one thing to assert that Jesus' path brings us into confrontation with the "absolute dimension." But it is something else to absolutize this way, this path, and present it as the only one. This leads automatically to the introduction of the category of imitation in the area of ethics.[24] But this category does justice neither to the particularity of the path taken by Jesus nor to the necessity Christians are under to assume responsibility for the historical routes they must follow themselves in their various situations. The scale of values we find in Jesus' praxis is one thing; the analysis by which Jesus arrives at the proclamation of these values is something else again. Clearly, Berkhof's portrait of Jesus lacks two things. First, what are his criteria in his search for the visage of Jesus? What is he looking for? What questions does he ask? Secondly, how is Jesus' place in the socio-cultural context of his age to be defined?

Nolan, it seems to me, takes these concerns into consideration, and is therefore in a position to present a Jesus who is much more particular and concrete. As we have suggested, is this not owing to the fact that he lives in South Africa? That is, Nolan places himself before a horizon that is supremely interested in the presence of a Jesus who has relevancy for the situation of exploitation and discrimination obtaining in his own country. Berkhof speaks of the "European experiment"—the fertilization of European soil by Christian elements as making Europe something different. Christianization makes Europe a place where we may observe the historical effect of the merciful lordship of God. Of course, this is not the only thing Berkhof says. He also speaks of the ambivalence in which the North Atlantic bloc finds itself, and its need for a clear option in favor of humanization. What he does not mention, however, is that the unique phenomenon that is Europe is able to exist precisely thanks to the existence of the peripheral countries, which are peripheral not by nature but by the coercion historically exercised by Europe in the successive phases of colonization.[25] In other words, Berkhof suggests that the particularity of which Nolan is speaking has little relevancy for European theology. I think he is mistaken on this point, and that it is precisely his theology with regard to the continent of Europe as an experiment in the Messianic spirit that reveals—although, I repeat, Berkhof does express himself with a great deal of prudence, and certain reservations—that he does not regard concepts such as domination, imperialism, and capitalism as important for an analysis of the reality of the world.

## OUR LATIN AMERICAN TASK

It is my opinion that Latin American theology has a part to play in the search for the historical Jesus. I think it ought to profit by the Copernican revolution now taking place and forcing the abdication of the sad reign of narrow individualism of the Bultmannian school

The first thing that needs to be done is to face up to the fact that popular images of Jesus in Latin America are invariably an invitation to escape from history. Jesus is seen as the personification of the senseless tragedy that is human life. His passion is experienced as the exteriorization of the resignation that most Latin Americans live throughout their whole life. Or again, Jesus is the symbol of the tragedy of a violent death. His resurrection has very little to do with life and history; rather it is a celebration of his escape from history. In a word, what is lacking in the great majority of these images is the relationship between the symbolism projected and the concrete, historical life of the historical Jesus.[26]

With all respect to the Protestant churches, it is to be noted in their case that this shortcoming is due in large part to an almost total disregard for the Old Testament. Jesus is approached from an individualist and liberal need, in which what is decisive are values such as immortality and future reconciliation. I believe that it is the Old Testament that must save the church from this implicit and explicit gnosticism, as it has so often done in history. Hence great emphasis should be placed on the Old Testament in catechesis and preaching.

It would be most meaningful, for example, to rethink the dialectic of the priestly, prophetic, and royal roles of the Old Testament, in light of Jesus' praxis and in the ecclesial reality of Catholicism and Protestantism in Latin America. For example, what is the sacerdotal without the prophetic? Ritualism. What is the royal without the prophetic? Triumphalism. In other words, one of the most important tasks in the area of christology is the remythologization of the central concepts of the Old Testament, for this is what will be of service in a reencounter with the concrete and daily impact of the praxis of Jesus. This is the way to lend the quality of "evangelical" to such titles as Lord, the risen Christ, Son of David, and so on, for they express the continued validity of Jesus' historical praxis.

Secondly, it is urgent that we redefine the relationship between Jesus and politics. Logically this has a great deal to do with a like necessity for reaffirming the bond that always exists between church and state. Research into Jesus' contacts with the political dimension evince the fact that the kingdom of God proclaimed by Jesus is a political reality of the here and now. Furthermore, it is now possible to recognize the falsity of the dilemma of Jesus as either a revolutionary or a pietist. Such a dilemma is of no good whatever for the articulation of the political praxis in which Jesus was continually involving himself. In other words, a biblicism of the left is as worthless as a biblicism of the right. The Old Testament can afford us an insight into the universal claim of the implicit lordship of Yahweh. It is this implicit lordship that constitutes the motive of Jesus' total inability to withdraw from the consequences of his preaching where the political problems of his time are concerned. But one must take account of the fact that Jesus is often dismissed as a "mere revolutionary" precisely in order to deprive him of his political relevance.

Thirdly, Latin America is that place in history where Jesus has been converted into an object of manipulation precisely via an abstract and falsely universal use of his titles of lordship. Latin American Christianity has rendered inestimable service to the privileged classes and to their need for a peace that is not the fruit of liberation but rather the result of resignation.[27] Taking a position within the hermeneutic of a search for the historical Jesus will allow us to contribute to the unmasking of official images of Jesus as a defense of vested interests. To take an example—Jesus' ascension has been deprived of its efficacy by means of a "spiritualization," instead of according it the force of a seal of approval on Jesus' concrete praxis as is done in the Pauline epistles. The ascension is not an invitation to withdraw from history. It is precisely an encouragement to historical commitment in the name of the Messiah. It is not a call to quietism, but a challenge.

I hold that Latin American theology stands to gain by developing an implicit and pneumatological christology—a low, not a high, christology—from a point of departure in the Old Testament, and not in the criteria of Hellenism—moving from the historical Jesus to the Christ of the kerygma, and presenting the kerygma as the mobilization of the universal meaning of the word of Jesus. I consider these observations to be important, given the fact that they imply a hermeneutical application of the biblical texts. If this is not done—and we shall see that it is not the only thing that needs to be done—christology will go on being a blind spot in liberation theology, a vacuum that can always be filled by the theology that happens to be prevailing. We must also be on our guard against abstractions of a leftist stripe. The weapons for defense against manipulable abstractions are to be found not only in hermeneutics but also in the effort to break a path to the historical Jesus via the new methods with which we are concerned here.

And yet all this is not enough, and it seems to me that this is abundantly evident in the thought of Berkhof. We must be wary of a set of presuppositions that tends aprioristically to determine the outcome of exegesis. It is worth the trouble, then, to explicate our premises and consciously to include them in our exegetical work. (We all include them; the only difference is that some of us say we do not.)

We can draw two important conclusions from what has been said. First, one must arrive at a hypothesis that can consistently explain the context in which one finds oneself. We have seen that Nolan does this by means of an analysis of the Achilles' heel in the capitalist system. It is equally clear that his analysis does not ignore socio-economic and political factors—that is, his analysis is not limited to an anthropologizing intimism. Nolan does not speak of *the* human being or *the* poor person. He tries to understand *these* human beings and *these* poor persons, in their particular situations.

It is my opinion that a hermeneutical explication such as that presented by the Latin American theology of liberation continues to be of great importance. The categories of domination and dependence—that is, the implicit contract between rich and poor countries—continues to provide an excellent frame of reference in which to be able to explain most of the phenomena that a serious analysis can encounter along its path.

These categories are not restricted to an epoch in which, with unshakable optimism, one could expect processes of emancipation—emancipation on a cultural, political, and social level—in the countries of Latin America. It is true that revisions are necessary within these categories. But this does not apply to the categories themselves. The revisions will concern rather a certain tone of triumphalism and a certain short-sightedness that have occasioned an insufficiently rigorous reading of reality in the peripheral countries. But the concepts of domination and dependence themselves are not married to an emotionalism (however understandable) determined by illusory expectations. Thus we must place ourselves in opposition to all those who seek to beat a strategic retreat in order to launch new models of interpretation—models that neglect the necessity of including the hypothesis based on dependence and domination within any broader synthesis that may be developed.

We must be on our guard against a certain new theological and philosophical trend that emphasizes "interiority" and "the discipline of the secret." I am not against interiority, nor do I oppose an interpretation of the Christian community as the church of the exodus, lacking basic links with "the world." But unless these notions are integrated into the broader horizon of rigorous sociological and political analysis, they will automatically lead to a new state of ahistoricity.[28] I believe that one of the things that simply cannot be combined with Christianity—in the sense of an adequate translation and application of the praxis of Jesus—is a retreat from responsibility for the world and its history. I am not opposed to the category of exile as a representation of the provisory character of the church. But everything depends on how one defines the attitude and praxis that correspond to an exilic period.

Abiding by the "great and small countries" analysis, as it might be called, will lead to a series of questions about the life of Jesus—questions that would be difficult to formulate within a context of a so-called pure and objective exegesis, for it conceals ulterior interests. (The Bible, as Tillich put it, answers no questions that are not asked.)

Taking his cue from Juan Luis Segundo, Nolan formulates one of these questions thus: In a situation of dependence—dependence in the total sense—what should one do? Struggle as fiercely as possible against the enemy? (That is, against the dominating country—Rome, in the case of Israel in the time of Jesus.) Nolan recognizes that the Proto-Lucan interpretation, too, has but little liking for a foreign hegemony and that it presents Jesus within a matrix of expectation of liberation from the clutches of the invader. But, as Nolan points out, the invader becomes more and more visible for Jesus in the imperial collaborators within Israel itself. Jesus expresses his opposition more and more against the representatives of the Jewish establishment who oppress their own compatriots, and in Yahweh's name to boot. In other words, Jesus "declares war" (the purification of the temple) on those who defend their status and perquisites without any concern for those who have no defense and no official recognition of their rights. In comparison with this oppression, the Romans are not so bad.

Once the validity of the hypothesis of dependence is accepted, the question of combative tactics can be posed. It is easy to make a centrist country the scapegoat and put all the responsibility for the situation of dependence on foreign agents infiltrating and defending the interests of their countries. (Not that I am unaware of the implications of foreign security organizations in the situation of misery characterizing the periphery.) But the struggle against the system must be waged at home as well. Simplistic references to the "enemy over there" can be converted into an excuse for the absence of conflict and struggle on one's own soil.

In other words, the romanticism of dogmatizing the struggle for liberation is a luxury we cannot afford. We must go in search of direct confrontation with the enemy at home. An escapism that defines the enemy as the other country has its altogether concrete response in the historical practice of Jesus, who surely did not turn his back on the enemy at home. To put it another way, there is no point in sitting back and waiting for the transformation of supranational structures, important as this may be. We must come to grips with the individualization and identification of the enemy in a local context— however conflictive *this* may turn out to be.

There is a second question. Clearly, the majority of churchgoers in peripheral countries belong to the upper and middle classes. How can the churches gain identification with the *'am ha'arets,* the masses? We must admit that such efforts are bound to be fruitless, given the very closed and antagonistic concept of social classes we retain. Nolan calls attention to the fact that Jesus, a member of the middle class, strove by every means to express his solidarity with the defenseless. He took his meals with them regularly and was evidently not much concerned about the alleged insuperable barrier separating the middle class from the laboring or marginalized classes. Of course, it is entirely logical that the poor would regard with suspicion any attempt on the part of the privileged to approach them. What, nevertheless, carries more weight: the compartmentalization of a classist society or an attitude of solidarity that seeks, and not in words only, a relationship with those who have all the reason in the world for doubting such demonstrations of solidarity? If we turn to the gospel for an answer to our question, we discover that the contagion of Jesus' solidarity with the marginalized is so original and creative that it becomes its own success. And at the same time, the tone with which Jesus invests his praxis makes it simply impossible to interpret this solidarity as populist demagoguery.

As to the concrete forms this solidarity should take, there is much to be discovered and invented. Naturally, it must express itself on many levels, including that of economic and political struggle. Nevertheless what is important to emphasize here is the ecclesiological aspect. Nolan points out that evidently the custom built up by the primitive church of the holy supper had its origin in the meals that Jesus was accustomed to share with "sinners," and it would seem that this same thing must be kept in mind in order to understand the community of goods reported in Acts. A rereading of the gospel from the point of view of concrete solidarity with those who have no rights therefore has a surprising result: without indulging in cheap biblicism, one can safely assert that the church departs from its tradition when it converts itself into a mere institution and no longer seeks to organize the "meal shared with others."

A second consequence of identification with the "great and small countries" hypothesis is the following. Obviously, the intent of this hermeneutic is to bring into focus not just economic dependence, but all dependence. And yet it accords a very special meaning to the economic aspect and seeks a most precise understanding of this structure in the totality of the structuring of society. Hence we also want to study the manner in which Jesus' preaching formed part of the social praxis of his time. New work in christology will be unacceptable unless it comprises this focus. It must be admitted that until now attempts at this sort of reflection have not been very promising. The studies of Kautzky and Puente are not very convincing.[29] Still, it is obvious that we have to move in this direction and hold before our minds the importance of what is called the "economic factor" in the tradition of the primitive church (the church of the first and second centuries).

But withal, it will not suffice simply to come to an understanding of the importance the politico-economic factor has for avoiding a platonizing reading of the gospel. It is equally necessary to form an exact idea of the totality of the social processes of Jesus' times and to see how his praxis is determined in this field of gravitation. I think there is room here for a Latin American contribution to the exploration of Jesus' life and history.

Let us borrow an example from Sobrino. In searching for images to use in retelling the story of Jesus, Sobrino says, it will be very interesting to develop the concept of Jesus' faith—not faith *in* Jesus, but Jesus' own faith, surely a much neglected concept in the history of theology. Sobrino attempts to do this from a Latin American point of view, where, among other particularities, the alternatives are not so much faith and unbelief, as an abstract faith and a renewing, or liberating, faith. He is also interested in the triumphal dimension of faith, which presupposes a situation or tone of conflict that arises when faith is proclaimed and exercised. Finally, it is not so much a question of the relationship between faith and God, but rather between faith and the kingdom of God.[30] Hebrews 12:2 has a very important place in these considerations—Jesus as the one who leads the pilgrimage to the kingdom. Sobrino notes the great conflict in the life of Jesus—the Galilee crisis, which results in Jesus' acceptance of suffering.

Not much argumentation is necessary to demonstrate the importance of understanding Jesus' faith for a christology that intends to reflect on the praxis of Christians in Latin America. Given the general absence of the proclamation of the good news here, faith takes on the aspect of a conviction that flies in the face of the facts. Faith in this sense means giving assent to a promise, and rending the spiderweb of fate. Then too, faith means cross and suffering—not masochistic suffering, but suffering as the price of discipleship. Finally, faith means striking a relationship with the one who leads the pilgrimage, along with confidence that such faith has nothing to lose. A faith that so lives, manifesting itself in love and hope, creates space for social conduct in community and solidarity.

In this fashion, from a point of departure in a practical accord with the values represented in the history of Jesus—in the historical Jesus—Christians in the Latin American context will discover more and more of the identity of Jesus. More and more they will be in a position to determine for themselves the titles he bears among them. The road passes by way of the particularity of the history of Jesus, and at the same time by way of the particularity of the contemporary situation.

It is impossible to arrive at an explication of universal realities in Jesus Christ without having discovered the implicit weight of his praxis, adequately translated for the time and space in which it is allotted to us to live. The locus of encounter with Jesus is the road he himself trod. We find him when we "join him on his way."[31] For the relevance of Jesus' praxis invites us not to repeat his history, but precisely to make our own. The handing on of his history is not the womb of nostalgia, but the megaphone that educates us to genuine historical freedom. Unless our titles for him make Jesus rich with our praxis, they will never be more than fetishes and idols.

# NOTES

1. See Severino Croatto's position on the relationship between authentic faith and liberation in "La religiosidad popular: un intento de problematización," *Cristianismo y Sociedad* 14 (1976): 46–47.

2. Basically I am referring to the work of Gutiérrez, Assmann, Miranda, and Segundo.

3. Hendrikus Berkhof, ed., *Christelijk Geloof* (Nijkerk: Callenbach, 1973); Eng. trans., *Christian Faith: An Introduction to the Study of the Faith* (Grand Rapids, Mich.: Eerdmanns, 1979), pp. 267–69.

4. See Wolfhart Pannenberg, *Grundzüge der Christologie* (Gütersloh: Mohn, 1964) Eng. trans., *Jesus, God and Man* (Philadelphia: Westminster, 2nd ed., 1977).

5. See Gutiérrez, *Teología de la liberación* (Lima: CEP, 1970); Eng. trans., *A Theology of Liberation: History, Politics and Salvation,* (Maryknoll, N.Y.: Orbis, 1973).

6. See Enrique D. Dussel, *Teología de la liberación y ética,* Caminos de liberación latinoamericana 2 (Buenos Aires, 1974), pp. 87ff; Eng. trans., *Ethics and the Theology of Liberation* (Maryknoll, N.Y.: Orbis, 1978), pp. 63ff.

7. See Pannenberg, *Jesus, God and Man,* passim.

8. See J. M. Robinson, *A New Quest for the Historical Jesus* (London, 1959; Naperville, Ill.: Allenson, 1959).

9. See Jon Sobrino, "Cristología y el seguimiento," *Christus* 41 (March 1976): 15–39.

10. Etienne Trocmé, *Jesus as Seen by His Contemporaries* (Philadelphia: Westminster, 1973).

11. Berkhof, *Christian Faith,* section 32, pp. 280–93.

12. See Hendrikus Berkhof, *The Doctrine of the Holy Spirit* (Atlanta: John Knox, 1976), p. 14.

13. Kurt Lüthi, "Systematische Theologie angesichts einiger Ergebnisse der neutestamentlichen Wissenschaft," *Theologisches Lexikon* 101:9ff.

14. See Edward Schweizer, *Jesus* (Munich: Siebenstern Taschenbuch, 1968), Eng. trans., *Jesus* (Richmond: John Knox, 1971).

15. The question is justified with respect to the necessity of certain ontological notions as an expression of a totalizing horizon. In the present case we would have to make a distinction between the ontological *modus enuntiandi* and the meaning itself.

16. Paul Ricoeur, *Le conflit des interprétations: Essais d'herméneutique* (Paris: Seuil, 1969); Eng. trans., *The Conflict of Interpretations: Essays in Hermeneutics,* ed. John Ihde (Evanston, Ill.: Northwestern University Press, 1974), esp. 381-88.

17. See Sobrino, "Cristología."

18. See Albert Nolan, *Jesus before Christianity: The Gospel of Liberation* (Claremont, South Africa: David Philip, 1976; Maryknoll, N.Y.: Orbis, 1978), pp. 121-24.

19. Sobrino is clearly following a line of thought of Assmann's. See his references to Assmann's *Teología desde la praxis de la liberación: Ensayo teológico desde la América dependiente,* vol. 1 (Salamanca: Sígueme, 1973); Eng. trans., *Theology for a Nomad Church* (Maryknoll, N.Y.: Orbis, 1976), pp. 60-61.

20. See H. M. Kuitert, *Gott in Menschengestalt: Eine dogmatisch-hermeneutische Studie über die Anthropomorphismen der Bibel* (Munich, 1967).

21. Berkhof, *Christian Faith,* p. 293. See also pp. 294–99 for what follows.

22. See note 18, above.

23. C. H. Dodd, *The Parables of the Kingdom* (1935); rev. ed. (New York: Scribners, 1961); "The Fall of Jerusalem and the 'Abomination of Desolation,' " *Journal of Roman Studies* 37 (1947), pp. 47-54; *The Founder of Christianity* (New York: Macmillan, 1970). Lloyd Gaston, *No Stone on Another* (Leiden: Brill, 1970).

24. Sobrino, "Cristología," p. 35.

25. See Berkhof, *Christian Faith,* sections 53–55 of "The Renewal of the World," pp. 507–20.

26. See *Cristianismo y Sociedad* 13 (1975), no. 43–44, devoted entirely to the images of Jesus in Latin America.

27. See Gulio Girardi, *Amour chrétien e conflit de classes* (Paris: 1970), p. 43.

28. I refer especially to Rubem Alves, *Tomorrow's Child: Imagination, Creativity, and the Rebirth of Culture* (New York: Harper & Row, 1972), and Leonardo Boff, *Teología desde el cautiverio,* Iglesia Nueva 23 (Bogotá: Indo-American Press Service, 1975).

29. Karl Kautsky, *Der Ursprung des Christentums* (Stuttgart, 1908); Eng. trans., *Foundations of Christianity: A Study in Christian Origins* (New York: International Publications, 1925; Monthly Review Press, 1972). Gonzalo Puente, *Ideología e historia: La formación del cristianismo como fenómeno ideológico* (Madrid, 1974).

30. Sobrino, "Cristología," pp. 18ff.

31. Ibid., p. 25.

# INDEX

*Compiled by William Jerman*